RESTORERS OF HOPE

RESTORERS OF HOPE

Reaching the Poor in Your Community
with Church-Based Ministries
That Work

AMY L. SHERMAN

CROSSWAY BOOKS • WHEATON, ILLINOIS
A DIVISION OF GOOD NEWS PUBLISHERS

Restorers of Hope

Copyright © 1997 by Amy L. Sherman

Published by Crossway Books,
  a division of Good News Publishers
  1300 Crescent Street
  Wheaton, Illinois 60187.

Cover design: John Lucas

Cover photo: Index Stock Photography, Inc.

First printing, 1997

Printed in the United States of America

Library of Congress Cataloging-in-Publication Data
Sherman, Amy L. 1965-
    Restorers of hope : reaching the poor in your community with church-based ministries that work / Amy L. Sherman.
        p.   cm.
    ISBN 0-89107-958-0
    1. Church work with the poor—United States—Case studies.
I. Title.
BV639.P6S524   1997
261.8'325'0973—dc21   97-25330

05	04	03	02	01	00	99	98	97
15	14	13	12	11	10	9 8 7 6 5 4 3 2 1		

*This book is dedicated to
my friends and co-laborers
in Abundant Life Ministries
and especially to Mrs. Lula Rogers,
whose living, most certainly,
has not been in vain.*

Contents

Acknowledgments

In God's wonderful providence, with new book projects come new friends. I am indebted to the many servants of Christ who work on the front lines in the ministries discussed in this volume. I could hardly name them all, but am grateful to everyone who consented to interviews, took me on ministry tours, shared their testimonies, acquainted me with their neighborhoods, and hosted me in their church services so that my research trips were fruitful and productive.

Also, I wish to express appreciation for several people who went above the call of duty in assisting me during my field research. In Chicago Wayne and Ann Gordon were especially generous with their time, and Precious Thomas made logistical arrangements smooth. In Detroit Bill Cash assisted in organizing my interview schedule, and Mary Jackson gave bountifully of her time. In Dallas Roberta Jones and LaFayette Holland helped coordinate my contacts. In Washington, D.C., Bob and Sharon Mathieu graciously gave time out of their extremely hectic schedules, and Tony Yates permitted me to accompany him on his daily sales rounds in Anacostia. In Phoenix Bob and Judy Moffitt showered wonderful hospitality, and Kit Danley and her family "adopted" me. Tim Ritchie and Gerald Austin in Birmingham have not only helped me with this book, but have also provided many hours of counsel as my own church imitates the Center for Urban Missions's ministry model here in Charlottesville. In Michigan Don DeVos and Virgil Gulker were especially eager to help, and they have provided useful feedback in my thinking about urban ministry. My thanks are also due to Linda Tracey, Elaine Metcalf, and Inez Fleming in Richmond, all of whom went out of their way to serve.

This book is far richer due to the testimonies of individuals served by the ministries profiled, testimonies that are intimate, poignant, and probably not easy to share with a stranger holding a tape recorder. I'm grateful that Luis Osoy, Sheila Anderson, Leslie Miller, Clarissa Crews, Denise Thomas, Ora Stinson, and many others shared so openly with me.

My thinking on these matters has been enriched through discussion with colleagues Ken Myers, Herb and Terry Schlossberg, Stanley Carlson-Thies, Marvin Olasky, Bob Osborne, Tim Ritchie, and, of course, my hardworking and thoughtful research assistant, Carol Sargeant. The important writings of Glenn Loury, Tim Keller, John Perkins, and Harvie Conn have also shaped my understanding of the problem of underclass poverty and the church's appropriate response.

Finally, my thanks are due to the Fieldstead Institute and the Ethics and Public Policy Center; without their financial and administrative support, this project would have been impossible.

Introduction

Three Who've Made It

When Ora Stinson first met Rev. Gerald Austin of the Center for Urban Missions ten years ago, she was living with her two young sons in Metropolitan Gardens, the largest public housing project in Birmingham, Alabama. Aerial photographs of this sprawling complex are alarming; Metropolitan Gardens looks more like a prison than a residential neighborhood. A few years back rates of crime and violence in "the project" reached such heights that police required residents to wear identification badges. That way officers could keep out nonresident gang members and drug dealers. The complex's three-story red-brick apartment buildings don't look too shabby from the outside, thanks to a face-lift in the 1970s, but the neighborhood was called America's poorest zip code in a 1986 government study.

When Ms. Stinson met Rev. Austin, though, violence and poverty were just two of her problems. She was a "lady of the streets" and an illiterate alcoholic. A troubled childhood and a painful divorce had left Stinson emotionally wounded and bereft of self-confidence. "I was a person who didn't care about anything," she explains, "because I didn't even think I had a right to be living."

Today Ms. Stinson lives in a ranch-style home in a quiet working-class community about a fifteen-minute drive from Metropolitan Gardens. She's sober, literate, and off welfare. She works two jobs and is an active member of New City Church, the congregation pastored by Gerald Austin. The church is closely affiliated with the Center for Urban Missions (CUM), which Stinson credits, along with God's faithfulness, for her family's transformation.

Ms. Stinson and I chatted in her modest living room where pictures of her two sons—one now a navy man—were proudly on display. CUM, she explained, provided her with a "community of caring" in which she learned personal responsibility and the vocational and life skills necessary to make it without welfare. CUM encouraged her to enroll in adult literacy classes and paired her with a private volunteer tutor. Male staff at CUM became "substitute fathers" to her two sons, and the ministry secured scholarships for both boys to attend private schools.

Most importantly, CUM helped Ms. Stinson decrease her thirst for drink and increase her hunger for God. Ministry staff encouraged her to become involved at New City Church and didn't give up on her when she'd backslide and go out drinking after the Friday night Bible studies. When Stinson was ready, CUM hired her part time to assist with programs at the ministry's "Family Care Center" in Metropolitan Gardens. Over time, CUM staff challenged her to assume ever-increasing responsibilities at the Center. They invested in her, and it paid off. "If it hadn't been for CUM and the church," Stinson admits, "I wouldn't have made it out of the projects. It hasn't been easy, but I've had the power of God and the church by my side."

Stinson hasn't forgotten where she came from. "I think God wants me to focus on the people in Metropolitan Gardens, and that's why I go back there nearly every day," she says. "I try to show [the residents] that there is something they can do to help themselves and help others. It's the most important part of my life," she emphasizes fervently. She has learned that God can "take a little bit of nothing and make something big out of it," and she wants to share that message of hope with her former neighbors. "I love talking to the parents who come into the Family Care Center." She smiles. "A lot of them feel that 'right here [in the projects] is as far as I can go.' But I don't believe that, and I tell them so. I tell them that Jesus is the Man who can take them farther than that."

✧

Today in Phoenix thirty-year-old Luis Osoy works with third to sixth grade boys in Neighborhood Ministries' youth program for underclass Latino kids. But Osoy wasn't always a churchgoer. He grew up on the streets of Guatemala City and gained notoriety there as a violent gang leader and drug dealer. Osoy came to Phoenix in 1989 and continued peddling and using drugs. "I used to drink and use cocaine and smoke marijuana all the time," he relates.

Then Osoy's nephew Edgar began giving Spanish lessons to Jeff Kanner, a member of Open Door Fellowship, the church that oversees Neighborhood Ministries. After Edgar and Kanner's first tutoring session, Edgar reported back to Osoy about Kanner: "This guy—he's a nice guy—but he likes to talk too much about God!" Edgar continued to "hang out" with Kanner, though, and Osoy got jealous. "I used to hate [Kanner]," Osoy admits now. "He was always inviting me over to eat; he always tried to shake my hand and be nice, and I got tired of his invitations." Eventually, though, Kanner's persistent friendliness in the face of Osoy's hostility piqued Osoy's curiosity.

One day Osoy rode his bike to the house where Kanner was living with some Christian friends. "I didn't go in," Osoy recalls. "I just tried to see him through the window. I kept thinking, *Why is that guy like that? Why is he different? What is different about these church people?* And I began to cry."

Even though he was beginning to want to change, Osoy was doubtful he could break away from his drug-dealing partners. "When you're a drug dealer, you can't just quit," Osoy explains. "You can't just say, 'Okay, I'm not going to sell drugs anymore. Bye.' You do that and, wow, something terrible is going to happen to you. I'm talking about death." Osoy continues, "So I thought, *Well, selling drugs is going to be the end of my life.*"

But Osoy believes God gave him an escape route. One night the police captured all the members of Osoy's drug-selling clan. With them in jail, Osoy saw a way out. He began spending more time with Kanner and church member Mike McBride and others from Open Door Fellowship who offered their friendship. "They talked a lot about God's love," Osoy recalls, "but to a gangster, *love* is a gross word." He kept meditating on God's compassion and forgiveness, though, and one night alone in his shabby apartment, Osoy bowed down before heaven and committed his life to Christ.

"Now I'm a church volunteer with the younger boys," he professes proudly. "I try to give the kids the advice I didn't have growing up. Also, I like to hang out with gangsters—not as a gangster anymore—but to get them to see the reality beyond gangster life." Osoy is enrolled in college, is a budding artist, and hopes to someday be involved in a counseling ministry. He is living proof to young gangsters that there are alternatives to pushing drugs on the street.

✧

After being taken from her abusive, drug-addicted mother at a young age, Leslie Miller spent most of her early life in group homes. At eighteen she was released from the state's care, attended college in Detroit for one year, and then just drifted, sometimes homeless, sometimes not.

She met Pastor Hamon Cross, Jr., of the Rosedale Park Baptist Church at a Campus Crusade for Christ retreat, which she attended with some college acquaintances. Cross listened to her history; challenged her to forgive her mother, herself, and God; and invited her to his church. "I grew up mostly in the streets because my mother did not take responsibility for me," Leslie Miller says. "I didn't really know my mother, but I knew abuse. Pastor Cross told me how to forgive. . . . We just talked a great deal, and he gave me a lot of personal attention at that retreat. It made me feel real good about him."

Shortly afterward Miller landed in jail on minor charges, and some young Christian women from Campus Crusade visited her. These women had been attending Cross's church since the retreat, and they promised to take Miller there when she was released. Remembering the pastor's kindness, Miller agreed to go. In the summer of 1986, she joined Rosedale Park Baptist Church. Now, after ten years of the congregation's straight talk and tough love, Miller has turned her life around.

Throughout the late 1980s, the church helped Miller pay her rent and fuel bills so she wouldn't be evicted. But she is quick to acknowledge that this sort of help was not the key to her transformation. "They weren't just giving me money," she explains. "They were reaching my seared heart."

Pastor Cross became the father Miller never had. "I was lazy at some points," she admits. "There were times Pastor Cross would come and bang at my front door and yell that he needed me to do some work for him. So I'd get up at 7:00 A.M., get dressed, and go over there. And then he'd say, 'I don't really have anything for you to do. I just wanted you to get up. You don't need to be sleeping all day.' I'd be so irate!" Miller laughingly confesses.

Cross exhorted Miller to strengthen her character and set goals for herself. But he always couched his moral challenges in a compassionate love expressed in concrete actions—like taking Miller out to dinner to celebrate her birthday. "We shared things," Miller says. "He became a real influential person in my life."

In March 1991 the congregation's faithfulness to Miller was put to an additional test when Miller, who was not married, became pregnant. The pregnancy devastated her. "I felt like I'd let Pastor Cross and God down."

Panicked, Miller decided to handle the situation the way she'd dealt with two previous unwanted pregnancies—she'd get an abortion. But Cross said abortion was not an option. "Pastor Cross took me into his office one day and said, 'What shall we do?' I said, 'It's my problem.' And he replied, 'We got a mountain to climb.'" Ms. Miller continues, "I made a lot of mistakes, and I had put him through a great deal. He had every right to say, 'We can't have you messing us up.' But instead he said, '*We* got a mountain to climb.'"

This acknowledgment of the church's willingness to partner with her in the midst of her trial won Miller over. She decided to have the baby. Cross's sister offered to be Miller's birthing "coach," and Cross's brother provided Miller with some much-needed financial support. Other congregants gave emotional and material support and offered parenting pointers. "The church just pulled together," Miller says, her voice beginning to break. "Even though I had put them all through so much."

Miller had a little girl, Stormy, who's now a playful four-year-old. Glancing at Stormy across the cluttered living room where we sit, Ms. Miller says, "The church has helped me to groom a young lady, to take responsibility for myself, and to teach my daughter love and responsibility—the things I didn't have growing up."

This support, Miller believes, helped her to escape from what many people considered her inevitably grim destiny. "I grew up with all kinds of abuse," Miller muses. "I've been abused by just about everyone possible you can think of. And they say the cycle continues, and, true enough, it can," she sighs. "But when you got a church run by a pastor who believes in God's vision of how the world should be, and how we should be, you can't go wrong.

"At ten years old I was told that I was either going to end up in jail or dead or in an insane asylum. And there's been many times that I almost ended up in all three," Miller admits, leaning back in her worn, dark chair. "I spent most of my teenage years as the wrong kind of leader. But Pastor Cross is teaching me how to be the right kind of leader."

✦

What do Ora Stinson, Luis Osoy, and Leslie Miller have in common? Each has been embraced by a RESTORER—a congregation of loving Christians dedicated to reaching out to broken people and broken places with a message of hope. Through God's power and the support of God's people, these three individuals have dramatically transformed their lives. Their success is rooted in the unique approach to mercy ministry employed by RESTORERS.

RESTORERS, unlike most government agencies, many secular programs, and even some well-intentioned but misguided churches, treat needy people personally, flexibly, and creatively. RESTORERS build friendships with the disadvantaged while addressing people's physical, emotional, intellectual, and spiritual needs. They challenge "can't-do-it" attitudes; they counteract cultural messages of hedonism, promiscuity, and moral relativism; and they build self-esteem, wield moral authority, and care for people in ways that encourage self-sufficiency rather than prolonged dependency. What they do *works*, as the stories of Ora Stinson, Luis Osoy, Leslie Miller, and countless others demonstrate. And since precious little else is working to help America's most disenfranchised, perhaps it is no surprise that, at long last, more of our nation's power brokers are beginning to admit that they have much to learn from the achievements of RESTORERS.

The Changed Welfare Debate

A few years ago, in an address entitled "Ghetto Poverty and the Power of Faith," Boston University economist Glenn Loury criticized the character of then-current discussions about welfare policy in the United States: "The fundamental assumption behind our public language about ghetto poverty is a materialist viewpoint: economic factors are supposed ultimately to underlie behavioral problems, even behavior involving sexuality, marriage, childbearing and parenting, matters which reflect people's basic understanding of what gives meaning to their lives."[1]

According to Loury, government-sponsored welfare programs have failed because they only address material or economic factors while ignoring moral-cultural factors.

Today the tenor of the welfare debate has changed. Of late, grave disappointment with welfare programs has led even secular commentators to note the effectiveness of faith-based welfare programs and to wonder aloud about the adequacy of projects that neglect spiritual matters. For example, admitting that what he was about to write might "seem strange from a not particularly religious writer in an utterly secular newspaper," *Washington Post* columnist William Raspberry recently argued: "[T]he most successful social programs are those that are driven—even if only tacitly—by moral or religious values. . . . Show me a program that helps people to change their lives (as opposed to merely feeding their physical hunger), and I'll show you a program with a strong element of the spiritual."[2]

Arguments have raged for years over the origins of America's underclass. At the risk of oversimplifying, there are two principal points of view. Both contain important truths. According to one side, factors within "ghetto culture"—such as an entitlement mentality, high incidence of illegitimacy, unwillingness to accept menial labor, substance abuse, materialism, and negative attitudes towards educational achievement—perpetuate poverty. According to the other side, America's social and economic structures keep the poor down through discrimination, lack of investment in "community infrastructure" (i.e., schools, security forces, medical facilities), an unfair judicial system, and the exercise of a brand of capitalism that encourages an ever-increasing gap between America's rich and poor.

The most accurate assessment of poverty in America falls somewhere between these two positions. The reasons for persistent poverty are many and varied. Ideologies that recognize *only* structural factors or *only* moral-cultural factors miss the mark.

In the 1960s and 1970s, the latter view on America's underclass predominated, to the neglect of the former. Some scholars even defended "ghetto culture" as a legitimate alternative to traditional bourgeois norms of family life, sexual behavior, work, and education. Ironically, as scholar Nicholas Lemann has noted, great migrations out of the inner city occurred more or less simultaneously with this celebration of ghetto life.[3] Indeed, as Lemann wrote, "of the millions of black Americans who have risen from poverty to the middle class since the mid-sixties, virtually all have done so by embracing bourgeois values and leaving the ghetto."[4]

This flight from the inner city gave weight to the arguments asserting that poverty was a problem of values, behaviors, and attitudes as well as a result of structural forces beyond any individual's control. In response, the structuralists cried foul and accused those willing to confront ghetto pathologies of "blaming the victim."

By the late 1980s, when it was clear that years of governmental spending on public housing, education, and job training—as well as governmental affirmative action programs and other measures aimed at eradicating institutional racism—had not succeeded in freeing the underclass from poverty, even more commentators sided with the behavioralists over the structuralists. The new debate centered not on whether ghetto culture was a problem, but on whether public assistance exacerbated this problem. Charles Murray's 1984 bombshell, *Losing Ground,*[5] made the most persuasive case that it did.

Two years later Congress passed the Family Support Act of 1988, the first significant reform in the federal welfare system in fifty years. The Family Support Act tackled the problem of the "dependency mindset" head-on, insisting that able-bodied welfare recipients attend job skills classes and find private sector employment.

More recently welfare reformers have gone even further in their attempts to address the cultural and behavioral factors contributing to long-term welfare dependency. Reform legislation in Virginia, Michigan, and Wisconsin directly confronts issues of illegitimacy, personal responsibility, and dependency. Virginia's law, for example, prevents welfare recipients from receiving additional benefits if they have additional children (the so-called "family cap" provision); makes aid contingent upon establishing a child's paternity; insists that able-bodied recipients find jobs within ninety days of applying for aid; and places a two-year limit on benefits (with transitional benefits available in the third year).

In 1996 Congress passed the Personal Responsibility and Work Opportunity Reconciliation Act, which includes similar provisions. While emphasizing actions that address the moral-cultural issues, the federal welfare reforms also recognize real structural obstacles that hinder poor families from achieving independence from welfare. For example, the new legislation earmarks more funds for subsidized day care for the working poor.

The now-accepted assumption that personal behavior, values, and attitudes impact one's economic prospects has led many people to ask what can be done to transform ghetto culture. Slowly more policymakers are recognizing what Loury has been saying all along: Even positive reforms in welfare policies, such as those aimed at "getting the incentives right," though necessary, are insufficient. Public policy changes alone cannot reform behavior; personal transformation requires more than legislative reforms. It requires "holistic ministry"— that is, attention to a person's "whole" being (his/her emotional, physical, mental, and spiritual state).

For many years numerous Christian organizations have conducted holistic ministry and have been remarkably successful in changing people's lives and lifting people out of economic dependency. But the efforts of these RESTORERS have only recently been noticed by policy-makers and opinion-shapers in the broader society. The new consensus doubts whether any welfare program that neglects moral and spiritual issues can offer long-term hope and argues that private organizations, particularly churches and faith-based ministries, must play a greater role in social welfare while the government must reduce its expectations of what it can reasonably achieve through its impersonal and bureaucratic public aid programs.

In sum, in today's welfare reform climate, enthusiasm for faith-based ministries is at an all-time high. Both Governor George Allen of Virginia and Governor John Engler of Michigan have summoned religious leaders and directors of faith-based ministries to welfare reform "summits" to discuss how church and state can work together more fruitfully. In Mississippi Governor Kirk Fordice has implemented a "Faith and Families" project in which churches mentor welfare families and provide them with the emotional support, tough love, practical assistance, and life skills that can help them exit public aid. In our nation's capital, many voices are now advocating increased funding for religious nonprofits.

The federal government already provides some 350 grant programs for social service nonprofits,[6] and most nonprofits receive considerable public sector financing. But some Republican legislators want to go even further. Senators John Ashcroft and Dan Coats have proposed legislation allowing individuals a dollar-for-dollar tax credit for donations made to charities—including religious groups—that serve the poor.

In this new climate, many churches are reconsidering their role in social welfare ministry and acknowledging the need to increase their outreach efforts. A few have been startled into action by talk of governmental cutbacks. More, though, have remembered the biblical call to serve the poor and the exemplary heritage of evangelical church-based social ministry prior to the imposition of the federal welfare state. *Nearly every church that desires to be more involved is asking: How can our church implement an effective, life-transforming mercy ministry among the poor?* This book seeks to answer that question.

Overview of the Book

Restorers of Hope describes and analyzes the work of several effective, biblically committed church-based social welfare ministries from around the country. Part I describes why these ministries (which I call RESTOR-ERS because they rebuild broken lives and broken places) are working. It explains how RESTORERS are overcoming the challenge of the streets and transforming lives by countering ghetto culture with biblical values, by deliberately incorporating evangelism and discipleship into their outreach efforts, and by "enlarging" the world of inner-city residents.

Part II offers some practical "how to" advice, from Christians on the front lines, to churches desiring to start (or strengthen) their own outreach ministries. According to leaders in the religiously based social service sector, many churches are uninvolved in mercy ministries because their diaconal vision has atrophied. Church leaders and lay people must recapture the biblical imperative to serve the poor. Chapter 5 offers some suggestions for reinvigorating a congregation's vision for outreach, as well as some guidelines for designing an outreach strategy faithful to the biblical teaching on mercy ministry. Chapter 6 describes some common barriers to outreach ministry and recommends ways of overcoming them. Chapter 7 examines how churches can make the shift from conventional "commodity-based" social service ministries to more effective relational, long-term ministries. And chapter 8 walks readers through the main steps churches must take to implement life-transforming, holistic ministries in their own communities.

Part III examines the larger context in which churches and faith-based ministries conduct their outreach efforts. Social ministry does not occur in a vacuum; it is affected by existing public policies. Currently, many outside the church (and some inside it) are advocating greater public-private collaboration in social services. Such collaboration offers both potential benefits and potential pitfalls; these are described in chapters 9 and 10. Some intriguing forms of collaboration are already underway in Mississippi, Maryland, and Virginia, and chapter 11 distills from these initiatives some insights for churches (and faith-based ministries) considering whether they should partner with government entities or secular nonprofits.

Who Are the RESTORERS?

While this book draws on examples, testimonies, and experiences of dozens of church-based and parachurch outreach ministries, its main conclusions emerge from my study of seven RESTORERS: Lawndale Community Church in Chicago; Anacostia Gospel Chapel in Washington, D.C.; Rosedale Park Baptist Church in Detroit; Strategies for Elevating People (S.T.E.P.) in Richmond; the Center for Urban Missions (CUM) in Birmingham; Neighborhood Ministries in Phoenix; and Oak Cliff Bible Fellowship in Dallas.

The Settlers. The first two ministries, Lawndale Community Church and Anacostia Gospel Chapel, could be labeled "settlers." They fit the standard model of Christian community development propounded by Dr. John Perkins and the Christian Community Development Association (CCDA).[7] They emphasize reconciliation between the races; relocation of families from other races and classes into a targeted economically depressed neighborhood; and redistribution of economic assets, opportunities, and skills. Staff in these ministries live and work in the communities they serve. They become residents there—"settlers"—and work for the transformation of these neighborhoods from the inside out. Both the Lawndale and Anacostia ministries have planted new churches in their respective neighborhoods, although other churches (which generally were not reaching out to the immediate community) already existed.

Chicago's Lawndale Community Church and its associated ministries is a premier example of Christian community development and one of the jewels of the CCDA. The "Lawndale miracle" began in 1975 when a young white small-towner named Wayne Gordon graduated from a Christian college and started coaching a Lawndale high school's wrestling team. He became the first teacher to move into the Lawndale community. "Coach" Gordon set up weight-lifting machines in a local storefront and began witnessing to his athletes about Christ. The Bible studies he and his wife led for neighborhood youth later blossomed into the Lawndale Community Church (LCC). Today the church is a nondenominational parish of some 300 members; the congregation is roughly 80 percent black and 20 percent white.

Considering the church's humble beginnings, the scope of LCC's outreach in Lawndale is astounding. Affiliated with the church are an economic development corporation that rehabilitates abandoned properties, builds affordable housing, and provides capital for new business enterprises; a learning center for elementary and middle-school children; a College Opportunity Program for high school students; a Christian medical center serving 4,000 patients each month; and a variety of benevolence efforts, family counseling ministries, substance abuse recovery programs, and job training courses.

Anacostia Gospel Chapel in southeast Washington, D.C., also traces its roots back to the efforts of one specific family called by God to urban ministry. Bob and Sharon Mathieu moved into Anacostia in 1971. "Brother Bob," as he's called, immediately sought out black evangelical leaders in the area, admitted he didn't know much about urban ministry, and asked them what he could do to help. Now, twenty-five years later, families from across Ward 8 (the geopolitical divisions used in Washington, D.C., are "wards") come to him for counsel and aid.

Back in 1973, when the Mathieus were first getting started, they established "Camp Dynamite," a summer camp program that now serves 300 D.C. youth annually. Later they began holding church services in their garage. Eleven years ago they moved their Anacostia Gospel Chapel to a modest meeting space in the community rooms of a red brick apartment building on Alabama Avenue S.E. Today seventy to eighty parishioners regularly attend the charismatic worship services. Two floors above the "sanctuary," about twenty neighborhood kids attend after-school tutoring sessions in the church's learning center. Brother Bob advises more children in his office at Ward 8's Terrell Elementary School, and he and his associate, lay minister Tony Yates, counsel drug-addicted adults, frazzled single moms, and troubled teens.

Though Anacostia's staff, budget, and facilities are far more modest than Lawndale's, its philosophy of ministry is the same—target a well-defined geographic area plagued with violence and drugs and discover and nurture its hidden assets. Both ministries reach out to whole families, not just to children; both seek cordial, cooperative relations with local school officials; both emphasize education; and both see the church as the core of their outreach efforts.

The Gardeners. Richmond's S.T.E.P. ministry, Birmingham's Center for Urban Missions, and Detroit's Rosedale Park Baptist Church could all be labeled "gardeners." These ministries view the neighborhoods they have targeted for outreach as extensions of their own churches (spiritual homes), in the same way that homeowners view their gardens as an extension of their houses. Some of the staff members and volunteers in these ministries actually live in the communities they serve, but most do not. All participants in the outreaches, though, have a deep sense of commitment to, and "ownership" of, the targeted neighborhoods; they want to share the burdens of the residents in these overgrown "gardens." They lovingly work alongside native gardeners—community leaders who heretofore lacked outside support—planting new seeds of hope, nurturing young lives, and combating the elements that would destroy and despoil the fruits of everyone's labors. Moreover, they introduce additional tools and "fertilizers," in the form of material resources and connections to job and educational opportunities, from outside into the targeted community.

In S.T.E.P.'s case, the garden—the targeted community—is across town. S.T.E.P. mobilizes suburban churches in Richmond to support the families living in Gilpin Court (a public housing development) and people attending Victory Christian Fellowship, an inner-city church in the heart of the Gilpin neighborhood. Richmond's S.T.E.P. began when a small group of suburban Christians and a few leaders from Victory Christian Fellowship decided to come together to design ways to serve each other and support those individuals (school officials, social workers, etc.) working for Gilpin Court's betterment. S.T.E.P. organized a tutoring center and a reading program; it also helped to refurbish a large community center, where Victory Christian Fellowship now holds services. S.T.E.P. encouraged racial reconciliation by organizing Family Friendship Teams composed of families from the white suburban congregations and families from the African-American Victory Christian Fellowship.

A few years ago, the ministry founded the S.T.E.P. Academy, a holistic educational outreach to Gilpin residents who wish to pursue either their GED or a community college degree. The Academy operates from 8:30 to midafternoon daily, and fifty-one students are currently enrolled. The curriculum includes a morning motivational /devotional talk; several hours of instruction in English, math, science, and history; and various discussion-oriented sessions on life skills and "values and personal growth." Students receive personalized tutoring and can join a weekly noon Bible study. As will be described later in the book, each student can also request to be linked with a "Family Share Team," a small group of Christian volunteers who meet regularly to encourage the student.

In Birmingham the garden—Metropolitan Gardens housing project—is just a few blocks away from the church. The Center for Urban Missions and its church affiliate, the New City Church, serves the 3,000 families in the housing complex through its Family Care Center. The Center offers numerous after-school and evening activities. About 60 children participate daily in after-school academic enhancement and creative arts programs, and over 150 enroll in the Center's eight-week summer day camp. Adults can also receive tutoring through the Center or hone their computer skills in the Center's computer lab.

Each Tuesday families can attend the Family Support Network. A staff member from the Family Care Center offers a biblically based lesson for parents on a relevant topic (e.g., child-rearing, dealing with stress, self-esteem) while the parents' children meet separately for their own program. Then the families join together for an evening meal.

All of the Center's programs are implemented by the Community Leadership Team, a group of Metropolitan Gardens residents (and ex-residents) who work alongside CUM staff. Team members receive modest stipends for their labors and must commit themselves to personal five-year plans for getting off public assistance. The Center also runs weekly junior and senior high school Bible studies as well as a special Scholars Club program through which aspiring youngsters can earn scholarships to private schools.

In Detroit Rosedale Park Baptist Church's garden is located literally in its own backyard; the church sits adjacent to a public housing development called the Smith Homes. Rosedale reaches out in a variety of ways. Men from the church coordinate sports leagues in which Smith Homes teens participate. Teens also participate in Rosedale's youth group, while younger children are enrolled in Sunday school classes and evening tutoring programs. One church member relocated into the Smith Homes and runs a weekly Bible club for about thirty neighborhood children; she also makes numerous home visits to encourage and advise parents. The church's women's group also sponsors special evangelistically oriented events for the young mothers in the Smith Homes. The church's counseling program offers free Bible-based counseling to neighborhood residents struggling to overcome, among other things, previous physical or sexual abuse, family problems, the stress of unemployment, and drug and alcohol addictions. In addition to these ministries, Rosedale's Pastor Hamon Cross has dreams of establishing a multifaceted Christian Family Center in the neighborhood.

The Shepherds. Neighborhood Ministries in Phoenix and the outreach center of Oak Cliff Bible Fellowship in Dallas could be labeled "shepherds." These ministries primarily serve one targeted population (poor Latino children and the working poor, respectively) rather than a specific geographic neighborhood. Neighborhood Ministries uses its old buses to travel about the city picking up children enrolled in its twice-weekly programs and summer camp. Oak Cliff's Alternative Adult Education Center draws adults from across Dallas's south side who are looking to improve their educational and job skills. Both ministries gather people together to provide them with "pasture"—places of refuge, nurture, and instruction.

Neighborhood Ministries (NM), like Anacostia Gospel Chapel, operates on a modest budget with very few paid staff. Open Door Fellowship, the church that sponsors NM, provides most of the NM volunteers. Open Door Fellowship is a nondenominational congregation of approximately 1,000 members, which has long been characterized by a commitment to cross-cultural ministry at home and abroad. Some suburban congregations are also actively engaged in NM's efforts, providing both financial support and volunteers. NM operates an after-school learning center called LifeShop, cooperates with the evangelical student ministry Young Life in reaching out to young Latino gang members, runs a food pantry and clothing closet to serve poor Latino families, and has helped to plant a Spanish-speaking church just across the street from Open Door Fellowship. NM is also in the process of establishing a small Christian medical clinic.

Oak Cliff Bible Fellowship is a large, primarily black, middle class congregation. Its Outreach Center is but one facet of Oak Cliff's community ministry; the church is closely affiliated with The Urban Alternative, a large-scale community development association that works throughout Dallas in the areas of youth ministry, economic and business development, mentoring, and family services. In this book, I focus only on the programs of the Outreach Center. These include the Adult Alternative Education Center mentioned earlier, as well as a job-matching service, counseling program, and a benevolence ministry that addresses people's short-term financial and material needs.

These seven RESTORERS differ in their size, diversity of activities, form, and location. One is a multimillion dollar ministry, most of the others have middle range budgets, and a couple operate just above the red. Some have been around for more than two decades; others are younger. Many focus on families on welfare; a few concentrate primarily on the working poor. Some are nondenominational, some denominational. Some of the RESTORERS' sponsoring churches are large, some small, some urban, some suburban.

Despite this diversity, these RESTORERS share a commitment to "distinctively Christian" mercy ministry; that is, ministry that emphasizes God's love in word (proclamation, evangelism, discipleship) and deed (meeting people's physical, social, and emotional needs). Though many of the RESTORERS focus on children, all are committed to being "whole family" ministries that aggressively reach out to parents as well as kids. All are solidly evangelical and orthodox in their theology. All believe that poverty is ultimately rooted in sin—both personal sin (i.e., moral failings) as well as social sin (i.e., institutional greed, racism, and materialism). And all believe that outreach to the poor and needy is not only a matter of obedience to Scripture, but also a necessary component of spiritual growth. In other words, they believe that they need the poor as much as the poor need them: They assert that their own spiritual health is impoverished if they are not entangling their lives with the lives of others different from themselves.

And Finally, a Word to the Readers

A friend recently told me of a sermon she'd heard in which the pastor confessed how difficult it was to preach to a diverse audience. Looking out at his flock, the minister said that he knew there were some pew-sitters out there who felt they were "pretty good Joes;" these folks lacked an adequate appreciation of their own capacity for sin and of God's immeasurable and awesome holiness. To counter these insufficiencies, these "pretty good Joes" needed a hard-edged sermon from time to time on God's holiness and humanity's depravity.

On the other hand, the preacher continued, other people in the church body had a tendency to be almost too conscious of their sin, and, as a result, they wallowed frequently in guilt and despair. These sheep needed to hear repeatedly the Gentle Shepherd's gospel of grace. According to this pastor, if he were to preach too frequently on either grace or holiness, he'd run the risk of frustrating the spiritual pilgrimage of either one or the other of these two groups.

To some degree, I've felt a similar dilemma as I've written this book. On the one hand, some readers will be go-getters, optimists, eager and ready to take on the challenge of initiating new church-based ministries among the poor. While such enthusiasm is laudable, it can be dangerous—especially if it is not wedded to a sober understanding of the challenges of mercy ministry. Being a RESTORER is long, hard work that requires tremendous patience and perseverance. I want those readers with an eager disposition to see clearly the difficulties that await them as they pursue their vision for urban outreach.

On the other hand, if I overemphasize the challenges of reaching out to the needy, I run the risk of dissuading those readers who already approach the topic of urban outreach with serious hesitation and pessimism. Some readers know all too well the difficulties of ministering to the poor and needy, and the persistence and time that are required to help transform people's lives. These readers may be too willing to give up before they've even gotten started! These pessimists need to hear a message of encouragement; they need to understand that people similar to themselves and churches like their own have made genuine progress in restoring broken lives and broken communities.

I don't know whether I've achieved the right balance between encouragement and sobriety in this book. You, the reader, know on which end of the spectrum you fall. So I ask that you pay special attention to those sections in this book that challenge you the most.

Every writer creates out of his/her unique experience, and I am no exception. I have written this book as an observer of—and a participant in—ministry among the poor. This dual perspective has helped me to appreciate both extremes of the encouragement/sobriety spectrum. When I return from a site visit in, for example, Birmingham or Chicago, I am often brimming with enthusiasm for what God has accomplished through willing Christians. Friends often ask me whether all my travels to our nation's ghettos have been depressing. For the most part, they have not. The light of hope that shines forth from the RESTORERS is so bright that it drives back the inner city's darkness of pain and despair. Walking around the section of North Lawndale where the Lawndale Community Church is located, I have the feeling that absolutely anything is possible. Reality checks in, though, several blocks north of Ogden Avenue. Here I'm overwhelmed by the number of abandoned buildings, and I'm a little frightened by the gangs of insolent young men hanging out on the street corners, dealing drugs. But as long as I'm near the church, where the evidence of restoration is so prominent, my optimism soars.

That boundless confidence sinks a bit when I visit Blue Ridge Commons, a low-income apartment complex in my hometown of Charlottesville, Virginia. Here I can only see the need for restoration, rather than the evidence of it. Here, instead of being an observer of the great things God has already accomplished, I'm a participant on the front lines. For nearly three years a number of us from my church have gotten together with several Blue Ridge Commons residents in order to pray and work, building relationships and designing plans, sowing vision and recruiting helpers. We don't have big renovated buildings to show for our efforts; we can't yet boast about the numbers of teens we've helped to attend college; we haven't posted photographs of women who have gone from crack addiction to wholeness in God's love or from welfare to full employment. The drug dealers still guard their turf at the complex's entrance; the truants loiter in the stairwells; and many single moms remain behind closed doors, feeling lonely, fearful, apathetic, frustrated, and hopeless.

Those of us at my church are just beginning to learn how to be RESTORERS, and the road ahead is long and steep. I'm thankful that my visits to Dallas's Oak Cliff Bible Fellowship, Richmond's S.T.E.P. Academy, and Detroit's Rosedale Park Baptist Church have given me a glimpse of what it's like to be farther along the road of urban ministry. RESTORERS in these cities don't claim to have reached the end of the road, of course; their dreams and God's power are too big to tolerate such complacency. But they are an example of progress; they inspire hope.

Sometimes, walking through Blue Ridge Commons, I close my eyes and see the single moms in our job-training program who sit in front of computers, learning marketable skills. I see families from my church and from the neighborhood praying together, laughing together. I see children proudly displaying certificates of accomplishment for completing educational programs. Dreaming about the future, I imagine men in the neighborhood who have found a renewed sense of purpose by establishing their own businesses. I see young men and women resisting peer pressures, staying out of drugs, practicing sexual abstinence, graduating from high school. I see members from my church learning to overcome racial prejudice, practicing a servant lifestyle, humbly receiving as well as giving. I see God's people restoring hope and—most importantly—fostering a spiritual revival. Then my own spirit rallies, and I remember that God is more than able to do in Charlottesville the mighty deeds He has accomplished elsewhere. He is more than able to do His work in your hometown as well.

It's my hope that the examples in this book will speak to readers at many different points on the "restoration road." Some readers are in congregations that have not yet set foot on the road. Others are in congregations that have just begun the journey. Still others are in congregations that may be well on their way, with years of experience in outreach ministry. Even these congregations may benefit from the examples of the RESTORERS profiled in this book.

I pray that we all will have the courage to count the cost of reaching out to the needy in our communities, as well as to exhibit great daring as we visualize the wonders promised by the God of Restoration.

Part One

The Challenge of
the Streets

JoVann Mills, thirty-three, became a single mother when her husband left her after the birth of their second child. This greatly increased the economic pressures on the family, and JoVann moved into subsidized housing in Richmond's Gilpin Court. She receives $347 each month in welfare payments and $319 in food stamps. But her life defies the unflattering stereotype of the "welfare mama" of the projects. Every day JoVann wakes at about 6:00 A.M., gets her children dressed, fed, and off to school; participates in five hours of GED classes in the S.T.E.P. Academy; picks up the kids after school and prepares them dinner; then heads off to work from about 5:30 P.M. to 11:00 P.M. at a janitorial service. She gets home late and catches about five or six hours of sleep before starting the routine anew.

Throughout the six years she has lived in Gilpin Court, JoVann has attended church. Her daily life attests to her willingness to make sacrifices now in order to give her children a brighter future. She's a hard worker, and she instills in her children a desire for a good education. She looks forward to the day when she can exit the welfare system and move out of the projects.

Sharron Corley is a seventeen-year-old resident of Brownsville, a decaying neighborhood in east New York portrayed in the recent book *The Ville: Cops and Kids in Urban America*. Sharron's a "pretty boy," according to the ladies, as well as a talented amateur singer and actor. He and his gang of friends call themselves the "LoLifes." They wear only expensive Ralph Loren "Polo" designer clothes, most of them stolen from department stores downtown. Sharron is consumed with his image and with amassing "props"—material possessions that help earn him "proper respect." He disparages menial labor since it diminishes his reputation on the street. Sharron is largely indifferent to educational achievement. For him, school is a theater for "presenting" himself, his style, his clothes, and his girlfriends. Sharron is not a "gangbanger," has nothing to do with drugs, and in many ways desires to stay straight and pursue his dream of a big-money future as a vocal star. Still, he believes in the "law of the jungle" and takes advantage of those weaker than himself when it suits him.

"Decent" and "Street"

JoVann and Sharron embody two different life orientations common in the ghetto—what residents call "decent" and "street." "Decent" families, explains urban anthropologist Elijah Anderson, "tend to accept mainstream values. . . . They value hard work and self-reliance and are willing to sacrifice for their children."[1] Many go to church, embrace traditional morality, employ strict child-rearing practices, and strongly encourage educational achievement. Many have a vibrant faith in God. They also have some faith in the larger society and believe a better future is possible if one is willing to work hard, persevere under trials, obey God, adopt a positive mental attitude, and be respectful and cooperative. Decent families are forward-looking. They seek to resolve disputes peacefully and eschew violence. They value loyalty to family and to community.

"Street" families, by contrast, shun traditional mainstream virtues and have no faith in the wider society. They "often show a lack of consideration for other people and have a rather superficial sense of family and community," says Anderson.[2] They find it difficult to sacrifice personal desires for the sake of their children's needs. They are narcissistic and exalt personal freedom and self-expression. They are preoccupied with their own survival in a world they believe has shut them out. They expect little and live in the present, having few dreams for the future. And they are disposed to employ physical violence to get their way.

To overcome the challenges of the street, RESTORERS reinforce decent families in distressed neighborhoods, while countering the destructive tenets of street culture. RESTORERS do this effectively because they understand the dynamics of street culture—and the underlying factors that produce it. By contrast, outsiders usually find inner-city horrors—such as teens gunning each other down over a pair of sneakers—utterly incomprehensible because they do not understand what Elijah Anderson calls "the code of the streets." Christians who would be RESTORERS need to comprehend the code and learn how the ministries profiled in this volume are combating the street's destructive values and behaviors.

The Sources and Content of the "Code"

The code of the streets is rooted largely in inner-city residents' profound distrust of the police and criminal justice system. Many low-income urban dwellers believe the police are incapable of providing security or unwilling to do so. Consequently, ghetto residents feel justified in taking extraordinary measures—including deadly violence and revenge—to protect themselves and their families. Anderson writes: "Lack of police accountability has in fact been incorporated into the status system: the person who is believed capable of 'taking care of himself' is accorded a certain deference, which translates into a sense of physical and psychological control. Thus the street code emerges where the influence of the police ends and personal responsibility for one's safety is felt to begin."[3]

In this environment, it is no accident that "respect—loosely defined as being treated 'right' or granted the deference one deserves"—is at the heart of the code.[4] Given inner-city residents' lack of faith in the police, "respect" assumes an exalted status because it is intimately associated with physical survival. "With the right amount of respect," Anderson explains, a person can "avoid 'being bothered' in public."[5] Since respect can deter aggression, being disrespected implies a genuine potential for danger, not simply a temporary personal embarrassment.

Many young people in the inner city view respect as an external quality that is "hard-won but easily lost."[6] Respect is in short supply, they believe; competition for it is considered a zero-sum game. One can lift oneself up only by putting someone else down. "Dissing" (disrespecting) takes several forms—stealing another's possessions or girlfriend, verbally cutting someone down, or physically attacking another person. The code of the streets sets forth rules that help inner-city residents negotiate this intense competition for respect.

In environments outside the "'hood," residents look to the police to provide security. Consequently, they have difficulty understanding how one inner-city teen could shoot another over a designer jacket. But confrontations like this in the ghetto are often really about perceived shifts in the quantities of respect—and hence security—possessed by different people. The teen who shoots the offender sends a clear signal to others that in the future he is "not to be messed with." While this explanation does not justify the teen's action, it does help us to comprehend why the murderer might be convinced that he acted in self-defense.

On the streets disputes are almost always settled violently. The code's tenet that "might makes right" is learned early. Violence in the home, as well as on the street, further reinforces the injunction that "toughness is a virtue, while humility is not."[7] Physical prowess is honored.

The reality of ghetto violence influences child-rearing patterns among both street and decent families. Many parents, even those disdainful of street culture, carefully instill in their children a suspicion of others, warning their kids to "watch their backs" and be ready to fight. Some children are even punished by their parents for being insufficiently aggressive. Parents believe that this is in the child's own best interests: The child must learn to be tough in order to survive.

In the midst of this violence, the code teaches young men to take self-protective actions. These include (among other things) carrying a gun, peddling stolen merchandise (this cultivates one's reputation as a fearless risk-taker who beats the system), and joining a gang or "crew." As Sharron Corley explains in *The Ville*: "If you are nobody and somebody shoots you, then nobody is gonna come back for you. You just go out. Simple. But if you got props, you got respect and you got a crew, people think twice about cappin' you, 'cause then there are people who are comin' back."[8]

Distrust and Alienation. Profound distrust of the police (and the ensuing violent competition for survival) is one source of the street code. An overwhelming sense of alienation from mainstream society is another. Racism, lack of employment opportunities, and poverty have led many inner-city youth to reject mainstream society, or at least these realities have squelched their hopes of one day fully integrating into it. Ghetto youth perceive life in the inner city as totally "other," fundamentally different from mainstream life.

Consequently, they view traditional mainstream values—such as educational achievement, respect for authority, determination to work steadily up the employment ladder—as irrelevant to *their* world. Instead, they exalt alternative values and norms, which they believe fit better with their life on the streets.

As already noted, respect is the ultimate value in this oppositional culture. Consequently, anything contributing to one's accumulation of respect is highly prized. Physical appearance—including clothes, jewelry, and grooming—"plays an important part in how a person is viewed," says anthropologist Anderson. "To be respected, it is important to have the right look."[9] As a result, street-oriented youth eagerly amass "props"—things that earn them proper respect. Props include possessions that visibly demonstrate the right image, as well as unique experiences, sexual conquests, or a reputation as a successful con man.

Street youth also work hard at presenting themselves in ways that inhibit others from "dissing" them. Their facial expressions, gait, and style of speech must all indicate a predisposition towards violence—a "don't mess with me" attitude. Owning and flaunting valuable, coveted goods—leather jackets, fancy jewelry, guns, designer clothes—is also important, as this reveals one's willingness "to possess things that may require defending."[10]

Sharron Corley's actions as described in *The Ville* clearly illustrate these oppositional values. Sharron is completely self-absorbed in his appearance. He showers with the door adjusted so that he can view himself in the mirror. He hangs large posters of himself on his bedroom walls. He carefully selects designer clothes to give to his girlfriend, since her appearance reflects on his own.

In addition, Sharron painstakingly cultivates his reputation on the street. He quickly quits his summer job bagging groceries when he realizes it threatens his image. He spends the first seventy-five dollars he earns from another job on a beeper, in part because it makes him look like a drug dealer. Sharron and his friends "have nothing to do with drugs," author Greg Donaldson reports in *The Ville*, "yet they don't seek to dispel the impression that they do, because dealers have props, and they 'get paid.'"[11]

Sharron also defends his image and reputation (and the security they purchase) fearlessly and incessantly. An anecdote from *The Ville* captures this well. Sharron is robbed of an expensive leather jacket he had recently shoplifted. When Sharron sees the perpetrators the following day, he responds to the earlier "dissing" by running to get his gun. Donaldson relates: "[H]e charged outside, lest it be said by anyone watching—and it is axiomatic for Sharron that people are watching—that he abandoned his spot on the corner at the sight of the two thieves."[12]

It is "axiomatic" for Sharron that people are watching because the zero-sum nature of the struggle for respect requires that everyone keep abreast of exactly where everyone stands in relationship to others. The security youth seek, which is dependent upon cultivating the right image and winning others' respect, proves elusive due to this constant nerve-wracking competition.

Fatal Materialism. A third source—this one from outside the ghetto—also undergirds the code of the streets. It is the media's constant proclamation of American society's "consumerist gospel": health, happiness, and status through material possessions. The pervasive low sense of self-worth felt by many ghetto residents makes them even more vulnerable to this message. And they are exposed to it unceasingly. As longtime community development activist John Perkins laments, "Even the poorest of the poor have access to TV, and they watch more TV than anyone."[13] Donaldson confirms this in his own research in Sharron's neighborhood:

> The teenagers [in Brownsville] are undereducated in most things, but they are connoisseurs of pop culture, ready receptacles for the jingles and scattershot imagery of television. Their speech is drenched in the verbal flotsam of television shows. The police are called Five-O's after *Hawaii Five-O*. They know the stars of the soaps and sitcoms as well as they know their neighbors. Brand names tyrannize the classrooms; prestige cars are worshiped.[14]

Kit Danley, executive director of Neighborhood Ministries in Phoenix, believes that harsh inner-city realities make consumerism's siren song more plausible to residents in the 'hood than it might be to people outside. Ghetto youth prize material possessions, she says, because these possessions make the kids feel valuable. They have had little experience of beauty in their home life and little love to make them feel good about themselves. Consequently, she argues, kids easily equate owning valuable things with being a worthwhile person. Such thinking is then reinforced repeatedly by the media.

Donaldson goes so far as to argue that consumerism has trumped every other path to meaning, significance, and identity in the ghetto. In *The Ville*'s most bracing passage, he asserts: "The world Sharron travels in is pure consumer culture; the LoLifes are more an outlaw consumer group than a gang. . . . The young black men of Brownsville indict society by their total belief in it. They trust what they have been told about image, status, competition, hierarchy, and the primacy of self-gratification. Their faith is lethal, mostly to themselves."[15]

Is it possible that inner-city youth, believing they are shut out from genuine participation in mainstream society (as exemplified by attending good colleges or obtaining promising jobs), seek a form of societal participation as pure consumers? Perhaps young people who feel inferior because they cannot seem to access opportunities in the wider society comfort themselves with the idea that they are "just as good" as the people outside the ghetto because they buy, use, and wear the same products.

Certainly, inner-city residents like Sharron Corley are not alone in their materialistic ways. Consumerism is a shared disease, characterizing mainstream America just as much as the "Other America." The difference is that the disease's effects are amplified in the ghetto. The inner city's isolation and alienation drown out voices that could engender skepticism towards the nihilism vigorously promoted in popular culture. Many mainstream Americans have an idolatrous faith in materialism, but it is tempered by opportunities (educationally and vocationally) to build their identities on something other than their possessions or appearance. While they too are consumers, they have the option to become more than *mere* consumers.

By contrast, many inner-city residents like Sharron cannot or will not access such opportunities. Consequently, "meaning" gets hollowed out of their world and replaced with "image." In this shrunken existence, kids literally kill each other for gold chains and leather jackets.

While materialism is dangerous for all people, Donaldson is right: It can be fatal in the ghetto.

The Problem of Dependency

Street culture is not only characterized by the code and oppositional values. It is marked as well by a culture of dependency. In recent years individuals from across the political spectrum have acknowledged that the welfare system has contributed to the development of dependency and an entitlement mentality. Not all welfare recipients stay on aid long term, but a significant minority experience multigenerational dependency. Welfare as a lifestyle—not desiring anything else nor believing alternate ways of living are possible—has become normal for some households. Welfare has, in the words of Rev. Gerald Austin of Birmingham's Center for Urban Missions, helped some people to "make peace with poverty."

Prior to the 1996 federal reforms, public assistance provided recipients with their basic needs—food, shelter, medical care—but gave little if any incentive for exiting welfare. Indeed, as such critics as Charles Murray and Robert Rector have argued, the old welfare rules actually discouraged marriage, responsible childbearing, work, and saving.[16]

Research scholars are not the only ones persuaded that the welfare system encouraged dependency. Inner-city residents themselves acknowledge some obvious flaws in public aid policies. Clarissa Crews, a resident of Richmond's Gilpin Court and a participant in the S.T.E.P. program, says the welfare system has created a situation wherein "half the women in Gilpin have the mentality: 'This is all I want.'" Crews declares, "They've made peace with the system. [They say] 'Give me my check, give me my food stamps, give me my Medicaid. I'm not gonna work.'"

The rise of "rights talk" in American society is reflected in the entitlement mentality of some (*some*, not all) recipients of public assistance. These individuals view aid as just remuneration for historical oppression or present discrimination. This mind-set, of course, inhibits any motivation for exiting the system. "They think somebody owes them something," laments Mary Jackson, an African-American church worker who relocated to the projects in west Detroit. And when a woman views the welfare check as "due" her, Jackson asserts, she has little reason actively to seek alternative ways of earning a living. Thus, dependency on the system becomes ever more entrenched.

Concentration Effects

The ghetto's oppositional culture is further fortified by what sociologist William Julius Wilson calls "concentration effects." In his important book about urban America, *The Truly Disadvantaged,* he explains, "The social transformation of the inner city has resulted in a disproportionate concentration of the most disadvantaged segments of the urban black population, creating a social milieu significantly different from the environment that existed in these communities several decades ago."[17]

In other words, urban neighborhoods that formerly included families from varying economic classes are now home only to the poorest and most disadvantaged. This social transformation was, ironically and sadly, one of the unintended consequences of the otherwise positive civil rights reforms. Antidiscrimination measures in housing opened up new residential areas for Blacks. Better-off families left their old inner-city neighborhoods for greener pastures, leaving the poorest families behind.

Other reforms also influenced this social transformation. In his book *Hardball: A Season in the Projects,* Daniel Coyle describes the decline of Chicago's Cabrini-Green community. When the red-brick row houses were first constructed there in the 1940s, the neighborhood was integrated, and "applicants were carefully screened to ensure two-parent, one-wage-earner households. Unseemly behavior such as littering or walking on the grass was punishable by fine."[18] Throughout the 1950s two supermarkets, a department store, a restaurant, and a bank were established in the neighborhood.

In the late 1960s, though, a combination of racial tensions, mismanagement and corruption by city housing authorities, well-intentioned but problematic legal reforms, and governmental intervention initiated the community's breakdown. The Chicago rioting and fires following the assassination of Martin Luther King, Jr., left large numbers of Blacks homeless. Many—even those with known gang affiliations—were quickly moved into available units in Cabrini-Green. Lawsuits by the ACLU crippled the housing authorities' ability to screen potential tenants. Then a 1969 congressional act fixing tenants' rent at 25 percent of their income drove working-class families out of the projects into cheaper housing in the private sector.[19] By the 1970s, snipers from rival gangs were shooting each other—and innocent bystanders—from the rooftops of the complex's drab high-rises. Cabrini-Green became a national symbol of urban decay.

Today many people in the inner city strive to follow the so-called decent path. But their ability to challenge street culture is limited. They are under siege, threatened by drug dealers, gangbangers, and addicts, and surrounded by a disproportionate number of the chronically unemployed or underemployed, school dropouts, pregnant teens, single-parent households, and families fully dependent on public assistance. The concentration of dysfunctional families in the inner city means that concepts like marriage, work, and fatherhood lose plausibility. In inner cities across America, as Richard John Neuhaus has written, "millions of children do not know, and will never know, what it means to have a father. More poignantly, they do not know what a father is. They do not know anyone who has a father or is a father."[20]

This is because ghettos are not only demographically homogeneous, but also demographically isolated: Nonpoor people from outside the inner city rarely enter in. New York's middle class subway riders don't cross over 96th Street into Mott Haven, the dismal and disadvantaged South Bronx community Jonathan Kozol writes about in his recent book *Amazing Grace.*[21] Taxi drivers won't answers calls from residents of Cabrini-Green. As one journalist explained, "Chicagoans routinely detour for blocks rather than drive through [Cabrini-Green]."[22] In small towns, too, the "bad neighborhoods" are isolated. In my own hometown of Charlottesville, Virginia, a modest city of about 40,000 residents, pizza deliverers won't enter Blue Ridge Commons because of frequent shootings there.

Overcoming the Challenge of the Streets

The multifaceted challenges of the street are daunting. Over the last thirty years, governmental attempts to win the War on Poverty have produced only a limited number of sustainable victories. But there is hope for the city, because some efforts *are* working. RESTORERS are successfully transforming lives and neighborhoods in urban America. Why are their strategies successful when so many other efforts have failed? The following three chapters seek to answer that question.

Transforming Culture

RESTORERS are effective because they accurately diagnose the ills of the inner city. They understand the influences inside and outside the ghetto that contribute to and sustain those ills. They avoid the pitfalls of seeing urban poverty as rooted exclusively in behavioral factors or exclusively in environmental factors. Their prescriptions, therefore, are inclusive: They neither preach without addressing material needs nor give bread without proclaiming truth and hope. They challenge the behavior and worldview spawned by the code of the streets, and they address the structural problems—high crime, high unemployment, limited affordable housing, poor schools—that contribute to the persistence of poverty. They do not impose cures from a distance; instead, they get up close and personal with the people they seek to serve. They include these people in the design, implementation, and evaluation of potential solutions. And they deal with people, in the words of Glenn Loury's most recent book, "one by one from the inside out."[1]

This chapter examines the general strategy employed by RESTORERS to transform inner-city culture by countering street orientation and the dependency mind-set. The following two chapters look more specifically at RESTORERS' efforts to address the personal and environmental factors underlying street orientation.

Tackling Street Culture

To counter street culture, RESTORERS reinforce decent culture in at least four ways: They strengthen families; they shore up neighborhood schools; they expose the myths of the consumerist gospel; and they break through the demographic isolation of the ghetto. To counter the problem of chronic dependency, RESTORERS engage in what Rev. Gerald Austin calls "responsible caring." Basically, this means challenging the entitlement mind-set and helping the needy in ways that promote self-sufficiency.

Strengthening "Decent" Families. RESTORERS know that there are more decent families in the ghetto than there are street families. Strengthening these embattled decent families is central to their work.

In Washington, D.C., members of the Anacostia Gospel Chapel testify to the ways the church and its outreach ministries have bolstered them. Evandalene Dorsey started attending the church eleven years ago. Recently divorced, she was looking for support in raising her three daughters and was attracted to the church's emphasis on children. "As a single parent, I've not had the daddy there to reinforce what I teach at home," Dorsey says. "I've depended on the consistency of the teaching here at church—that's been my real backup at home."

Single mother Joyce Peebles agrees. She says the church's pastor, "Brother Bob" Mathieu, has been a substitute father for her girls. He mediates disputes between the teens and their mom, accompanies the girls to job and school interviews, and exults in their academic achievements. Each year the church throws an extravagant graduation banquet to honor students completing high school. In light of the pressure common in the 'hood against scholastic achievement and ambition, church leaders believe it is imperative to reinforce decent parents' pro-education messages to their children.

Tenth grade student Wayne Keys says that Anacostia Gospel Chapel reinforces parental counsel in additional ways. Keys admits that he was running with "the bad crowd" before he got involved in the church. He hung out with older guys who drank a lot. "With them, girls were pieces of meat," Keys reports. "Now I see them as young ladies. My mom taught me that difference," he continues, "but I never really put it into effect until I got into the church."

In Birmingham parents involved with the Center for Urban Missions praise the ministry for helping them rear their kids. CUM's Family Support Network, says Delois Walker, "helps you learn to be a better parent." Her three children are enrolled in programs at the Family Care Center. She reports that she has benefited from CUM's teaching on appropriate discipline techniques. She also finds the opportunity to get together with other parents encouraging. "We talk about problems that you may feel you can't talk about," Delois says, "but then you find out that someone else has that problem [too]. So we help each other find the solution."

CUM's children's Bible classes have also strengthened her family, Delois adds. "I have seen a big change with my kids. I used to have a harder time disciplining them, but now it's not so difficult." She says her kids enjoy learning about the Bible: "They are really being inspired by that. Where we live at, it's hard to have an uplifting attitude." Like many other single moms, Delois is especially grateful for the male role models the ministry provides for her children. "[My children] have plenty of role models to talk to [at CUM]. That's good, because I might not have the answer to everything, and maybe someone [here] will have some answers. It's good to know that [my kids] can go to someone that I can trust, who will tell them the truth," Delois says. "It's a very caring place."

Bolstering Neighborhood Schools. In cities across the nation, RESTORERS are shoring up local schools as well as strengthening families. Linda Moody, president of the Washington, D.C., Board of Education, reports that a number of schoolteachers in the southeast district come from the Anacostia Gospel Chapel (including Rev. Mathieu's own adult son and daughter). And Mathieu himself has an office inside the Terrell Elementary School where he can offer one-on-one advice and encouragement. Moreover, Moody says Brother Bob and other preachers like him reinforce the "values education" program that the D.C. school district inaugurated a few years ago. The program aims to build character among the students. "There's little training in the household as far as values are concerned," remarks Moody. Since the schools can't do this job alone, Moody believes preachers like Brother Bob help tremendously by teaching young people old-fashioned morality.

Mallory Coats, principal of Phillips High School in Birmingham, applauds the Center for Urban Missions for the enthusiasm it generates for educational achievement. Coats says he witnesses daily the positive effects of CUM's work. "I see students in their program who are doing better [in school]. I see more visits to the school by parents involved in their programs—parents who perhaps otherwise I would not have seen."

Hector Placencia, principal of Kenilworth Elementary School in Phoenix, has praise for the help Neighborhood Ministries provides his school. He explains that many of the low-income Latino children at Kenilworth bounce around from one dilapidated, insecure rental unit to another, and that this mobility "brings with it tremendous social needs." Placencia emphasizes that "although we are here to educate the mind, there's a lot to the rest of the body that needs to be looked at. Sometimes I feel like I'm just putting a little Band Aid on a big wound." He says regretfully, "You can't feed the mind if the kids are bleeding or if you can't stop the hurt and pain they come to school with."

Consequently, Placencia credits Neighborhood Ministries for accomplishing many things that need doing, things the school has no resources to do. He mentions, for instance, the church's counseling and referral services as well as the ministry's food and clothing drives for Kenilworth children and their families. And he says that Neighborhood Ministries director Kit Danley often is able to share useful information about the students and their families, because she and

Neighborhood Ministries volunteers visit the students' homes and are in frequent contact with the children outside of school.

Countering Consumerism. RESTORERS also intentionally challenge the false promises of materialism sung regularly on T.V. and educate participants in their programs to be wise consumers. For example, Oak Cliff Bible Fellowship's job-readiness training course, called "KEYS to Personal and Professional Success," includes classes on personal money management. Instructor Jim Talley reports that he not only shares basic budgeting tips, but also tries to help the students eschew the "wantitis"—want this, want that—mentality. Talley is also developing a more in-depth curriculum on personal finances designed specifically for families making the transition from welfare to work. His aim is to help families unlearn what they've picked up from the media.

"They've been taught that you just live for today," Talley laments. "The media has duped us into believing that if you want it, if it makes you feel good, go ahead and get it, and don't think about what's going to happen next week." He cites an advertisement for a furniture rental company that calls itself Rentco—"The Go Ahead and Get It Store." Such companies make their customers believe they can have whatever they want with no problems, Talley says. Meanwhile, customers do not realize that they will pay far more to rent the furniture at the "low weekly rates" than they would if they saved and bought the furniture outright. And they fail to see the consequences of spending money on furniture rental while other bills may be more pressing. The company's sales strategy appeals to the human desire for instant gratification. So Talley's goal is to equip students to withstand the temptations of living for the moment and to reject the false notion that material things will bring happiness.

RESTORERS also vigorously counter the consumerist message of "you are what you wear." Birmingham's CUM insists that the children in their summer camp wear uniforms donated by local businesses. This not only promotes group identity but relieves children of the pressure they often feel from peers to wear a different expensive athletic suit every day. Finally, as is discussed in greater detail in chapter 3, RESTOR-ERS help young people build their self-esteem on the solid foundation of God's love rather than on their appearance or possessions.

Overcoming Concentration Effects. RESTORERS in Chicago, Detroit, Dallas, and other cities are overcoming the demographic iso-lation of the ghetto by relocating Christians of other races and socio-economic backgrounds into impoverished communities. This increases the number of families in the neighborhood pursuing a decent life-orientation and encourages community residents who long felt alone in their struggles against the forces of the street. The reloca-tion strategy also helps to make concepts such as marriage, fatherhood, and work more common and more plausible in the ghetto.

On the southwest side of Chicago, the Lawndale Community Church has recruited a number of white and black middle class fami-lies to make their homes in the Lawndale neighborhood. Rev. Carey Casey, the church's African-American co-pastor, remembers talking with some local kids after he and his wife moved into the area a couple years ago. "We came out of the house and were talking to some little children," Casey recalls. "They asked my wife, 'What's this ring on your finger?' And my wife said, 'That's my wedding ring. I'm married to Pastor Casey.' And they said, 'You're *married*? He's your *husband*?' It was as though we'd told them we'd come from the moon."

Ann Gordon, wife of Lawndale Church's co-pastor Wayne Gordon, tells similar stories. "One woman who is about our age . . . who grew up in the neighborhood came to our house one night at dinner-time. When she knocked on the door, we were all sitting around the dinner table eating, and she said, 'Do you all do this every night?' It was such a weird thing to her. It seemed to her like a big event, whereas to us it was just part of family life and very normal."

Because church families are now sprinkled throughout the Lawndale neighborhood, local kids are seeing far more daddies getting up every morning and catching the bus or train to work. They're seeing families sitting down together for the evening meal. They're seeing homeowners caring for their houses and lawns. According to church staff, this visible witness of simply living "normal" lives is just as important as the church's multiple education and job-training programs.

William Little, a recent college graduate who returned to his home in Lawndale to work with the church's community development corporation, remembers the influence of Pastor Gordon's "alternative role models." Little's uncle and cousins "hung out" with Gordon (who's called Coach). These guys were Little's heroes. "It was cool to play ball, to be in Bible studies, to be with Coach," Little recalls. "That was cool and I wanted to be like those guys." Back then Coach Gordon's bunch provided an alternative to the gangs; today the church continues to offer a place to belong and a different set of values to live by.

RESTORERS who do not pursue a relocation strategy but, nevertheless, do acknowledge the importance of overcoming the ghetto's demographic isolation design alternative ways of bringing inner-city and suburban residents together. In Richmond the S.T.E.P. Academy accomplishes this through its innovative "Family Share Teams." The Teams are composed of three to six Christians from suburban churches who are paired with one inner-city woman enrolled in S.T.E.P.'s GED training and college support programs. Family Share Teams meet twice monthly in order to develop a friendship with the student and her family. These cross-racial, cross-class friendships bring people together who might otherwise never have met.

Pastor Harold Wilson, Jr., of Victory Christian Fellowship (S.T.E.P.'s local urban church partner) struggles to articulate some of the many intangible benefits of the Share Team friendships. "There's just something about a student living here in Gilpin Court knowing that there's a woman way out in the West End suburbs, from an entirely different lifestyle, who cares for her and has a genuine interest in her," he says. And beyond this, he comments, the relationship can have an indirect socioeconomic payoff. He explains, "The more exposure you get to a wide gamut of people, the more prepared you are to deal with the marketplace at large. It draws you out of your little closed community, brings you into situations where you talk to people of different mindsets, different educational levels, economic levels, and colors of skin. That's good."

Responsible Caring

Besides aggressively combating street culture, RESTORERS also fight the dependency mind-set by refusing to help people in ways that encourage further dependency. CUM founder Gerald Austin explains, "We do not feel that we should be a surrogate welfare program. We must attack that system because it is so destructive." Instead, he argues, "We challenge individuals not to make peace with poverty. Poverty can be overcome if we encourage goal-oriented behavior that is consistent with true self-sufficiency."

CUM and the other RESTORERS encourage such behavior with incentive-based programming throughout their ministries. Each student enrolled in CUM's programs at the Family Care Center, for example, is given a CUM "Metro Economy" bank account. Through good behavior, regular attendance, and academic achievement, students earn "Metro bucks" that can be spent in the Center's "Metro store." Suburban churches supporting CUM provide goods for the store, which sells everything from candy and gum to sports equipment, clothing, and Barbie dolls. Students can also save and earn 10 percent interest on their Metro bucks by leaving them in the "Metro bank." A minimum number of Metro bucks are required for a student to be eligible for entrance to CUM's coveted summer camp. Students thus have a variety of incentives to earn Metro bucks. The system encourages good behavior as well: Kids are assessed "Metro taxes" if they break the Center's rules.

CUM's incentive-based programming also shapes the Center's relationship with the parents of students. Not only do children need to earn a minimum number of Metro bucks in order to gain admission to the summer camp, but their parents also have to work a certain number of volunteer hours throughout the academic year. Parental involvement is also expected in CUM's various educational programs. For example, kids can apply through CUM for scholarships to attend private schools, but parents must provide $500 of the tuition each year.

Outside observers as well as program participants recognize that this incentive-based approach distinguishes CUM from state agencies. Principal Mallory Coats reports that other organizations working in the ghetto have a "social work" mind-set that gives freely but expects nothing in return. CUM makes the youths work for what they get, he says, and this avoids creating dependency, discourages an entitlement mind-set, and promotes dignity. By keeping enrollment in the summer camp limited, for example, CUM teaches children that their participation in it is a privilege, not a right. This also helps in maintaining discipline. Kids know that by failing to obey the rules, they risk losing their place in the camp to someone on the waiting list. CUM is also helping families on welfare in Metropolitan Gardens to "realize there is more," asserts Coats. "CUM doesn't let them get comfortable [on welfare]; it pushes people forward and provides them the vehicles to help them out [of the ghetto]."

Metropolitan Gardens Tenants Association president, Louise Shufford, supports CUM's incentive-based approach. She too feels the welfare system has harmed the community by "giving too much." She argues that when the residents do not have to pay their rent, for example, they do not take care of their units. "Anything you have to pay for, you'll take more pride in," she states.

In Chicago, Lawndale Community Church's approach to mercy assistance also reflects "responsible caring" and encourages self-reliance. Instead of giving away food or clothes for free to able-bodied recipients, the church asks such people to work for a short time for what they receive. Those needing a bag of groceries, for example, are asked to spend a little time vacuuming carpets or setting up chairs in the sanctuary. In this way, the ministry treats people with dignity, reminding them that they are capable of earning what they need if they are given the opportunity.

Rosedale Park Baptist Church in Detroit follows a similar approach. Parents from the Smith Homes who want their children enrolled in the church's summer camp program are asked to pay a fifty-dollar registration fee. And from the pulpit at Rosedale and all the RESTORER churches, chronic dependency on welfare (by the able-bodied) is discouraged.

A Two-Pronged Attack

RESTORERS directly confront the symptoms of street culture through a strategy of reinforcing decent culture and caring responsibly, and they also seek to address the underlying personal and environmental factors that sustain the street worldview. The next chapter describes the RESTORERS' focus on reforming individuals' thinking—countering the assumptions that undergird street behaviors with biblical truths. Then chapter 4 explores the ways RESTORERS enlarge ghetto residents' worlds so as to counteract the structural causes of persistent poverty in the inner city.

Reforming Hearts, Renewing Minds, Refreshing Spirits

In 1992 Sheila Anderson had hit rock bottom. She was hopelessly addicted to crack cocaine. She'd sold everything she had—even the beds from under her children—for drug money. She'd been homeless. She'd had her children taken from her. She was selling her body in the back of a car for $10 per "client" so she could buy cheap rocks of crack. She hated herself for all the unfulfilled promises she made to her children.

One night she heard a preacher on the television set. "He said, 'If anyone is miserable and feels like nothing in their life is working out, put your hand on the TV and repeat after me,'" Sheila recalls. "So I put my hand on the TV, and I started praying. I asked Jesus to forgive me of my sins and to come into my life and be Lord of my life."

Afterwards Sheila began losing interest in her old drug buddies. She began thinking more about her children. She got sick of being poor. She quit smoking crack. At night, when the drug's siren song would call her, God gave her the power to resist. She started attending church and heard God tell her to go back to school. Upon the encouragement of friends in the congregation, she joined the S.T.E.P. Academy.

Today Sheila Anderson is in college majoring in early childhood education. She has her children back and has become a pillar in her church—counseling, teaching Sunday school, and evangelizing on the streets. She returns to the S.T.E.P. classroom at the beginning of each new year to share her testimony with the new students. I first heard her in the fall of 1995. She planted herself at the front of the classroom, smiled at the two dozen students, and then began singing in a deep baritone about the power of God to keep her on the narrow road. After telling her story and relating how all of her previous attempts to turn her life around with the help of secular organizations had failed, she concluded with these words:

> What I found [that] was so great about [S.T.E.P.'s] program was that it dealt with problems that are deeper than educational [ones.] I had problems with *me*. I didn't feel good about me. But I got involved in the Bible study, and I got around different women and I didn't feel inferior—they didn't say they were better than me—and I blossomed. So if you're looking to be changed, this is the place to be. Because not only are they going to teach you the educational thing, they are going to teach you about Jesus. At a time like this, we need Jesus, especially when we've tried everything else, and nothing has worked.

Bible-Centered Ministry vs. Postmodern Spirituality

The most basic reason why the RESTORERS are effective is that they lead people to Jesus Christ—the source of salvation and the power for self-transformation. RESTORERS emphasize a reformation of the heart and a renewal of the mind. The spiritual growth they encourage is directed and specific. It is centered on Jesus and the Bible.

These days it's fashionable to assert that successful social programs are those with a "spiritual component." While there is truth to this claim, it is important to note that there is a difference between ministries with a spiritual component and those that are distinctively Christian. RESTORERS do not permit their participants to pursue *any* spiritual journey that might suit their fancy. The spiritual component of RESTORERS' ministries has a definite content that resists the common postmodern credos that "individuals are free to chart their own spiritual journey according to their felt needs" and that "all spiritual journeys are equally valid."[1]

RESTORERS lead people to Jesus, not to a "spiritual encounter." In so doing, they provide people a moral anchor, a transcendent referent by which to judge their choices. RESTORERS encourage people to submit to God's guidelines for healthy, faithful living. Once people do, RESTORERS obtain moral authority and can hold new converts accountable to the objective truths in God's Word. In the typical "spiritually sensitive" postmodern approach, individuals design their own methodology of recovery, believing that the god they have fashioned for themselves will bless their efforts. Such spirituality leaves humans in charge, trusting in their ability to decipher a way out of their predicaments. Postmodern spirituality does not challenge people to conform their behavior to an objective standard of morality; it encourages them to do whatever they *feel* helps them. By contrast, RESTORERS insist that individuals submit to Christ and His ways and then follow Him as He leads them out of their darkness.

True Path to Recovery

The difference between distinctively Christian social ministry and spiritually informed social work is perhaps most pronounced in the efforts to help substance abusers. For example, while twelve-step Alcoholics Anonymous and Narcotics Anonymous groups encourage people to admit their need for a "Higher Power," they do not include a requirement for recovering addicts to forgive those who have hurt them. By contrast, Christian counselors encourage addicts, on the basis of Scripture, to forgive past wrongs. Doing so is often an important element in the addict's recovery.

In addition, the counseling offered by RESTORERS insists that clients take some responsibility for their own healing. This may involve forsaking sinful behaviors. Chaplain Leo Barbee, who runs Lawndale Community Church's substance abuse counseling program, is realistic about the addicts with whom he works. Some are "just sorry; they're not ready to repent. They're sorry about last night, but they're not really ready to give up."

This demand that clients recognize their personal responsibility and repent of their mistakes distinguishes RESTORERS' "tough love" from the therapeutic social work of other organizations. Sabrina Black, director of Rosedale Park Baptist Church's counseling ministries, explains that when clients come to the church for help, "We don't just say, 'Well, just show up for your next appointment, and we'll tell you all the answers.' Instead, we say, 'Go home and work this through and try some new principles. Christ will always do His part, but you need to do some things as well.'" Black reports that her clients receive much more homework in the church's counseling program than they ever received in previous therapy groups.

Moreover, while Rosedale's counselors seek to provide loving care and support to their clients, they also encourage clients to get beyond a victim mentality:

> In other [programs], clients can go into counseling and say, "Well, you know, it was the way my mother reared me," or "It's the system's [fault]," and those types of things are acceptable answers. But [we say], "Yes, you have had a hard life, but now what?" [Our approach] isn't that Let's-get-stuck-in-the-past-and-reanalyze-all-the-things-that-have-ever-happened-to-you. We definitely deal with those things, but still, it's how you respond to them that is the key.

Counselors teach clients how to respond based on biblical principles. They offer support groups for clients dealing with similar problems but argue that "renewing the mind" is the most important key to healing.

Teaching Biblical Values

Rev. LaFayette Holland, Outreach Pastor of Oak Cliff Bible Fellowship in Dallas, agrees. "Getting an individual to think the way God thinks is the key to having an impact. The world has one way of thinking, and the church has an alternative way," he argues. RESTORERS unabashedly present the Bible as the governing rule for life and behavior. They demonstrate how biblical principles apply to every area of daily living. And they offer straight talk from God's Word about three of the biggest obstacles to godly living—sin, self, and sex.

RESTORERS do not deny that environmental factors contribute to the persistence of poverty. Many of their efforts (as will be described in chapter 4) address the structural problems faced by the poor. However, RESTORERS argue that behavioral factors are equally, if not more, important in explaining poverty. Consequently, RESTORERS are not afraid to talk about sin and to exhort individuals to change their behavior.

When I visited the Lawndale Community Church, the bulletin announced that Pastor Carey Casey would preach that night on Psalm 51. Casey titled his sermon: "When You Feel Like a Total Failure Because You Are." That evening Casey acknowledged in prayer: "We know it's a fact that our hearts are wicked apart from Your grace." Other RESTORERS are equally matter of fact. Rev. Anthony Marciano, who directs the Central Union Mission serving homeless men in Washington, D.C., acknowledges candidly: "[Everyone] needs to reckon with their own sinful nature and surrender it, and their life, to Jesus Christ."[2]

In Detroit Pastor Haman Cross's preaching style demonstrates his agreement. "I gotta hurt ya before I can help ya," thundered Cross from the pulpit when I visited Rosedale Park Baptist Church one Sunday. This proclamation foreshadowed the blunt sermon on sin that followed. Cross's church takes sin seriously, exercising church discipline against errant members. Any engaging in sinful activities—such as using drugs or having sex outside of marriage—are visited by church leaders and exhorted to repent. If after three such visits the member remains unrepentant, he or she is barred from taking Communion. If sinners do repent, they may be asked to confess their sins before the congregation.

Some organizations—both secular and religious—that serve the poor bristle at the words *sin* and *repentance*. Father Robert Krueger, priest at St. Andrew's Catholic Church in an impoverished area of Portland, Oregon, argues, "Often it's not [the poor's] behavior that needs changing. What they need is full employment at decent wages."[3] Liberal scholar Jonathon Kozol's analysis of poverty in Mott Haven (a decaying section of South Bronx) reduces the problem of poverty to root causes outside of the neighborhood—lack of compassion by the "haves," racism, and fiscal tight-fistedness by government. He uses the language of sin only to denounce the "principalities and powers" in rich, white America that oppress the poor.[4]

RESTORERS eschew reductionist diagnoses of urban ills that identify the root causes of poverty as exclusively "environmental"—or, for that matter, exclusively "behavioral." At the risk of political incorrectness, they argue that poor people, like *all* people, need moral reformation under God's power. The problem, they explain, is not that poor people are necessarily more sinful than non-poor people. The problem is that sinful behaviors—sex out of wedlock, refusal to work, drug addiction—have consequences that can stimulate, exacerbate, or prolong poverty. In short, RESTORERS are not afraid to make what scholar Glenn Loury calls "hard-edged judgments about decency and personal morality."[5]

True Compassion

Lest it be thought that RESTORERS are self-righteous and coldhearted in berating the poor, let me add quickly that the "hard-edged" judgments they make about others' behavior are no different than the judgments they make about themselves. Here again we see the importance of biblically based rather than merely "spiritually sensitive" approaches to inner-city ministry. In Christian ministry everyone—ministry staff and ministry participant alike—is held to the same standard—God's Word. Sexual sins are not considered more grievous than attitudinal sins of greed or pride. Everyone is treated as equally capable of breaking God's laws—and equally capable of being empowered by God to keep His laws. This biblically based approach enhances rather than degrades the poor. It dignifies them by asserting that they are able to change their behavior.

Unfortunately, in avoiding saying or doing anything that might be construed as "blaming the victim," some organizations engaged in urban ministry never challenge their clients. They worry that to do so would not be "compassionate." This, however, displays a (perhaps unwitting) condescension; it implies that people, like animals, cannot control their behavior. Kozol's book repeatedly exemplifies this false "compassion." One scene he references is a littered park in Mott Haven where drug addicts and prostitutes come to receive free clean needles from (ostensibly well-intentioned) volunteers.

But true compassion doesn't hand out clean needles that enable people to continue in their self-destructive behaviors. True compassion establishes a ministry that befriends the addicts and hookers, invites them to change their lifestyles, provides biblical instruction in a better way to live, and lovingly assists over the long, long transition from homelessness and destitution to self-sufficiency. And true compassion is not a fiction. RESTORERS such as the Detroit Rescue Mission Ministries, the Lawndale Community Church, and Birmingham's Center for Urban Missions are living it out daily.

Teaching Biblical Self-Esteem

RESTORERS don't just talk of human sinfulness. They also vigorously seek to instill in people a healthy sense of self-worth based on God's love for His creatures.

This emphasis on strengthening the self-esteem of inner-city residents is no capitulation to the therapeutic culture that dominates American society. It is a necessary response to the "profound sense of psychological depression, personal worthlessness, and social despair" widespread in the "Other America."[6] Many forces contribute to the pervasive problem of low self-esteem in the ghetto—abuse and neglect, lack of opportunities, and a bleak environment, to name a few. Street culture also contributes to the problems because it defines persons in ways that can degrade or distort. For example, in the street worldview, drug dealers are accorded status, academic achievers are mocked, and women are viewed merely as objects. The media, too, exacerbate the problem by portraying unfair stereotypes of inner-city residents, focusing exclusively on "welfare mamas" or gangbangers or crack addicts, to the neglect of the hardworking and law-abiding citizens.

Effective neighborhood organizations encourage their participants to broaden their self-understanding beyond the stereotypes common on the street and in the media. As Keisha, a young woman in a particularly successful inner-city Girl Scout troop explains, "Outside [on the streets] it's like we're not ladies."[7] Men on the street, according to Keisha, view girls as trophies: "It's like they [are] markin' down how many babies they got and each girl they got pregnant." Inside the Girl Scout troop, though, Keisha and her friends gain a new sense of self-worth "in opposition to the largely negative images fostered by many boys and men." They also begin to see themselves as "givers," by participating in community service projects organized by the troop's leader.[8]

At Rosedale Park Baptist Church, youth minister Dennis Talbert laments how the media tells kids that "their worth is based on what they own. Therefore they go out and buy $500 gym shoes. Take the gym shoes off their feet and they feel like h___. Put the gym shoes on and they feel like God." So Talbert encourages the kids to turn off the TV for a month and to fast during the time they'd otherwise be planted in front of the tube. Consequently, for a short time they avoid exposure to the barrage of image-distorting advertisements. Meanwhile, Talbert teaches the kids Scriptures demonstrating that their self-worth is based on their value in God's sight, not on their possessions.

Dereck Jackson, CUM's director of high school outreach, says that the teenagers with whom he works are "continually bombarded with music that is conducive to immoral activity—drugs, sex, doing as you please, doing what you feel." He notes one song that he particularly dislikes, even though the language in it is cleaner than in most popular songs. For him, the song embodies the street code's mantra of "self-worth through possessions:"

> The singer is saying he has a truck with a hydraulic lift on it, and because he has this, he has it all. This is everything—I pull up in my truck, and people look at me and watch me and see me, and that's what these kids want. They want to be seen, they want to be watched, they want to have it all. And this song is saying that a truck with hydraulics on it is "all." These songs twist and lower the standards, and the standards are already sub-level.

Jackson says that when he argues against this mind-set, the teens are quick to recognize the difference between what the street teaches and what CUM preaches. "They always say, 'The people at CUM is crazy! You don't think like normal folks,'" Jackson reports. But the kids are intrigued and keep coming back. "Some of them are still searching, trying to find their identity," Jackson says. CUM and other RESTORERS are helping youth find their true identity and worth in God's sight.

Outreach staff members at Dallas's Oak Cliff Bible Fellowship emphasize similar teaching. In one class session of "KEYS to Personal and Professional Success," for example, church worker Annie Roberson uses Proverbs 31 to exhort the female students to remember that their worth stems from their inner character, not from their outward appearance or dress.

"Seeing Me as a Person"

Clarissa Crews, a participant in Richmond's S.T.E.P. ministry, reports that the affirmation S.T.E.P. students receive from the staff and volunteers plays a critical role in boosting the students' self-confidence. She herself has benefited from such encouragement. Crews came to Gilpin Court, Richmond's largest public housing project, in the early nineties with her three children after fleeing a drug-dealing husband. In 1992 a medical problem forced her to quit her $4.85/hour job making hats, and she applied for welfare. Later she started volunteering in S.T.E.P.'s tutoring program and joined Victory Christian Fellowship. When tutoring director Ann Green resigned from her position, she offered Crews her job. "I said, 'Uh oh, I can't do this!'" Crews relates. "But Ann pulled me, she pushed me. She didn't see me as some Black woman in the projects that didn't want to change; she looked at me as a person. And that's so important to me and the other students." Crews took the job, and the program flourished.

Similarly, in Detroit Pastor Cross tells his congregants that they can be "winners." This message is music in the ears of parishioners from the Smith Homes, a public housing project next door to the church. "You are always on God's mind," Cross reminds his listeners as he paces across the sanctuary's worn burgundy carpet. Holding up his Bible, Cross plants himself at the top of the center aisle. "There are promises in here that you can believe. You *are* going to make it!"

Countering Promiscuity

In addition to plain talk about sin and the self, RESTORERS maintain what is considered by street youth as a "radical" view of sex. RESTORERS aggressively counter permissive views of sexual behavior and teach biblical norms of chastity and modesty.

Like the problem of materialism, the problem of sexual license is not unique to the inner city. The ghetto environment, though, is characterized by widespread illegitimacy, high rates of teen pregnancy, and the equation of manhood with aggressive—even predatory—sexual behavior. In these conditions, the message of abstinence is difficult to hear.

RESTORERS are confronting the problem of promiscuity head-on. At Anacostia Gospel Chapel, lay minister Tony Yates pulls no punches with the youth group. He gives fire and brimstone sermons, like the one entitled "Don't Get Caught with Your Pants Down." And he jealously guards the young women in the group, watching over them like an overly protective father. In her classes at CUM's Family Support Network, teacher Celita Holt counsels against immodest dress. She explains to the women in the class that inappropriate clothing proclaims loudly to watching men that "you can have it with me." Both Tony and Celita emphasize the importance of young people having self-respect and enough self-confidence to realize that they do not have to give in to peer pressure and engage in premarital sex in order to be liked or to be "cool."

RESTORERS also directly confront the issue of adults living together outside of marriage. Cohabitation is a pervasive problem in the ghetto. When cohabiting couples come to Oak Cliff Bible Fellowship's outreach office for assistance, long-time staffer Roberta Jones gently asks them why they are living together and whether they realize that doing so is sin in God's eyes. In Birmingham CUM's single parents' Bible study curriculum includes a chapter on cohabitation. It forthrightly identifies this as sin in God's eyes (even though it is largely accepted in today's society). It guides people in thinking through the effects of this arrangement on their relationship to God and on their children. The Bible study also includes lessons on maintaining sexual purity as a single parent. These offer counsel to single parents on how to recognize their emotional vulnerabilities, avoid tempting situations, practice a pure thought life, dress modestly, and seek the support of other Christians trying to obey God's commands in the midst of our permissive society.

Explaining the Bible's View of Work

RESTORERS also teach a biblical view of work. Negative attitudes towards work stem from at least two sources. The first is the street's devaluing of daily nine to five labor as demeaning, boring, and uncool. The second is the lack of economic incentives: Some welfare recipients believe it's not worth it to work, since the total value of their aid benefits may outweigh the salary they can expect to receive from entry-level jobs. RESTORERS challenge both these ideas.

At Oak Cliff Bible Fellowship's "KEYS to Personal and

Professional Success" class (a Bible-based life and job skills course), teachers explain that work was created by God as a good thing. Though many subconscious messages in society suggest otherwise, they argue, work is not a curse. Not only this, but God commands work; it isn't optional. And, KEYS instructors stress, God says that *all* work, not just that which is deemed "high status" by humans, is significant and valuable. Any legal employment conducted faithfully and responsibly is dignified by God's approval.

Work for Your Soul. This emphasis on the dignity of labor and God's intention for all people to work provides a coherent, persuasive, positive perspective on work that undercuts the attitude of the street. Fortunately, the new welfare reforms are also changing the destructive disincentive toward work created by the old public-aid approach. Nonetheless, while much needed, these reforms are insufficient. Front-line activists contend that individuals must be motivated to work for reasons other than economic gain alone. "We have to convince people that there is a point to working, whether or not it makes economic sense," says CUM's Tim Ritchie. "That it's important for their children to see them working. That it's important for the community. That it's important for their soul." He adds, "You have to see it as an emotional and spiritual matter as well as an economic matter." Jim Talley of Oak Cliff Bible Fellowship agrees. "It really boils down to a spiritual thing," he says. "An individual has to come to the point where he understands that work isn't necessarily a dollar-thing; it's about what God wants me to do with the talents He has given me."

Pastor Carey Casey of Lawndale Community Church tries to encourage this expanded understanding of work among his congregants. In his sermon "Don't Give in to Sin," Casey argues:

> In Lawndale and other urban areas we say, "But there ain't no jobs!" Now listen to this. When we're talking about this work thing, we're not just talking about when you get paid to work. . . . The word *work* means giving of ourselves. Some of

us without jobs need to be working even when we are not paid. We literally need to be doing volunteer work. . . . Some of you say, "No. Sit. Let the system take care of us." I'm not cracking on you if you're on welfare. What I'm saying is this: We are supposed to work, to use our bodies; to get up in the morning, not lay around in bed even if we don't have a formal job [to go to]. . . . We are supposed to work. Young people, maybe you can't find a job. But there is *something* that you can do to get prepared [for formal] work.

Such biblically based teaching on work is having an impact. Outside observers of RESTORERS' job-training programs say they see a difference in the attitudes of those who've gone through the churches' training programs versus those who have completed secular programs. Shelton Pinnix works for TRC Staffing Services in Dallas and recruits temporary employees for firms in the area. Pinnix visits Oak Cliff Bible Fellowship's outreach center each week to interview applicants—most of whom have completed the church's "KEYS" class. Pinnix speaks highly of the job candidates he finds there: "They are eager to learn; very few are looking for a handout." He reports that they have a "higher quality of attitude and motivation" than applicants he meets at government-sponsored job-training programs. And they have learned valuable interpersonal skills and the "do's and don'ts" of office procedure through the KEYS class.

In addition to teaching the spiritual benefits of working, RESTORERS also draw attention to the long-term economic gains of making the shift from welfare to work. Jim Talley of Oak Cliff Bible Fellowship believes that welfare recipients who realize the long-term advantages of working will accept a short-term economic loss as an investment in a better future. "They may have to take a step down and take a job that does not give them as much [money] as they would have if they stayed on public assistance," Talley explains. "But eventually they can move up to better-paying jobs and end up doing better than they would on welfare."

Thomas Worthy, director of Lawndale Community Church's

Imani job-training program (*Imani* means "faith" in Swahili), tackles this issue up front with the men who come to him for help. He explains that he tries to get the men to articulate what they want out of a job and what realistic goals they can set for themselves. Worthy relates the following story to illustrate this process:

> A young man came in here and said he wants to work. I asked him, "Why?"
>
> He said, "I want to earn money."
>
> "How much money do you want?" I asked him. "How much is enough? Do you have a budget?"
>
> He says he wants to buy a car. I say, "Do you know how much a car costs?"
>
> He [said], "$14,000."
>
> I said, "No, you can buy a car for $2000. How much money do you need to make?"
>
> "About $10 an hour," he says.
>
> "Do you have $10 an hour skills?" I ask him. We deal with realities here; we can't play games; there's not enough time. We're in a short window when it comes to economics, so we have to get to [reality] immediately. I said to him, "How about a $6.50 an hour job, forty hours a week?"
>
> "That's not enough money," he says.
>
> So I say, "How much money do you need?" We have to get back to that. Then I broke it down for him and showed him the mathematics of eight-hour days, forty hours a week. I showed him how he could have a $2000 car in three months. If he takes an additional part-time job . . . he could have the $2000 car plus money in the bank.
>
> So he begins to see this. He begins to say, "If I do this, I can have a car and this much money in the bank," and all of a sudden he's really *thinking*, where he wasn't thinking before.

Keeping That Job. Of course, Worthy adds, a positive attitude is as necessary for retaining a job as in deciding to search for employment in the first place. Worthy says finding the job is "the easy part. It's what happens after they get the job that I'm concerned about." In the *Imani* program, Worthy stresses character and spiritual development as much as skills training. "Obedience [to God's Word] is the number one thing we push at *Imani*." Worthy continues, "I may give a guy a job, but the biggest challenges he may have are personal." For example, if an unemployed man has a drug problem, Worthy knows that finding employment is not the correct first step.

"Foundationally, what I'm trying to do is build leadership character in individuals," Worthy explains. He addresses topics such as dealing with tough situations in the workplace—for example, encountering racist attitudes. He suggests parameters for his students' dress, while explaining what's expected in the workplace. He also works with the men on their communication and negotiation skills.

As for the women in the program, Worthy has found that he needs to equip them to deal with the "interpersonal sabotage" they may face from other women. "When a woman who's a second or third generation welfare recipient tries to go out and do something good, others will ask her, 'Why do you want to work? You're gonna cut your benefits off.'" That's a "big challenge" for the women, Worthy says.

The Crucial Role of Personal Support

In the process of reforming hearts, renewing minds, and encouraging positive change, solid biblical teaching is critical. RESTORERS know that such teaching, though, has to be accompanied by persevering, loving support. Richmond's S.T.E.P. ministry exemplifies the priority RESTORERS give to meeting this need.

"A lot of people don't realize [what] it takes to get to the point where [welfare recipients] are ready to venture out," warns Gloria Simms, a middle-aged mother of four, who recently graduated from S.T.E.P. Academy's GED (general equivalency degree) program. S.T.E.P. Academy coordinator Inez Fleming explains how vulnerable these women are. "These are women who've thought, *As long as I'm hidden behind these walls, I'm nothing, but nobody but me knows it.* To step out, they need to be sure they're ready to take whatever comes and stand naked before the world." And that's a huge step.

Simms relates how she promised friends and family for nineteen years that she would return to school and complete her GED. However, she explains, "you have to not only want it, but act on it." What inspired her, and many of her fellow classmates, to act was the personal support she knew she would receive through S.T.E.P.

"I didn't have much confidence," Simms admits. "There was fear. Last time I'd been in a classroom was twenty years ago. I knew I needed encouragement." She'd tried other GED programs. But one offered no personal support or private tutoring; another mixed in disruptive teens with the older nontraditional students, and she could not concentrate. The S.T.E.P. program offered personal tutoring, a more controlled learning environment, and best of all (in Simms's opinion) a "Family Share Team."

As described earlier, Family Share Teams are composed of three to six Christians who meet twice monthly with an assigned student and her family. Their role is simply to be a friend. Simms requested that her Team include a teacher, because she "couldn't stand math." She got her wish. One member is a teacher, and two others are math whizzes.

S.T.E.P. staff repeatedly emphasize that because of the complexity of problems inner-city residents face, personal emotional support is absolutely essential in helping them to exit the system. S.T.E.P. executive director Linda Tracey recalls a recent conversation with one student. "She'd been a victim of domestic violence, and in the midst of our conversation she just listed off [problems], not making a big issue of these things, [saying], 'When my younger brother died' and 'when my daughter died,' and 'my cousin was a crack addict.' She just presented these things like that's the way life is."

Inez Fleming reports that the two most common issues the students deal with are domestic violence and substance abuse (their own past addictions or the drug use or drug dealing of family members).

Many bounced between foster homes as kids. Depression and loneliness abound. The S.T.E.P. Academy's application asks students who they think loves them. "We find out that some of the women think that no one really cares about them," Fleming sighs.

Some of the women "are so desperately in need of some love and care that they just launch right in" to their relationships with their Family Share Teams, Fleming continues. First-year student Anita Jones told me she could hardly wait to meet her Share Team, explaining that she came from a painful alcoholic home. She's been clean from drugs for a year and has a newfound interest in God. She believes her Share Team will offer her the personal support that's been lacking from her family.

Other students, though, initially have trouble trusting their Teams and building cross-racial friendships. Second-year student Lisa Richards says at first she was nervous about meeting regularly with her Team. "But when I got to know them," she explains, "I'd never in my life met so many nice white people. They care, they help me when I need it, and if I need encouragement, they give it to me." She credits S.T.E.P. and her Share Team for teaching her to stand up to her party-loving siblings who would regularly dump their children on her to baby-sit for days at a stretch.

Though S.T.E.P. asks the Share Teams to meet twice monthly with their students, often Team members spend more time than this with their new friends. Share Team member Carolyn Dunaway stops by Lisa Richards's apartment once a week on her way home from work. Gloria Simms relates how her Team visited her when she was in the hospital and brought by groceries while she was recovering. Academy student Sheila Anderson gets misty-eyed talking about the loving support she received from her Team when her mother passed away. Then she smiles, recalling how one of the men on her Team taught her seven-year-old son to swim.

A Mutually Refreshing Ministry. The benefits of the relationships between the students and their Share Teams are numerous—on both sides. Suburbanites are exposed to inner-city realities and sometimes find their stereotypes of welfare recipients shaken. Elaine Metcalf serves as a consultant to the S.T.E.P. Academy and is active in recruiting volunteers from suburban congregations. She reports that the suburbanites appreciate having opportunities to minister as a whole family and to expose their children at a young age to interracial relationships. "It's also a wonderful check on the materialism in our society," Metcalf adds. "When you're thinking you have to get your kid a second jacket and realize that the people you know don't have a good first jacket, a dissonance sets in."

For their part, Academy students report that they are making major life changes and growing stronger in their Christian walk. Through the combined influence of S.T.E.P., the teaching at Victory Christian Fellowship (the urban congregation most closely affiliated with S.T.E.P.), and the Share Team, Clarissa Crews decided to kick out her live-in boyfriend. Sheila Anderson is continuing to abstain from crack cocaine, and Lisa Richards is regularly attending church.

To help individuals get out of the ghetto—and to build friendships across the divides of race and class—S.T.E.P. board member Scott Oostdyk explains that ministries must offer a vehicle for spiritual and economic transformation. The kinds of friendships forged through the Family Share Teams rarely occur spontaneously in American society. The Teams, whose objective is to encourage the urban students to successfully complete the Academy, offer a structure and focus for these relationships. And the Academy and Victory Life Fellowship provide the students the necessary moral exhortation, spiritual encouragement, and educational training for socioeconomic betterment.

A New Set of the Three "R's"

RESTORERS, such as Richmond's S.T.E.P. Academy, are helping individuals like Sheila Anderson transform their lives through ministry based on a new understanding of the three "R's." They *reform* hearts, they *renew* minds, and they *refresh* spirits. RESTORERS proclaim the Gospel and offer people the chance to receive a new, clean heart from Jesus Christ. They present the Bible not as a collection of suggestions for self-improvement, but as God's authoritative, objective truth that lights the path to healthy, holy living. And they embrace hurting individuals, one at a time, offering personal support and encouragement that refreshes struggling individuals and sustains them on the narrow road that leads to life.

Enlarging
Worlds

A humorous billboard promoting the Charles Hayden Planetarium at Boston's Museum of Science reads: "Visit Our Planetarium, You Tiny, Insignificant Speck in the Universe."[1] The overwhelming vastness of God's cosmos does shrink our own personal worlds down to size. The world of many inner-city residents, though, has become *dangerously* constricted in at least three ways.

First, the world of the 'hood is isolated. Inner-city neighborhoods are cut off from many institutions and opportunities commonplace in mainstream society. Instead, the ghetto's own peculiar rhythms and scenery are shaped by the destructive forces of violence, drugs, crime, dependency, and discrimination. Moreover, as mentioned earlier, some residents of inner-city areas rarely venture into neighborhoods beyond their immediate surroundings and have limited—if any—association with individuals of other races and socioeconomic classes.

Second, this isolation, the concentration effects discussed in chapter 2, and the perception of limited opportunities work together to truncate many ghetto residents' aspirations. Numerous children and adults prune their hopes down to a "realistic" size. Thus, even the world of dreams shrinks.

Third, social life in the inner city is atomized. Associational activity is limited. Social contacts are often restricted, as fear, violence, and criminality cause residents to remain behind closed doors, suspicious of one another.

The ghetto's isolation, alienation, and social disorganization all contribute to the persistence of the "code of the streets." For residents separated from mainstream America, the ghetto's code of oppositional values offers a plausible, alternative way of thinking and living. In a world of shrunken aspirations, the code's emphasis on the present makes sense. In neighborhoods bereft of a sense of community, the code teaches indispensable keys to personal survival. In light of these various manifestations of the ghetto's "shrunkenness," another key to the RESTORERS' success is their ability to "enlarge" ghetto residents' worlds in several ways. This chapter describes how they do it.

The Isolation and Otherness of Inner-City America

Though many negative aspects of inner-city life are simply exaggerated expressions of social ills common to the whole society, certain every-day realities in the ghetto are quite shocking to mainstream Americans.

In inner-city Chicago, for example, fire drills are far more complicated affairs than they are in most suburban communities. Author Daniel Coyle explains why in his lively and moving "Bad News Bears from the Inner City"-type story entitled *Hardball: A Season in the Projects.* The Edward Jenner Elementary School on Oak Street in Chicago, he reports, unfortunately is situated on the boundary between two rival gangs—the People and the Folks. "To compensate," Coyle writes, "the school [is] careful to keep the students' comings and goings arranged by gang affiliation, using separate entrances and allowing teachers to divide their classes during fire drills: People out one door, Folks out another."[2]

Here in the "Other America," as some social critics have labeled the inner city, gunfire is discussed like the weather: "Better go shopping early, because they're gonna shoot tonight. They sure were shooting last night, weren't they? They was shooting early this morning, but then it let up, and I got to go to my grandmama's."[3]

Here fourth grade children in an impoverished South Bronx community complete safety exercises like this one related by Jonathan Kozol in his book, *Amazing Grace:*

> "What are these holes in our window?" asks the teacher at Public School 65.
> "Bullet shots!" the children chant in unison.
> "How do the police patrol our neighborhood?" the teacher asks.
> "By helicopter!" say the children.
> "What do we do when we hear shooting?"
> "Lie down on the floor!"[4]

In *There Are No Children Here,* a gripping portrayal of life in Chicago's Henry Horner Homes, author Alex Kotlowitz reports that although the projects are only about a mile from downtown, it might as well be 100 miles. Gang rivalries, shootings, drug dealing, and bloodshed make the area a virtual combat zone. Many of the residents do not allow their children to play outside. Instead they crowd all the furniture against one wall in the living room to try to give the children a play area.[5]

Gang activity and violence are not the only things that make the "Other America" so "other." Inner-city ghettos are different in that they often lack the typical mainstream institutions many Americans take for granted. The neighborhood around the Henry Horner Homes, for example, has no banks, no public library, no movie theater, no skating rink, no bowling alley.[6] Darcy Frey, in his book about high school basketball players in ravaged, destitute Coney Island, describes the area this way: "On this peninsula, at the southern tip of Brooklyn, there are almost no stores, no trees, no police; nothing, in fact, but block after block of gray-cement projects—hulking, prisonlike, and jutting straight into the sea."[7]

Frontline workers in inner-city areas report that they sometimes encounter residents who have never traveled outside the five or ten dismal blocks surrounding their homes. This geographic isolation severely limits the aesthetic experiences and encounters with natural beauty available to poor urban residents. Ministry staff know urban children who have never stood beside a pond or swam in a lake, gazed at lush mountains, hiked through a thick forest, or strolled along a sandy beach.

Overcoming Isolation

In their book *Urban Sanctuaries: Neighborhood Organizations in the Lives and Futures of Inner-City Youth*,[8] authors Milbrey McLaughlin, Merita Irby, and Juliet Langman profile six organizations, from three cities, that are effectively overcoming the ghetto's isolation and enlarging ghetto youths' worlds. These successful groups and the RESTORERS I visited have several characteristics in common.

First, they offer physical and emotional safety in the midst of the ghetto's turmoil and danger. RESTORERS provide sanctuaries, safe havens, for ghetto kids and their families. These ministries hire security staff and install alarm systems in their facilities—not so much to protect their property as to give neighborhood participants a sense of security. For inner-city parents like Delois Walker, a resident of Metropolitan Gardens whose children attend the Center for Urban Mission's "Family Care Center," it's a relief to know they have some place good to go. "Around here you're afraid to let your kids go out because of the violence and the drugs," Delois explains. "Every day you're afraid to let your kids go away from you. But here [at the Family Care Center], they are safe. It feels good to have your kids safe."

Adolescents, too, are attracted by the secure and loving environment RESTORERS provide. Kit Danley, director of Phoenix's Neighborhood Ministries, reports that even gang members come to the church for its Monday evening outreach program. She asked one of the gangbangers why he attended so consistently. He said, "Every day I feel like I'm looking over my back and wondering who is looking for me. I wonder if this is the day I'll be shot. I have a lot of enemies. Monday night is the only time I feel safe. I know that when I'm at church I'm safe. No will hurt me there."

Second, RESTORERS are careful to include local residents in the design of their programs, because the residents have firsthand knowledge of the inside realities that church leaders from the outside cannot know. This includes physical knowledge—such as the location of the crack houses—as well as emotional knowledge—what the residents feel about their lives in the community. McLaughlin et al. found in their research that organizations that did not adequately take into account the "daily rhythms, pressures, and ferocity of the inner cities" did not have a significant impact on the ghetto's young people. "The actual world in which inner-city youth struggle to survive and grow up exceeds the imagination of most mainstream Americans," they explain, "even those considered expert in issues of youth policy or urban environments. Even when the gritty facts of urban life are intellectually understood, it is impossible for an outsider to know what it *feels like* when siblings are murdered, abuse occurs daily, crime and violence are the norm, and messages of rejection are everywhere."[9] Thus, RESTORERS listen to the advice local residents offer regarding security policies, program priorities, disciplinary strategies, and other critical elements of the outreach ministry.

Third, effective ministries provide their participants with an alternate form of group affiliation. In inner-city communities fractured by violence, the desire for security compels many youths to seek gang affiliation. Though gang membership makes one a target for attack by rival gang members, remaining independent from any group is perceived as even more reckless. Consequently, some RESTORERS offer membership in groups that imitate certain aspects of gang life—such as initiation rites and distinctive clothing. This provides not only a sense of belonging, but serves the practical purpose of identifying the individual as part of a larger group—a group that would protect and defend him/her. Such group membership means that a potential attacker might face retribution not only from the victim, but from the victim's friends—and such a possibility serves as a deterrent to attack.

Exposure to the World "Out There." In addition to providing a place of physical and emotional safety, effective ministries offer inner-city families the opportunity to overcome the ghetto's geographic isolation by traveling outside the 'hood. These ministries offer trips to downtown museums, shopping malls, and historic buildings, as well as to country horse farms, camp grounds, and swimming holes. Middle and upper class families who enjoy a wide range of recreational options and who reside in more aesthetically pleasing areas may not recognize how depressing bleak urban environments are. Certainly Christian ministries should be concerned about providing *more* than just recreational activities and programs that get poor children out of their dismal neighborhoods; such efforts alone will not meet all the children's needs. But such programs are genuinely valuable and legitimate, as the grateful comments of inner-city parents signify.

In Birmingham the Center for Urban Missions (CUM) holds an eight-week summer camp for youngsters from Metropolitan Gardens, the city's largest public housing project. Each Friday the children take some sort of field trip—to the swimming pool, the museum, the science center. Berthean White, whose grandchildren have participated in the summer camp for the last few years, calls CUM "a ray of sunshine for the kids." It gives them "something different than the neighborhood." Other parents agree. Joanne Denny tells how CUM has offered her sons experiences that would otherwise have been unavailable to them, given her own limited income. Her boys have gone camping, hiking, and even river rafting with male staff and volunteers from CUM.

Truncated Lives

The isolation of the inner city—as well as the ghetto's shortage of opportunities—often produces truncated lives. Imaginations shrink, dreams shrivel, and self-esteem sinks.

Lyetta Matthews, tutoring director at Neighborhood Ministries in Phoenix, illustrates this with an anecdote about the ministry's

Christmas program. Before the holiday Matthews had asked the Latino children in her after-school program to complete a Christmas wish list. (The lists are then shared with suburban churches who support the ministry by purchasing gifts for the children.) Matthews showed me the forms one day, lamenting, "They're all the same. Shoes, socks, shoes, clothes, shoes. No toys, no books, nothing to build, nothing to make." It's as though the children have trouble hoping for anything beyond daily necessities.

Moreover, these children of the Latino underclass live life in what Matthews calls a "compressed band of reality." Inside that band, being "cool" means everything. "In school," Matthews reports, "kids get picked on if they're smart. It's just not acceptable."

The same sort of thing has been reported among the African-American underclass. Evandalene Dorsey of Washington, D.C.'s Anacostia Gospel Chapel reports that her two teenage daughters experienced persecution in high school because of their desire to excel academically and attend college. "It wasn't easy for them. They were considered 'nerds' and 'strange.' They were called names for having 'white' values," Dorsey sighs. The *Wall Street Journal*'s portrait of Cedric Jennings, a high school student from southeast Washington, D.C., tells a similar story. "Cedric is often taunted at his nearly all-black high school for 'talking white,'" the reporter writes. "Cedric's studiousness has earned him threats from gang members with guns." He is ostracized by his peers, "who see his ambition as a sign of 'disrespect.'"[10] As a result of pressures such as these, many inner-city youth severely limit their vocational aspirations.

Peer pressure isn't the only factor contributing to ghetto children's low aspirations. The stark fact of limited opportunities plays a role as well. In *Amazing Grace*, author Jonathan Kozol visits one inner-city school where the smartest kid in the class wants be an X-ray technician when he grows up. Kozol wonders why he doesn't hope to become a doctor. "Many of the ambitions of the children," the school psychologist replies, "are locked in at a level that suburban kids would scorn. . . . Boys who are doing well in school will tell me, 'I would like to be a sanitation man.' I have to guard my words and not say anything to indicate my sense of disappointment. In this neighborhood, a sanitation job is something to be longed for."[11]

Limited imaginations are not new among young people in the ghetto. Sociologist Douglas Glasgow, who conducted research over ten years ago in Watts, an inner-city Los Angeles community, found that "for young urbanized people, mainstream culture is not necessarily the center of orientation. Ghetto youths relate principally to their daily environment, and much of their socialization is geared to surviving in that context."[12] In other words, training for the kinds of jobs available in middle class America was considered useless by the young men in Watts. The schools attempted to prepare the youths for mainstream society, but the students "did not believe that they would ever depart from Watts into a new middle class life on the other side of town. Thus the agents of education were experienced as antagonistic elements in these youths' socialization, rather than as facilitators of their goals."[13]

Still, despite the hostility of street culture toward big dreams, some inner-city residents dare to aspire to mainstream goals—a college education, a decent job, and a home in a stable neighborhood. The obstacles these strivers face are considerable. Two recent books, Frey's *The Last Shot* and Ben Joravsky's *Hoop Dreams*, depict what a Herculean task it is for the youthful basketball players they portray to gain admission to college. For many middle class kids, going to college is taken for granted, something everybody does. For the young men of Coney Island and Cabrini-Green, it is a fragile dream that can be shattered at any moment.

In the film version of *Hoop Dreams*, one of the main characters, Arthur, plays in the state basketball tournament at the University of Illinois at Champaign-Urbana. During one afternoon Arthur's parents and younger brother stroll about the campus, marveling. Arthur's mom comments that the campus "sure is nice, sure is different." With wide-eyed wonder, Arthur's younger brother retorts, "It's *beyond* different."

For many young people in the Other America, a two-parent family, a school without guns, a job at more than five dollars an hour, a chance to go to college, and a gang-free neighborhood are so unknown, so inaccessible, as to be "beyond different."

Some inner-city residents have limited aspirations not only for their vocational future, but for their future, period. In *There Are No Children Here*, author Kotlowitz describes how one mother, LaJoe, is so concerned that her two (healthy) sons, ages nine and twelve, will not make it to age eighteen that she purchases burial insurance for the boys. In Phoenix, Neighborhood Ministries' director Kit Danley reports that when one of her favorite teens, a fourteen-year-old named Johnny Lopez, was gunned down in a lonely back alley, he had already planned his funeral and provided appropriate instructions to his relatives. "It's not unusual for young teens to know in detail what they want for their funerals," Danley laments. "It's like the Anglo kid planning a wedding."

Expanding Horizons

RESTORERS overcome the truncation of imagination by exposing youths to more ambitious vocational aspirations and providing excellent educational programs to prepare youths for better jobs. For example, Monica Johnson, a physician from Rosedale Park Baptist Church, directs a "medical mentoring" program that exposes eighteen students to career opportunities in the medical profession. The program links the students with Christian volunteer mentors with whom the students meet weekly. Under Dr. Johnson's supervision, the teens visit hospitals, nursing home facilities, and physical therapy and rehabilitation centers, thereby gaining a hands-on feel for such institutions. Participating teens may observe in the emergency room, watch a surgical procedure, and talk with hospital administrators, nurses, and doctors. Dr. Johnson thinks it is important for her students to have such experiences and encourages the teens to visualize themselves in these work settings.

Some of the students are doing just that. Kareem, an eleventh grader and program participant who grew up in the Smith Homes, wants to be a physical therapist. Donald, a recent high school graduate from a poor family in the neighborhood, longs to be a surgeon. When I interviewed Dr. Johnson, Donald was in his first year of college, but he had already begun studying for the MCAT exam he'll take in three years as part of the entrance requirements for medical school. Johnson's mentoring program is helping students like Kareem and Donald to set their vocational sights much higher than they might have otherwise.

Making Quality Education a Reality. RESTORERS not only encourage young people to set their vocational sights high, but they also provide quality academic enhancement programs that help equip youths with the skills they will need to prepare themselves for their chosen fields. This involves offering rigorous educational programs and personal tutoring. More importantly, it means creating an atmosphere where academic excellence is encouraged, legitimated, and affirmed.

In Birmingham, CUM's Scholars' Club provides a supportive environment for inner-city youths who want to gain entrance to high-quality private and magnet schools. The Club meets weekly. Tutors provide individualized attention to the students, helping them with their homework and providing them with a separate challenging course of self-paced study to supplement their lessons from school. Those who excel in the Club can earn scholarships to attend private Christian schools in the suburbs of Birmingham. Berthean White has a granddaughter who attends Briarwood, a private Christian school, on a CUM scholarship. White says the school is "a whole new world" for her granddaughter, a place where she is being exposed to new experiences and new ideas.

Of course, ministries that offer such programs quickly learn that it can be difficult for some inner-city kids to adjust to private suburban schools. These students sometimes find the academic work overwhelming compared to what they've been used to in the city public school system. CUM's Scholars Club helps to alleviate this hardship by providing the students with extra tutoring.

In Birmingham the availability of scholarship aid and the existence of the Scholars Club help families residing in Metropolitan Gardens realize that they need not settle for only one educational choice—the local public school. CUM provides information on city magnet schools and their entrance requirements, as well as information on private schools. It also sponsors field trips for parents and their children to visit various schools and talk with teachers and administrators. The idea is to show that real, concrete opportunities do exist and can be pursued. This helps to raise the educational aspirations of both parents and children.

In Chicago the Lawndale Community Church is making university attendance a realizable dream for local youths. Lawndale's College Opportunity Program (LCOP) recruits eighth grade students from the neighborhood for the challenging five-year program. Any young teen with a serious desire to attend college can apply for admission.

Lawndale's program is demanding. From eighth through twelfth grade, students enrolled in LCOP attend twice-weekly liberal arts classes at Lawndale. The curriculum focuses on a particular subject each month—for example, creative writing, algebra, Spanish, or ACT preparation. Students in each grade level also participate in mentoring and spiritual development activities; each grade has its own mentor/coordinator who tracks students' grades, visits their respective schools, and makes home visits. Students must maintain a minimum grade point average in school each semester and can be suspended from the program for failure to do so. They can also lose their spot in the program if they fail to attend required classes and activities.

In addition to their academic classes, students in LCOP participate in a sixteen-week entrepreneurial development program that teaches them how to start and operate their own businesses and instructs them in money management. LCOP participants must also complete various community service projects. In the summer LCOP students are eligible for employment in paid internships in various professions including health care, journalism, and community development. After meeting all the program's requirements, LCOP participants receive a $3,000 per year scholarship to attend college at a participating university. LCOP staff take students on visits to various college campuses and help them select a school.

LCOP gives Lawndale youth who want to pursue a better future tremendous support and encouragement. When I visited, forty Lawndale church youth were enrolled in college. While on the streets talk of college may be ridiculed—or is nonexistent—inside the church community, talk of going to college is common and youth discover that their dream of university attendance is accepted as a normal and achievable goal.

Providing educational opportunities for young people is a clear priority in most effective Christian community ministries. Some RESTORERS also focus on assisting adults to enhance their skills.

Adults with shared dreams of improving their job skills or getting their high school or college degrees find their aspirations applauded and supported, rather than demeaned, at Richmond's S.T.E.P. Academy, CUM's "Family Support Network," and Oak Cliff Bible Fellowship's GED program. In each of these programs, adult participants have succeeded though they'd previously failed in secular programs.

In Dallas, for example, Oak Cliff's GED students assert that the atmosphere in the church's program is much more conducive to success than in any previous programs they'd attended. At Oak Cliff, the students are not surrounded by half-clad women; they do not have to try to tune out the noise of street fights, hot rods, and ghetto blasters or study in rooms with overflowing trash cans and broken beer bottles. Instead, they work inside quiet, air-conditioned rooms in the neatly kept, beautifully carpeted church building.

Moreover, most of Oak Cliff's large staff have offices in the building in which GED classes are conducted. This means that each morning, as the students arrive for their classes, they rub shoulders with several Black middle class professionals. This provides a further benefit in that students are exposed to role models they might otherwise never have known. Such exposure helps minority students cultivate ambitious aspirations: It helps them see that other members of their race are occupying the professional ranks.

In Richmond the S.T.E.P. ministry targets its educational programs to the heads of households, believing that by improving the job skills and life skills of parents, entire families will benefit. It, like Oak Cliff Bible Fellowship, offers a GED program in a context where alternative GED classes are available. As in Oak Cliff's situation, students in S.T.E.P.'s program report that they are having a better experience in S.T.E.P. than they did in other programs. Most of the S.T.E.P. students are nontraditional and need extra support and encouragement to return to school after a long absence. Students who are succeeding in S.T.E.P.'s program say that the government-sponsored classes they previously tried failed to provide a quiet learning environment and didn't offer instruction during the times convenient for them as mothers of young children.

These anecdotes illustrate that the educational programs offered by effective neighborhood organizations are characterized by attention not only to academics, per se, but to the needs of the whole student— needs for a conducive learning environment, for incentives, and for personal support and affirmation. Notably, some RESTORERS began their own educational initiatives in neighborhoods where such programs already existed, but were not effectively serving the community.

While church-based ministries should be careful not to unnecessarily duplicate services in a neighborhood, the experiences of these RESTORERS demonstrate that the mere existence of a program does not guarantee that it is meeting the community's needs. Churches that determine they may be able to offer an educational program should certainly investigate what programs are already available. If residents are dissatisfied with existing programs, ministry leaders should determine what the specific complaints are.

In S.T.E.P.'s case, staff designed its GED program to run from 8:30

to 3:00 (the time when the women's children were in school), offered daily tutoring assistance, and ensured an orderly classroom decorum. S.T.E.P. also added a few of its own unique elements (such as a weekly life skills discussion, daily motivational talks, and a Thursday noon women's Bible study) to further distinguish it from the available GED programs.

The Problem of Atomized Neighborhoods

The world of the ghetto is not only shrunken by its isolation and the truncated aspirations of some inner-city residents; it is also highly atomized. It has lost its sense of community and social cohesiveness. The problem of atomization in distressed neighborhoods is even more difficult to address than other manifestations of the inner city's restricted world. For instance, isolation of the inner city can be surmounted by taking inner-city residents outside the 'hood and exposing them to new experiences and people. Truncation in poor neighborhoods can be overcome by providing an atmosphere that encourages confidence and high aspirations and by offering creative opportunities by which these dreams can be realized. But atomization—the relational barrenness of the ghetto—requires nothing less than the "re-neighboring" of a community.

Fear, violence, and criminality in inner-city areas create an atmosphere of distrust. People remain indoors, keep their children inside, and do not often venture out to meet their neighbors and make friends. In his description of the Henry Horner Homes in Chicago, author Alex Kotlowitz portrays this disconnectedness and alienation. "Exacerbating the isolation," he writes, "was the fact that nearly half of the families in Henry Horner . . . had no telephone." And those without phones often did not know anyone in the building who might let them use a phone.[14]

One of the most surprising things I discovered in visiting several inner-city communities was the pervasive loneliness. Although I realized that many residents would experience fear in their crime-ridden neighborhoods, I assumed that they still would know some of their neighbors and have at least a small circle of friends. Repeatedly, though, women would admit to me that for years they had remained inside their homes, unwilling to venture out and forge new friendships. These women left home only to take their children to school or to go to the grocery mart. Otherwise, they remained behind locked doors— many of them cut off not only from their neighbors but also from their own families. These women were desperately hungry for loving, supportive relationships.

In my discussions with women who participate in CUM's programs at the Family Care Center in Metropolitan Gardens, many admitted that before enrolling in the programs, they hardly knew any of their neighbors. Numerous women reported that before the Center opened, they rarely left their apartments and often did not allow their children to play outside. They said they spent long hours before the television set and "didn't get out much."

Today's fractured ghettos were not always so atomistic. Kotlowitz quotes one mother in Chicago's Henry Horner Homes as she described life in the projects when the Homes were originally opened in the late 1950s. At that time the neighborhood included a Boys and Girls Club with a gym and swimming pool, a youth drum and bugle corps, and a bustling chapter of the Girl Scouts. In addition, the neighborhood association energetically fought for better schools and health clinics, and the local Democratic party organization was active, as were the Black Panthers and members of the local Congregational Baptist Church. But by the late 1980s, when Kotlowitz conducted his research, almost none of this activity was observable.

The decline in civic life in the inner city—volunteer organizations, recreational clubs, church-based activity—has been paralleled by a decline in *any* sense of community connectedness and mutual responsibility. Several residents with whom I spoke in various inner cities could remember a time when "community parenting" was a reality. Youngsters

caught misbehaving by neighbors would be disciplined by those neighbors, who would also report the misbehavior to the children's parents.
Now families keep to themselves. Tony Yates, a long-time resident of the
Anacostia neighborhood in southeast Washington, D.C., offered this
appraisal: "Things didn't get like this until drugs infested our neighborhood. It used to be quiet. A good place to raise a family. When you spoke
to another person's child, they listened to you. Now you speak to them,
and they're gonna cuss you out or throw rocks at you."

Sociologist and urban researcher William Julius Wilson confirms
this unfortunate trend. In his study of urban Chicago, he concludes that:

> In both the housing projects and other inner-city neighbor-
> hoods, residents have difficulty identifying their neighbors.
> They are, therefore, less likely to engage in reciprocal
> guardian behavior. Events in one part of the block or neigh-
> borhood tend to be of little concern to those residing in other
> parts. These conditions of social disorganization are acute
> because of the unprecedented increase in the number of
> teenage and young adult minorities in these neighborhoods,
> many of whom are jobless, not enrolled in school, and a
> source of delinquency, crime, and unrest.[15]

Rebuilding Community

Church-based ministries throughout the country are rebuilding community through efforts to improve both the physical and social environment. That is, they are working to make inner-city neighborhoods
safer, and they are offering forums through which friendships among
neighbors can be encouraged.

RESTORERS are improving the physical environment of the
ghetto in several ways. In Chicago, for example, Lawndale Community
Church members have reinvigorated block clubs. These clubs set policies for their block (regarding noise and loitering), aggressively dis-

courage drug use and drug sales, and cooperate in neighborhood crime watch activities.

The Lawndale Community Church and RESTORERS in Atlanta, Detroit, Los Angeles, and other cities are also involved in home rehabilitation and home-ownership programs that enable community residents to purchase their own homes. This increases people's pride in their properties and contributes to better upkeep and maintenance. It also helps people to have a greater stake in their neighborhoods, stimulating their involvement in block clubs and other community improvement initiatives. Home ownership, in short, produces community ownership in that residents begin to care about the welfare of the neighborhood (since they now have an economic investment in it). This stimulates greater local participation in community affairs and associations, thus bringing neighbors together in common efforts for the betterment of the community.

In Washington, D.C., and other cities, RESTORERS sponsor prayer marches throughout their target communities. Residents of all ages, from infants to grandmothers, gather in the evening for a slow walk around their neighborhoods' trouble spots. Participating Christians sing and pray against drugs, violence, and despair—often right in front of the prostitutes, drug dealers, and gang members! Joyce Peebles from Anacostia Gospel Chapel reports that certain street corners where the prayer marchers have gathered, which formerly were major centers of drug dealing, are now peaceable and passable.

In Chicago's West Garfield Park neighborhood, Bethel New Life Church went even further in its efforts to take back the streets. Bethel, in conjunction with a local city alderman, organized a forty-day campaign against drugs and violence. The campaign was kicked off with a twenty-four-hour prayer vigil and march through the neighborhood. Bethel also recruited families from around the neighborhood to provide a "human chain" that cordoned off a safe corridor through which local children could walk to school.

During the forty-day period, Friday Evening Family Fun Fests were organized, complete with snow cone and popcorn vendors, children's games, musical entertainment, and gin rummy competitions. Other events during the campaign aimed to provide better opportunities for youths likely to fall into the hands of gangs. Job fairs and substance abuse counseling sites were set up.

Bethel also went door to door seeking residents' support for various public works initiatives aimed at curbing drug traffic. These included designating certain streets one-way roads, putting up fences around vacant lots, tearing down abandoned buildings, replacing broken street lamps, and passing a law that would allow newspapers to print the names of individuals arrested for purchasing illicit drugs in the neighborhood.

Efforts of this kind foster a sense of security in inner-city neighborhoods and pave the way for greater interaction among community residents, because residents feel more comfortable when out and about. Additionally, many RESTORERS recognize the need for deliberate efforts to provide places where neighbors can meet. Faith-based ministries have adopted a number of creative strategies for such re-neighboring of their communities.

In Detroit the Rosedale Park Baptist Church facilitates fellowship among community residents through special events such as neighborhood picnics. Rosedale church's women's group has hosted "Ladies' Days" and baby showers for women, many of whom are single moms from the Smith Homes (the public housing project next door to the church). During Ladies' Day, women enjoy beauty consultations, group fellowship, and individualized brief counseling/prayer sessions with church members. Through this initiative, women can participate in a fun event, meet their neighbors, and receive information about the Rosedale Church and its community services.

In Birmingham, CUM's Family Support Network gathers together weekly those families who participate in the various programs of the Family Care Center. Adults receive biblically based instruction and have a prayer and sharing time while their children meet separately in another room for their Bible club. Then all the families sit down together for a fellowship dinner.

"You'd be surprised to know that in this community of 3,000 people, so few people know each other. Our society has made a radical shift towards individualism and anonymity," says CUM's Gerald Austin. "No one wants to bother with each other. So what we're trying to create at the Family Care Center is a network of families who do care about each other."

The effort is working. CUM participant Joanne Denny says her involvement with the Family Care Center has made her "more aware of my community, my neighbors." Angie Lewis, who serves on CUM's Community Leadership Team, says her participation has increased her loyalty to the community. Lewis oversees many of the children's activities at the Family Care Center, for which she receives a modest CUM stipend. But, because of her increased community consciousness, Lewis puts in many extra hours. "It's not like I'm here [at the Family Care Center] and clock out at 5:30," she explains. "When I get out there on the streets, I've still got a job to do with those kids." Chuckling, she reports that local kids get nervous if they're "doing something wrong" and she spots them—even on her off hours—because she's unafraid to discipline them.

As previously noted, CUM's Family Care Center not only helps connect neighbors with each other; it also provides a place where similarly forward-looking people can come together to support and encourage each other. According to Bridget Dorsey, a resident of Metropolitan Gardens since 1993, this is critical. Dorsey attends the Family Support Network meetings every Tuesday night and also uses the Center in the afternoons to complete her homework from her community college courses. She hopes to finish college, secure a better-paying job, and eventually buy a house. Most of her neighbors don't have such motivation, she says. But the other parents she's met through CUM do. Their encouragement helps her to deal with the ridicule and criticism she sometimes has to take from neighbors who disapprove of her efforts to better herself.

In Washington, D.C., the Anacostia Gospel Chapel encourages fellowship among neighbors by organizing evening worship services in the so-called community rooms of various apartment buildings. The weekly program is called "Church in the 'Hood." These services provide an opportunity for prayer and fellowship in a small group setting. They also give interested apartment dwellers a chance to learn about Christ and the Bible outside of the traditional church context. Ministry leaders at Anacostia Gospel Chapel are finding that people who are reluctant to darken a church door on Sunday morning feel more comfortable attending a small group fellowship right in their own building.

Creating a Family Feel. The most important way effective ministries overcome the ghetto's atomization is by making participants feel as if they are part of a new family, rather than disconnected students in a jobs skills or other class. It is possible for people to participate in a common program for years without ever developing a sense of belonging. Consequently, RESTORERS think as much about relationships as they do about programs.

RESTORERS deliberately design their outreach ministries to foster a sense of group identity and affiliation. In Phoenix, Neighborhood Ministries cultivates a sense of belonging among the children enrolled in its tutoring and Christian education programs by tracking the children as they move from one address to another. This is necessary because the Latino underclass in Phoenix is highly transient. The church-based programs of Neighborhood Ministries thus provide a rare sense of stability in the midst of the children's tumultuous worlds. "Hanging on" to kids is hard work, as it requires the ministry to invest enormous efforts in transporting children from all over the city to the church's twice-weekly programs.

As I drove about the city one day with Neighborhood Ministries' director Kit Danley, she would often spot a little girl or boy and say,

"That's one of *our* kids." This sense of ownership displayed by ministry staff and volunteers gives the kids the feeling of belonging they so deeply crave.

Youth minister Dennis Talbert sees the same longing among the kids involved in Rosedale Park Baptist's tutoring program. Talbert relates a story he heard from Cheryl Miree, a volunteer tutor working with junior high girls. "Cheryl told me that one Sunday, one of the girls pulled her aside and said, 'Miss Miree, how come you don't own me?' And Cheryl said to her, 'What do you mean, *own* you?' The girl replied, 'When you introduce me, you introduce me as Tamia. But when you introduce your son, you introduce him as "this is my son."' So Cheryl asked her, 'Does that bother you?' And Tamia said, 'Yes, it does.'" Talbert explains: "Tamia says this because she wants the connectedness. These students are wise enough to realize that they come from a disjointed surrounding at home, and they're looking for something solid to hold on to."

Christ Community Church in Franklin, Tennessee, does one simple thing to encourage bonding between their volunteer tutors and the children enrolled in their tutoring center. Before the start of the academic year, staff take Polaroid pictures of each of the students. Then they present the photos to each child's tutor, along with some brief information about the children (e.g., about their family members, their hobbies, interests, and favorite teams). Tutors are asked to begin praying for their children by name before the program commences. In this way, the participating adults begin thinking about and caring for "their" children even before they actually meet them.

RESTORERS recognize that adults, as well as children, need the emotional support of feeling connected to a network of friends. Consequently, they incorporate social and recreational aspects even into programs designed principally to enhance skills (for example, educational programs or job skills classes). S.T.E.P.'s GED program in Richmond, for example, includes monthly fellowship dinners and an annual retreat.

Moreover, volunteers and staff in effective ministries treat program participants in ways that give the ministry a family feel. This involves learning people's first names and the names of their children, taking time before and after class to converse, warmly greeting participants when they arrive for an activity or class, paying home visits, and sending encouraging notes.

Finally, RESTORER ministry sites themselves engender a feeling of warmth and security. The sites I visited were typically neat and decorated in a pleasant fashion, avoiding an institutional feel. The Detroit Rescue Mission Ministries' Genesis House is particularly impressive. Homeless women, most of them recovering from drug addictions, live together there with their children. The basement has been converted into a brightly painted day-care center with plenty of toys and space for romping about. Each bedroom in the house has been decorated by a Christian group—for example, a women's ministry of a particular church—which takes financial responsibility for the upkeep of that particular room.

A quick tour through the house suggests that the various groups are determined to outdo each other in their decorating! All the bedrooms are neatly painted and/or wallpapered, with matching curtains and comfortable furniture, nice paintings or prints on the walls, and such "homey" touches as dried flower arrangements or handmade baskets. The kitchen and living room areas of the house are also tastefully done. Inside Genesis House one certainly does not have the sense of being in a homeless shelter.

Other ministries I visited make their premises feel homey by posting photographs of program participants, volunteers, and staff on bright, readily visible bulletin boards. And staff at the S.T.E.P. ministry in Richmond even assemble a photo album with pictures of each student with her Family Share Team, as well as photos of special group events such as field trips, graduation ceremonies, and the annual retreat. Then each program participant receives a copy of the "family photo album," further reinforcing the idea that the students have not merely completed an educational degree but have joined a supportive, loving community.

Summing Up

Effective community ministries enlarge worlds by exposing their participants to new experiences and opportunities, often outside the local neighborhood. They also overcome the isolation, segregation, and alienation of low-income communities by diversifying worlds—bringing people of different socioeconomic classes and races into such neighborhoods. They improve the physical appearance of neighborhoods through redevelopment efforts and anticrime initiatives. Most importantly, they encourage a reconstruction of the social landscape by facilitating new relationships among neighbors and engendering renewed community consciousness.

Part
Two

Laying the Foundation

What's working in Detroit, Dallas, Richmond, Birmingham, and other cities where RESTORERS are active can work in your community too. The ministries described in the previous four chapters operate according to different models and carry out their work in varying environments. But they share a common commitment to renew hearts, transform culture, and enlarge worlds by ministering holistically in Jesus' name. Regardless of your setting—urban, suburban, or rural—your church can adopt a suitable model of outreach ministry and be effective. This chapter, and the three that follow, aim to show you how.

The first step in becoming a RESTORER is to lay the foundation for your church-based ministry. As I write this, noisy construction vehicles are circling about outside, moving earth. I live in a hilly neighborhood, and the foundation for each new town house must be carefully laid if these homes are not to tumble down. Machines dig out the hillside and then pack down the remaining soil into a large flat surface on which to pour the concrete. Such careful, hard work is crucial for the future stability of the home. And it's equally crucial in building a community development ministry.

Anyone interested in establishing an effective church-based ministry among the poor must help his/her congregation understand *why* the church is taking such a step, *what* it hopes to accomplish, and *how* to begin. The answers to these three questions constitute the foundation on which the ministry will be built. This chapter offers some suggestions on thinking through these three questions. Chapter 6 describes the barriers we all too commonly face in outreach ministry and offers recommendations for overcoming these barriers. Chapter 7 offers advice on how your church can make the shift from traditional "commodity-based" mercy ministries to more effective, long-term relational ministries. And chapter 8 outlines the action steps a congregation can take to begin its own holistic ministry in a targeted neighborhood.

Knowing God's Passion

Outreach ministries will have little chance of success if they are not motivated by the participants' deep conviction that loving others is a central, essential aspect of the Christian life. Unfortunately, many congregations suffer from the disease of inwardness—that is, an exclusive focus upon the needs of the congregation itself, rather than an outward focus that considers the needs of those outside the body. Consequently, the first task for those who want to start (or strengthen) their church's mercy ministry is to inculcate their congregation with a deep awareness of Christians' responsibility to love their needy neighbors.

In 1 John 4:19 we read, "We love because he first loved us." Our love toward others is rooted in God's mercy toward us: We return thanks to God for His love in part by demonstrating love and mercy toward other people. We can also paraphrase 1 John 4:19 by saying, "We love the poor because God first loved them." This is the most basic answer to the question, "Why should our church begin an outreach ministry among the poor?" Our highest calling is to imitate the ways of God. Consequently, we must know and share His passions. And one of His deepest passions is His sustained and tender concern for needy people.

The Biblical Call to Love the Poor

The place to start getting acquainted with God's heart is, of course, His Word. Many people are surprised to learn that over 400 verses in the Bible speak of God's concern for the poor, vulnerable, and disadvantaged. God's compassion for needy people is illustrated scripturally in several ways.

In the Old Testament Law, God enacted special provisions to protect those on the bottom tiers of society. Deuteronomy 14:28-29 describes God's instruction that every third year, the Israelites were to bring the tithes of their produce to the towns. There the Israelites would distribute the produce to two groups—the Levites (who did not own their own land) and "the aliens, the fatherless and the widows." Deuteronomy 24:19-21 describes God's further provision for widows, orphans, and aliens (refugees). There He instructs farmers not to pick repeatedly over their fields during the harvest. Rather God admonishes them to harvest once and then to allow the poor to glean from the fields the remaining produce. God's tender concern for the poor is revealed as well in Deuteronomy 24:12-15. Here He teaches that hired laborers should be paid at the conclusion of each work day, since they are counting on their wages to provide daily bread for their families. And God tells those who lend to a poor man not to retain the man's cloak as a pledge overnight, since the man will need it to sleep in.

God's heart for the poor is also demonstrated in the way He equates mistreatment of the poor with a *personal* affront. Proverbs 14:31 says, "He who oppresses the poor shows contempt for their Maker, but whoever is kind to the needy honors God." Jesus' teaching in Matthew 25:40 comes quickly to mind when we consider this principle. There we learn that God sees Himself in "the least of these." Kindness shown to the poor, the sick, the naked, and the hungry is considered kindness showered upon God. And, Jesus warns, whatever we do not do for "the least of these," we do not do for our Lord.

Similarly, God often defines Himself in relation to His loving actions on behalf of poor people. He calls Himself the One who defends, protects, and rescues the poor (see, for example, Ps. 9:9; 12:5; 35:10; 72:12-14). As Psalm 68:5 says, "A father to the fatherless, a defender of widows, is God in his holy dwelling."

Moreover, God considers care for the poor a critical component of personal righteousness. In a memorable passage in Ezekiel 18:5-9, God defines a righteous man as one who avoids idolatry, remains sexually pure, and does not oppress the poor or lend at usury; one who faithfully follows God's laws and gives food to the hungry and clothes to the naked. Such themes are repeated in the Psalms. In Psalm 37:25–26, the righteous are defined as those who are generous and lend freely. Psalm 112:9 says that the righteous man is one who has "scattered abroad his gifts to the poor." Leaders in society have a special responsibility to be righteous in this regard. God, speaking through the prophet Jeremiah, defines a righteous king as one who does what is right and just and defends the cause of the poor and needy. Indeed, God says, this is what it means to know Him (Jer. 22:15b-16).

All of these passages of Scripture clearly establish the principle that if we are to honor God, we must imitate His concern for the poor. When we ignore the poor, we are as guilty as the Israelites whom God rebuked through His prophets. The prophetic literature is saturated with God's condemnation of both the individual and corporate sins of the Jews against the poor and vulnerable in their midst. God castigates the Israelites for their conspicuous consumption and their callous disregard for the poor (Isa. 3:14-17; Amos 5:11-12; 6:4-7), both of which were perpetuated by the Israelites' corrupt political and legal system (Mic. 7:3; Jer. 22:13-14; Ezek. 22:23-29).

The New Testament reiterates this principle that love for needy people is an irreducible part of true religion. When asked which was the greatest commandment, Jesus replied that it was to love God and neighbor—this summed up the whole Law and the Prophets (Matt. 22:37-40). The apostle James was so blunt as to write that "Religion that God our Father accepts as pure and faultless is this: to look after orphans and widows in their distress and to keep oneself from being polluted by the world" (James 1:27). And John wondered how the love of God could dwell in us if we have material goods and see our brother in need but do not take pity on him (1 John 3:17).

Understanding God's Intentions

As we realize just how frequently Scripture emphasizes our obligation to love our needy neighbors, we will repent of the times when we have loved only with "words or tongue" but not with "actions and in truth" (see 1 John 3:18). But learning to share God's *passion* for the poor is just the first step. After this, we need to understand His *intentions* for the poor (indeed, for all His people). This will then guide our ministry efforts. The answer to the question, "What are we trying to accomplish through our community ministry?" is simply this: Our goal is to help those we serve realize God's intentions for themselves.

This goal makes biblical development models distinct from secular ones. Secular approaches to development are premised on the question, "What are your needs?" Biblical approaches ask, "What are God's intentions for you?"[1] Clearly, Christians should not ignore people's "felt needs." Felt needs are legitimate concerns. We should be careful, though, because "felt needs" are "not *necessarily* reliable indicators of actual need."[2] For example, drug addicts have a "felt need" for heroin, and some American teenagers have a "felt need" for a new car. Focusing only on what *we* think we need fails to take into account that by nature we are rebellious toward God.

The goals of biblical development reflect God's intentions for us. As Phil Reed, pastor of an inner-city church in Jackson, Mississippi, explains, "We should not just have goals and objectives or a set of isolated programs we are operating for the betterment of society."[3] Rather we need an "overall picture" of what God wants to do in places of brokenness, such as the inner city. We find that picture in His Word.

As Reed notes, God's intentions are revealed in the early chap-

ters of Genesis, when Adam and Eve were living in Paradise under
God's watchful care. There in the Garden God communed regularly
with His children. Clearly, He created people to have a relationship
with Him; without such fellowship, we are "not truly human."[4]
Consequently, loving our needy neighbors will involve evangelism
and discipleship. We want deliberately to address people's spiritual
needs by encouraging them to establish a relationship with their
Creator through Jesus Christ.

God also intended that people be in right relationship with each
other. He gave Adam a companion and helpmate in Eve, and He
blessed their union. After the Fall that relationship was damaged.
Consequently, our ministry will involve restoring marriages and restoring people to right relationships within their families.

Third, Reed reminds us, God intended that people pursue fruitful, meaningful labor. God gave the first humans a job—to keep and
care for the garden. Work is God-given, not a result of the Fall.[5]
Consequently, Christians should be eager to help their needy neighbors find productive work. And not only that, but our goal should also
be "to develop people to the point that they are using their God-given
skills and abilities in satisfying work that is also benefiting the community."[6]

Man has a purpose—to "glorify God and enjoy Him forever," as
the Westminster Confession of Faith puts it. Ultimately, our efforts to
serve needy people are directed toward this goal. This requires us to
focus more on the needy *person* than on the need. If we are "need-
focused," our ministry runs the danger of becoming centered on *programs* that meet needs. If we are "person-centered," our ministry is
more likely to focus on the development of a *relationship* with the
needy person. In the context of this relationship, we will address "felt
needs" but also instruct the person about God's intentions and purposes. In this way, we share new life—"the life that truly is life" as the
apostle John puts it—with others, rather than merely making someone's current life more tolerable by providing goods and services.

Biblical and Historical "How to" Guidelines

In some instances, Christians may need to repent that they lack God's passion for the poor. In other cases, the problem might be that, although Christians understand their responsibilities and desire to help needy individuals fulfill God's intentions, they are at a loss as to how to proceed. Consequently, those wanting to start or strengthen their church's outreach to the poor need to teach their fellow congregants *how* to love the needy. Once again, Scripture offers numerous helpful insights. Additionally, the church through the centuries has grappled with its responsibilities to love the needy, and we can learn a great deal by reviewing church history. The church fathers and the reformers, for example, gave significant attention to the church's mercy ministry and offered many relevant guidelines and strategies for conducting an effective and biblically faithful outreach among the poor. Several guidelines drawn from Scripture and from the example of the "saints gone before us" are discussed below.

Having the right motive and attitude for doing mercy ministry is crucial. God looks at our hearts as well as our external actions. When we serve others, we should do so eagerly, cheerfully, humbly, and compassionately; we should not serve others to gain approval or a self-satisfied feeling for ourselves (see Matt. 6:2-4; Gal. 2:10; 1 Cor. 8:12). In the Sermon on the Mount, Jesus warns against giving publicly in order to gain man's applause. Instead we should seek to give secretly. In our financial giving, Clement of Alexandria, one of the early church patriarchs, reminds us that we should not give "mechanically."[7] Giving ought not to be a routinized, indifferent act. We should also beware of giving only our money, rather than our time, our talents, and ourselves. Money may be the thing a needy person most wants, but not the thing most needed. The church father Ambrose taught that nonmonetary help was more noble and of greater long-term consequence than financial aid, since money is easily spent, but good counsel can never be exhausted.[8]

Though mercy is to be shown to all, Christians have a special obligation to minister to needy people within the body of Christ. Paul instructs the young church of Galatia to do good to all, but especially to the household of faith (Gal. 6:10). In another letter, Paul commands believers to share with fellow Christians who are in need (Romans 12:12). It is legitimate and appropriate to minister to fellow Christians; we simply need to be careful of the danger of forgetting to help the lost.

Mercy ministry should be deliberate, thoughtful, and planned, not haphazard, careless, or sporadic. This instruction rings strange to our modern ears. In our culture we are taught to value spontaneity. As the popular bumper sticker reads: "Practice Random Kindness and Senseless Acts of Beauty." One problem with "senseless" mercy ministry is that it runs the risk of doing things that feel good but that fail truly to help. For example, it may appear to be an act of "random kindness" to give a homeless person ten dollars. But if that homeless person is only enabled thereby to purchase more crack cocaine, the kindness wasn't kind at all.

The other problem with practicing random acts of kindness is that we may *feel* we have adequately discharged our obligations to the needy when we have not. Surely, spontaneous giving of money or of ourselves can be appropriate in some instances. For example, suppose a missionary comes to your church with wonderful accounts of God's work in Romania. He also tells how children are suffering in orphanages that lack adequate supplies. Moved by this testimony, you reach into your wallet and add fifty dollars to the offering plate. Here your spontaneity is appropriate. We are, Scripture teaches, to be "hilarious" givers. In part, this means avoiding an attitude that would say to the Romanian missionary, "Sorry, but I've already given my tithe offering today." Spontaneous giving—*over and above our planned giving*—delights God's heart.

The danger with the bumper sticker mentality, though, is that our spontaneous giving—or spontaneous "random acts of kindness"—will substitute for planned, deliberate, sacrificial outreach. As fallen creatures, our tendency is to pat ourselves on the back for some "senseless act of beauty" we performed, rather than to compare our *lifestyle* with the sacrificial, servant life of Christ. If we focus on our random and spontaneous kindness, we are easily self-satisfied; if we focus on Christ, we are convicted. Disciples of Jesus aim to discipline their whole lives in light of Christ's example, giving up their lives in loving, daily service. The bumper sticker mentality allows us to keep our lives under our own control, while now and then practicing some feel-good act of mercy when the mood strikes us.

Paul's teaching on giving in 1 Corinthians 16 reinforces the importance of deliberateness. Paul counsels the Corinthian believers prayerfully to decide what they are going to give and then to set aside these funds at a specific time (in this case, at the beginning of each week). Scripture teaches that our giving is important to God. We honor Him by undertaking our giving responsibilities thoughtfully and by deliberately setting a schedule for giving. An actual accounting of our spontaneous giving usually reveals that the giving was not done in biblical proportions and that there was little sacrifice involved. Scripture presses us to be regular givers. We must avoid subjectivity in giving and become more intentional.[9]

Paul's teaching on the church's care of widows shows again the need for deliberateness in conducting mercy ministry. Consider these excerpts from 1 Timothy 5:3-10:

> *Give proper recognition to those widows who are really in need. But if a widow has children or grandchildren, these should learn first of all to put their religion into practice by caring for their own family and so repaying their parents and grandparents, for this is pleasing to God. The widow who is really in need and left all alone puts her hope in God and continues night and day to pray and to ask God for help. . . . No widow may be put on the list of widows unless she is over sixty, has been faithful to her husband, and is well known for her good deeds, such as bringing up children, showing hospitality, washing the feet of the saints, helping*

*those in trouble and devoting herself to all kinds of good
deeds....*

We can derive several guidelines from this passage. First, the
church should investigate needs and ensure their validity. Verse 3
shows that not all widows are due the church's care, but only those who
are "all alone." Second, verses 4 and 8 indicate that the church should
be considered the "third resort." The needy person herself (in this
instance, the widow) is the first one responsible for meeting her own
needs. If she is unable to, her family should assume responsibility. If
there are no family members, or they are unable to fulfill their obligation, then the church is called upon to help. Third, the passage suggests
that it is appropriate to put certain qualifications or preconditions on
material aid. According to verse 9, only widows who are over sixty years
of age, who have been faithful to their husbands, and who are known
for their good deeds of hospitality and service qualify for the church's
assistance. Charity is not to be indiscriminate; rather the church has to
make distinctions among those who are truly needy and those who are
not. In this way, it can focus its resources and energies on those with
genuine needs.

*Mercy ministry should be relational; it requires getting "up close
and personal" with the needy person(s).* As we've seen, developing relationships is one of the keys to the effectiveness of the outreach ministries profiled in Part I. The word *compassion* means "to suffer with."
It is difficult to be compassionate from a distance. As Gregory of Nyssa,
a church father living in the fourth century, taught: "Mercy is a voluntary sorrow that joins itself to the suffering of others. . . . Clasp the
afflicted man as if he were gold. Take the sufferer in your own arms."[10]

The reformers (e.g., John Calvin, Martin Luther, Martin Bucer)
stressed that anyone who was assisted by the church should be personally known by and visited regularly by a deacon. Such a policy was
necessary for at least three reasons.

First, it allowed the church to verify the validity of the need.

Abusers of charity are nothing new, as we see by examining church history. A common saying among the Christians in the early church was: "Let your alms grow damp with sweat in your hand until you know who it is you are giving them to."[11] The church fathers counseled congregations to adopt what might be called the "three-day rule." If a stranger in need of food and lodging sought the aid of a Christian community, the community would take him in. It would provide free lodging and meals for up to three days. During this time the stranger was to seek employment and take the necessary actions to settle down in the community. If he/she was unwilling to work or to attempt to meet his/her own needs, the Christians would terminate their aid after three days.[12]

Second, personal relationships with the recipients of aid allow the church community to understand better poor families' deepest needs and tailor its assistance accordingly. In the nineteenth century, as scholar Marvin Olasky has described, Christian charities employed this relational approach. They followed what Olasky calls the principles of "affiliation" and "bonding."[13] Affiliation means asking the question: Who is bound to help this person? As noted above, the needy individual herself was the first one responsible; after this, her family and friends were supposed to provide care. In the nineteenth century, church workers tried to reaffiliate needy individuals into the natural support systems available to them—namely, their family, friends, and neighbors. If the needy person lacked this support, then she was paired up with a small group of volunteers who could provide such support.

In addition, volunteers were encouraged to spend ample time with a few needy people, rather than spending little time with large numbers of poor people. Within the bonds of friendship, trust would grow, and volunteers would gain the "right to be heard," thus having the opportunity to provide spiritual and moral instruction and encouragement.

Finally, getting up close and personal is important because it shows genuine love, acceptance, and concern. Outreach efforts that become bureaucratized or routinized are dehumanizing and demeaning. They may provide for a person's temporary physical needs, but they do not transform lives. Sometimes we prefer to keep our outreach "sanitized" or "clinical," protecting ourselves from seeing and feeling someone else's pain. It is easier to write a check to a homeless shelter than to hug a smelly homeless person. It is easier to plan a large-scale Christmas toy giveaway for 200 needy children than to commit to a personal relationship over time with one little orphan girl, getting attached to her and having our hearts wrenched when we learn how she was abused and abandoned.

Jesus' method for ministry was up close and personal. He interacted and ate with the outcasts of society because they were needy and sick. In Luke 5:12-15, Jesus heals a leper by reaching out his hand and touching the man. The leper in this story knows he is a social outcast; he knows how others flee from him in horror and indignation. He knows he can hardly dare to hope that anyone will have compassion on him. Thus, when he approaches Jesus for help, he does not question Christ's *power* to heal him, but rather Christ's *willingness*. In His response, Jesus breaks all social customs by reaching out and touching the leper. We too must reach out and touch the unlovely and the outcast.

Mercy ministry should be holistic, ministering to people's spiritual needs as well as their material needs. Here again, Jesus' example is instructive. In His interactions with needy people, Jesus' approach is comprehensive, addressing physical, emotional, mental, and spiritual needs. In Mark 5:25-34, for example, Jesus does not allow the woman with the flow of blood simply to touch Him and leave. He wants to interact with her.

In Luke's account (Luke 8:40-48) we are told that the woman realizes that "she could not go unnoticed" by the crowd because of the fuss Jesus is making over someone having touched His robe. So she bolsters up her courage and tells her story before all the people (see verse 47).

Remember the context: Jesus is walking toward an important

man's home—Jairus, the synagogue ruler—in order to heal Jairus's fatally ill daughter. A large crowd is following Him closely. There is an air of urgency; they need to arrive at Jairus's house before it is too late.

In the midst of this, a woman who has been bleeding for twelve years touches Jesus' garments. Not only is this woman suffering from her physical ailment, but her condition has rendered her perpetually "unclean." In touching a great teacher, she has made Him unclean. So the last thing she wants is to be noticed by a crowd that will likely condemn her, a crowd that most likely has a low opinion of her in the first place, thanks to her illness.

Jesus, in His great wisdom, decides not only to heal her physically but to touch her emotions and her sense of self-worth as well, to show His acceptance of her before the crowd. Jesus stops the crowd, in effect placing the sick woman on the same level of importance as the mighty Jairus. Jesus is indicating that in His estimation, this lonely, long-suffering woman is just as worthy of His attention and concern as someone of higher social status. He further honors the woman after she relates her story by commending her faith in front of the crowd.

Other stories reveal Jesus' holistic approach. In Mark 9:17-27, Jesus deals not only with the boy who needs healing from demon possession, but also with the boy's father, who needs spiritual encouragement. After describing his son's condition, the man says to Jesus: "If you can do anything, take pity on us and help us." Jesus notices the man's lack of faith. He replies with gentle incredulity, "'*If* you can'?" and then instructs the man that anything is possible for those who believe. In another example of Christ's holistic concern—John 6:1-59, the feeding of the five thousand—Jesus meets the crowd's physical need for food but sees their spiritual needs as well. He challenges those who follow Him only for bread and encourages them to long for the spiritual "bread of life," which is, of course, Himself.

Ministering holistically is important, first, because of its eternal significance. But addressing people's spiritual and moral natures also has "this-worldly" benefits. In some instances, people's nonbiblical values, attitudes, and behaviors perpetuate their poverty (as in the case of substance abusers, the able-bodied who refuse to work, or "ne'er-do-wells" who gamble their earnings away). Our choices about work, about consumption, about pleasure, and about sexual behavior can have direct economic consequences. Often poverty can be overcome (or avoided) by changing our habits and choices.

Consequently, instruction in the biblical virtues for daily living should be an integral part of mercy ministry. Sinful patterns must be challenged and godly patterns affirmed and reinforced. The practical wisdom of Proverbs can be especially useful. In Proverbs we are enjoined to work hard, to manage money wisely, to be temperate in all things, to save and plan ahead, and to obey God's commands regarding marital fidelity and sexual purity.

Mercy ministry should respect the dignity of aid recipients and treat them as human beings capable of improving their situation. Since God created all people in His own image, all are endowed with dignity and are deserving of respect. Everyone stands equal before God. Sometimes it may be difficult to see the image of God in needy persons if they are disheveled, homeless, addicted to drugs, or engaged in prostitution. Nonetheless, God sees each life as sacred. The idea of the sanctity of life and human dignity is made clear in the Old Testament Law. (For example, God considers the taking of human life so heinous a crime that He institutes capital punishment for murder.) We must be careful to conduct our charitable activities in ways that protect and respect people's dignity. We must do nothing that dehumanizes people. These guidelines emphasize again the importance of keeping our ministries as personable and relational as possible; to bureaucratize implies that we are treating people as numbers.

Treating people with dignity also means that we assume that they can take responsibility for their actions and can play a part in meeting their own needs. We must be careful not to do for people what they can do for themselves. Our mind-set should be that of coming alongside a needy person, not taking charge of him or her. Our efforts should aim to encourage self-sufficiency. Doing otherwise can foster unhealthy dependency on the caregiver.

As we saw earlier, in the Old Testament Law, God instructs His people to give the poor opportunities to meet their own needs. The gleaning regulations are perhaps the best example of this principle. This law shows that God expects those with resources to share those resources and that He expects the poor to take initiative to meet their own needs. In this way, the more prosperous members of society can fulfill their obligation to be generous toward the poor. Rather than just giving the poor a handout, however, they provide the poor with an opportunity to help themselves. Thereby, the recipients maintain their dignity while practicing some initiative.

During the Reformation, Protestant church outreach encouraged self-sufficiency and gave people the opportunity to help themselves. The able-bodied poor were given the tools or materials they needed to earn their own living. Able-bodied refugees who had had to flee their homes and shops due to warfare, persecution, or famine were offered loans from the church to reestablish their businesses.[14]

In our society, given the small percentage of people engaged in farming, we have to be creative in applying "the gleaning principle." The S.T.E.P. ministry in Richmond offers one thoughtful approach. In the early years of its work among low-income residents of Gilpin Court, the ministry asked its suburban church partners to deliver holiday meals and Christmas toys to needy inner-city families. While this usually made the suburban volunteers feel good, it also caused some embarrassment and shame among the urban recipients. They were reminded of their own inability to provide for their children.

So S.T.E.P. changed its approach. It asked suburban churches to purchase new toys, leaving the price tags on them. Then it set up a small store in Gilpin Court for the three weeks prior to Christmas. S.T.E.P. hired local residents to run the store—taking inventory, serving as cashiers, keeping the books. The toys were made available for sale at half-price to local residents, and the store employees were paid in vouchers enabling them to purchase gifts for their own families. In this way, parents could earn what they needed to purchase the gifts and had the fun of choosing presents for their kids.

Summing Up

The prayerful, careful work of reflecting on the why, what, and how of mercy ministry may be unattractive to those action-minded souls eager to follow Nike's philosophy of life: "Just Do It." Without an adequate biblical foundation, however, even well-intentioned outreach efforts can backfire painfully and do more harm than good.

If Christians do not understand the reasons *why* they should be involved in mercy ministry, they may participate for the wrong reasons, such as guilt. Guilt is a lousy motivation. It causes us to focus more on relieving our guilty feelings than on truly helping the poor. Such a focus cripples our ability to evaluate our charitable acts. Giving a needy family money to pay their electric bill, for example, may make us feel less guilty about the fact that they are poor while we are rich. But such an act may not be truly beneficial to the family. Perhaps it will shame and degrade them. Or perhaps the reason the parents have no money to pay the bill is because they have wasted it on drugs and alcohol. In such a case, paying the bill only enables them to continue in self-destructive behavior. When we serve the poor out of guilt, we evaluate our ostensibly charitable deed by assessing whether our guilty feelings are gone, not by judging the impact of the deed on the recipient.

Understanding *why* we Christians should be involved in mercy ministry is essential, but it is not sufficient. We must also have a clear understanding of *what* we are trying to accomplish. This understanding keeps us focused on our mission and helps prevent our churches from becoming just another social service agency.

Take, for example, the family whose electricity has been turned off due to unpaid bills. In this case, the church will have to decide whether or not to pay the bills. Answering the question, "What are we trying to accomplish?" helps us to focus on the needy *people*, rather than on the needs, thereby providing some guidance on how to proceed. Rather than simply meeting the "felt need" (paying the bill), we'll talk with the family about the circumstances that led up to the loss of electricity. Have the bills not been paid because the father is unemployed? Because a family member has been ill, and medical bills have drastically reduced the family's income? Because the parents have misspent their money? Such questions will help identify the underlying needs beneath the "felt need." If the family lives in chronic financial instability and stress, concerned Christians will want to walk alongside them in a caring relationship. Together the family and the Christian volunteers can try to find solutions that will act as a hand-up to a permanent change in the situation—rather than settling for temporary "solutions" that are mere Band-Aids. Sustainable solutions in this case may entail substance abuse treatment, classes on biblical principles of money management, job skills training, or employment creation.

Moreover, because what we are trying to achieve—namely, helping people to know God, walk in His ways, experience wholeness in their relationships, and be faithful stewards of their God-given gifts and talents—is comprehensive and ambitious, we will quickly recognize that our outreach ministry should initially focus on serving a small number of families. Thinking through the "what" question will help us avoid creating mercy ministries that are a mile wide in breadth but only an inch deep in impact.

Finally, taking the time to think through the "how-to" guidelines listed above is an investment with a significant return. Loving others—especially those different from ourselves culturally or racially or socioeconomically—is not an impulsive or simple task. Every successful construction project requires definite blueprints to guide the placement of walls and doors and beams. Scripture and the examples of Christian mercy ministries throughout history serve as the blueprints for our outreach initiatives today. They guide our plans and help us to evaluate our efforts. For most churches, venturing into the inner city for ministry is a confusing and challenging task even *with* a blueprint! Without one, even the most enthusiastic supporters of outreach ministry among the poor can become discouraged and feel as if they are groping in the dark. Time spent on the seemingly passive task of laying the theological and philosophical foundations for the ministry will bear rich fruit during the active stage of getting the ministry up and running.

Overcoming the Barriers
to Reaching Out

The transition from reflection (studying God's concern for the poor and developing a theology of outreach) to action (actually engaging in mercy ministry) isn't automatic. When we try to "put feet" to what we have learned about loving others, we often collide with various obstacles. These barriers can be internal—the fears we have of going into unfamiliar surroundings—or external—the class and cultural differences between ourselves and those to whom we hope to minister.

Encounter at the Well

The story of Jesus' encounter with the Samaritan woman at Jacob's well illustrates some of the most common barriers to outreach. As the apostle John relates in John 4:4-42, Jesus deliberately chose to travel through Samaria on His way to Jerusalem. On this occasion, while His disciples went to buy food, Jesus came upon a Samaritan woman at Jacob's well. He asked her for a drink of water, thereby initiating an unlikely conversation.

Although most Jews purposefully avoided Samaria, Jesus knew that in order to minister to the woman at Jacob's well, He had to go to her. Often in Jesus' ministry, people came to Him for help; in this instance Jesus went to the need. And it was in a place that Jesus' own people considered unattractive. The first barrier we will have to overcome in ministering to the needy is our reluctance to go where they are—those locations on the "wrong side of the tracks" that are unattractive and unfamiliar to us.

Jesus also chose to speak to the woman—an act that amazed her. By speaking to her, Jesus broke down barriers of religion, culture, and gender. Jews had no dealings with Samaritans because the Jews considered them religious heretics. The Israelites considered the Samaritans half-breeds and despised their cultural and religious practices. And in the custom of the day, men didn't speak to women in public, as women were considered inferior. Jesus overcame all these common prejudices, intentionally reaching out to someone very different from Himself. He chose to minister to someone whom others of His religion, His culture, and His gender would have ignored or even despised. Today as we seek to reach out, we will also have to cross divides created by racial, religious, and cultural differences.

Jesus overcame other obstacles to ministering as well. He chose to help the Samaritan woman even though she was a sinner. Being omniscient, He knew that she was living in sin (see verse 18). Such knowledge did not prevent Him from reaching out. The woman was also most likely an outcast. According to the custom of the day, women would rise early and go to draw water together. But this woman had come to the well at midday all alone. This suggests that she did not feel welcome in the company of others. Probably the women in her village knew of her lifestyle and consequently shunned her. Jesus, by contrast, chose to speak with her rather than scorn her.

As we begin reaching out to needy people, we may discover that their own actions or lifestyles have contributed to their problems. And we may be tempted to ignore their needs, sensing that they are receiving the just deserts of their sinful choices. Jesus did not whitewash the woman's sin. On the contrary, He confronted her about it. But He did not allow her sin to impede His ministry to her. We may legitimately acknowledge another's sin and exhort this person to change his/her behavior, but we must be careful that our judgments do not prevent us from reaching out.

Jesus also overcame the barrier of personal inconvenience. He Himself was (we can assume) hungry—since the disciples had gone to buy food and had not returned yet. And John tells us that Jesus was tired from the journey (see John 4:6). These "internal" obstacles of hunger and weariness did not prevent Jesus from reaching out. Too often, however, physical needs inhibit our own actions. In contrast to us, Jesus was quick to perceive others' needs and often sacrificed His own personal comforts by meeting those needs. At Jacob's well, Jesus ministered to the woman even though He was tired and hungry.

Elsewhere in the Gospels, we find Jesus healing the sick and demon-possessed late into the night; we find Him footsore, traveling on long journeys from town to town spreading the Good News; we find Him comforting His disciples and praying for them the very night of His own arrest. In sum, we find Jesus regularly inconveniencing Himself for the sake of others. To follow in His footsteps, we will have to overcome the obstacles of our own weariness, selfishness, and desire for personal comfort.

The final barrier Jesus overcame—and perhaps the one we feel most keenly—was time pressure. As far as we know, Jesus did not carry a day timer! But His days were not aimless—He had a purpose and a plan. On the occasion of Jesus' encounter at Jacob's well, He was traveling to Jerusalem. His ministry to the woman at the well, however, initiated a change of plans. The woman ran to others in the village, urging them to come and listen to the man "who told me everything I ever did." So they came and listened to Jesus and begged Him to stay on with them longer to teach them. Many became believers. Jesus ended up remaining in Samaria for three extra days. He was flexible and available, ready to reorder His travel plans to address the needs of the Samaritan villagers.

Today our busyness can create a rigid schedule that leaves no room for such availability and flexibility. It is often difficult, however, to schedule mercy ministry, to confine it between hour-long time slots in our day timers. Effective mercy ministry is relational. And relationships take time; they sometimes require spontaneity. Our busyness and tight schedules become barriers to outreach when there is no margin, no room for responding to needs that present themselves at unplanned times.[1]

Overcoming the Barriers

Recently, the oversized headline of our daily paper proclaimed: "Gunfire Greets City Police Officers in Outreach Program." I quickly realized the shooting had occurred in Blue Ridge Commons, where our church is initiating a new community ministry. So my first anxious and droll thought was, *Boy, this will be just great for volunteer recruitment!* At a meeting later the chairman of our Urban Ministry Team said wryly, "I guess the volunteers we get will have to be prepared to meet their Maker a little earlier than they might have planned."

In all likelihood, it wasn't easy for Jesus to go to Samaria. The disciples probably thought He was crazy. Samaria was clearly the "wrong side of the tracks." But sometimes God calls His followers to do things that seem crazy.

In Jeremiah 32 God tells the prophet to purchase a field near a place called Anathoth. As Mark Gornik and Noel Castellanos have pointed out,[2] in human terms, this was an extremely foolish investment. The property Jeremiah was buying was behind enemy lines. The Babylonians had invaded the country and laid siege to Jerusalem. God had clearly told Jeremiah that the Israelites were going to fall to these conquerors. Yet He wanted Jeremiah to buy this plot of land—a field to which Jeremiah would lack access, a field devastated by warfare, a field whose ownership would likely not be respected, a field that wouldn't produce crops anytime soon. Jeremiah obeyed God, though, because God had promised that one day He would restore the fortunes of the

Israelites. "For Jeremiah," Gornik and Castellanos argue, "[B]uying this piece of land was above all an act of hope in the face of despair, a renewal of normal cultural activity that witnessed to a greater reality. In light of God's Word (Jer. 32:8-14), the investment in this land was a down payment on the Restorer's promises of a renewed city with its accompanying vibrant economic and cultural activity."[3]

God is still calling His people to make these kinds of investments in places of brokenness, violence, and despair. In the world's eyes, it does appear foolish for our church to embrace a community like Blue Ridge Commons when most everyone else is trying to avoid it. RESTOR-ERS are those who listen to the Restorer's great promise to revitalize these distressed places—and who start investing themselves there with joyful anticipation. Listen to the words God spoke to Jeremiah regarding His intentions to bless the Israelites after their captivity:

> *You are saying about this city, "By the sword, famine and plague it will be handed over to the king of Babylon"; but this is what the Lord, the God of Israel, says: I will surely gather them from all the lands where I banish them in my furious anger and great wrath; I will bring them back to this place and let them live in safety. They will be my people, and I will be their God. I will give them singleness of heart and action, so that they will always fear me for their own good and the good of their children after them. I will make an everlasting covenant with them: I will never stop doing good to them, and I will inspire them to fear me, so that they will never turn away from me. I will rejoice in doing them good and will assuredly plant them in this land with all my heart and soul. (Jer. 32:36-41)*

Who knows what blessings God is waiting to pour out on Blue Ridge Commons—and the places behind enemy lines in your own city! We do know that He Himself is the Great Restorer, and we ought not to abandon the places He has neither forsaken nor forgotten.

Get Exposed. To overcome the divides of race and class, we need to learn to step into the shoes of those different from ourselves. Since we want to minister to others out of true compassion and concern, and not just out of mechanical obligation, we must develop a compassionate and empathetic understanding of the poor and disadvantaged. Often this empathy can be encouraged by simply exposing ourselves to neighborhoods we might otherwise avoid, or by engaging in activities commonplace to the poor but unfamiliar to us.

People of different income levels, for example, are often isolated from each other. We live in different communities and shop at different stores. Those interested in becoming more involved with mercy ministry may find it helpful to:

* get acquainted with rough neighborhoods by shopping there, driving there, and walking there;

* ride public transportation for a week rather than driving;

* spend a few hours in the waiting room of the local Department of Social Services office;

* volunteer at a homeless shelter;

* attend a few church services in a poor community.

Activities like these can foster appreciation of the daily realities faced by those we wish to serve. We might discover how inconvenient and tiresome it can be to rely on public transportation. We'll probably discover that grocery stores within walking distance of rough neighborhoods have high prices and low quality and selection. We may experience the irritating noise and the unsettling "dis-ease" of inner-city streets. And we may begin to perceive the indignities of being just a number in the massive welfare bureaucracy. All these kinds of experiences can help us relate to the poor and be more sympathetic about the daily grind they endure while we who are more fortunate enjoy comfort and convenience.

For many suburban congregations, ministry among the urban poor will involve crossing racial divides. Consequently, congregants should be encouraged to pursue racial reconciliation. After prayer, self-searching, and repentance for underlying prejudices, our next step is educating ourselves. As Chris Rice and Spencer Perkins note in their important book on racial reconciliation, *More Than Equals*, minority Americans must learn much about white America, but whites often know little of the experiences and histories of minority groups.[4] Christians desiring to pursue racial reconciliation should learn more about the history of African-Americans in the United States or about the civil rights movement or about the experience of Latinos and other immigrant communities in America. Being reconciled to those of other cultural and racial groups involves taking the time to learn about them. Our studies tangibly demonstrate our respect for these groups' contributions and experiences.

Admit, Submit, Commit. Frontline activists emphasize that racial reconciliation has to be made personal and specific. "Don't try to take on the giant problem of 'racial reconciliation,'" counsel Gerald Austin and Tim Ritchie of CUM in Birmingham. "Just become committed to a specific person."[5] Here again we see the crucial importance of *relationship-based* ministry. Commodity-based approaches to mercy ministry never challenge us truly to cross the racial divide and pursue biblical reconciliation with those who are different from ourselves.

Here in Charlottesville, our Community Leadership Team is a kind of experimental laboratory where individuals from our church and from Blue Ridge Commons are building unique friendships. The interracial nature of the team sends a clear signal to the neighborhood that racial reconciliation is a key part of the community development efforts we are initiating. By working together, members of the team build specific relationships with each other within the context of designing and organizing community outreach events. The opportunity to focus together on a common goal is bringing teammates into relationships that otherwise we may not have initiated on our own.

Sometimes a real barrier to racial reconciliation is the simple fact of our separateness. Even if we desire to pursue interracial friendships, we do not naturally come into contact with people of other races in forums that permit sincere exchange. Tragically, many of our churches and neighborhoods are segregated. By working together in this ministry, we share a common interest on which to begin building friendships.

In *More Than Equals,* Perkins and Rice offer helpful advice on how to take these new friendships even further. They suggest viewing racial reconciliation as a three-stage process. The first step is to admit that racial tensions still exist and that we are probably guilty of wearing "racial blinders." We have to be courageous enough to take a long, hard look at our own underlying attitudes toward people of other races and admit that these may fall severely short of Christ's standard.

One of the racial blinders God convicted me of wearing had to do with Black self-esteem initiatives. Since I am generally suspicious of the "therapeutic overload" in our culture (and worried about the triumph of the therapeutic in the church), I was initially turned off by ministry programs aimed at strengthening the self-esteem of minority inner-city residents. I remember feeling that this was a capitulation to an unhealthy cultural trend.

What I didn't realize (due to my racial blinders) was that hundreds of years of oppression and discrimination have taken a serious toll on the self-esteem of many Blacks. I had not thought about the fact that Sunday school curricula rarely feature pictures of Black children. I had not considered that we often inadvertently associate colors with moral judgments (e.g., "washed as white as snow;" "cleansed from darkness;" "having a black hole in my soul"). While adults may recognize that such phrases have nothing to do with race, little children may find such distinctions confusing.

Once I realized these things, I grew more aware of other things that undermine Black children's self-esteem. Probably the most prevalent example is the dominance of negative media stereotypes of inner-city Black neighborhoods. Now I'm beginning to see such things a little more clearly, and my suspicions about efforts to strengthen self-esteem have waned.

A second blinder that whites often need to admit is a "fix-it" mentality. This looks at people as problems that need to be solved or cases that need to be managed. Our motivation in serving others ought to go beyond the idea that "we are going in there to help them." This condescending mentality fails to see that "we" may need "them" as much as "they" need "us." It fails to see their capacity for designing their own solutions; it looks only at needs rather than at assets. At the very first meeting of our Community Leadership Team, I facilitated a group discussion on the needs *and* assets of the neighborhood. Right from the start, I wanted our team to recognize that broken communities do have assets that should not be overlooked.

By focusing on building specific relationships, we can move beyond a caseworker mentality, because we begin to really see the people we are helping. We begin to see beyond their needs alone to their personalities and strengths and idiosyncrasies and histories and achievements. We begin to recognize that we are receiving from them—wisdom or encouragement or new ideas and perspectives. We begin to see that they are helping us.

The second step Perkins and Rice recommend is to submit. This means candidly acknowledging before God and others our inability, in our own strength, to love others as He loved. It means submitting to His Word and authority and following Him on the road of racial reconciliation. And it means submitting to one another—being willing to learn rather than only to teach, being willing to receive rather than only to give.

Finally, say Perkins and Rice, we must commit for the long haul. We must decide to stick with the cross-cultural friendships we're forging even when they cause pain and stress. Committing means sharing leadership responsibilities, even when we feel it would be easier if we just did everything ourselves. And it means that we make "intentional kingdom choices" that help us live out the pursuit of racial reconciliation. Such choices include exposing ourselves and our children to cross-racial experiences and interactions, choosing to participate in activities that afford genuine cooperation among races, organizing interracial committees, and hiring a racially diverse staff.

Social Capital. The primary way to confront our own judgmentalism—which hinders our outreach to those whose own sins exacerbate their poverty—is through prayer and repentance. We must ask God's Spirit to reveal our deep-seated prejudices and cleanse us from them. We can frequently reflect on Jesus' parable of the unmerciful servant (Matt. 18:23-35) to remind ourselves that we who have received great mercy should show great mercy.

Under God's discipline, I've been embarrassed to realize that I have a more critical spirit than I would like to admit. It became especially clear to me as I was working with a low-income family that lives on the outskirts of our city. The wife does not keep house in a way that conforms to my standards; the children are not groomed the way I think they should be; and the family doesn't spend its money according to the guidelines I think are best. To the extent that my judgments are based on scriptural principles, they are valid. Scripture strongly encourages us to be free from debt, for example, and to pay our debts honestly. When the family spends money for cigarettes and trips to McDonald's instead of paying the rent or the electricity bill, my criticisms are legitimate. The problem is that I did not give enough attention to understanding why this family lives the way it does and makes the choices it does.

When I did start to think about this, I realized that I have been blessed with some "social capital" that this family lacks. By "social capital," I refer to the training I've received from my parents, peers, school, and church that has equipped me with some valuable life skills. I was not born knowing that it's best to pay bills before paying for pleasures. Someone taught me this. I wouldn't have known the dangers of buying "rent to own" furniture if these dangers hadn't been pointed out to me. Additionally, someone had to teach me how to set up a budget and how to shop in money-saving ways. In short, I was taught many helpful lessons in the areas of personal hygiene, house cleaning, and money management.

This family, however, was not. Recognizing this has tempered my critical spirit and made me more sympathetic. I still believe that the family would benefit substantially from a transfer of the "social capital" I and others at my church have received. But instead of internally condemning this family because it "doesn't live and function normally," I'm trying to be more patient now.

Not My Own. To counter the barrier of our selfishness, we can meditate on the truth that we are no longer our own. The Heidelberg Catechism gloriously captures this truth in answer to its first question: "Christian, what is your only hope, in life and in death?"

> That I belong, body and soul, in life and in death, not to myself, but to my faithful Savior, Jesus Christ, Who at the cost of His own blood, has fully paid for all my sins and has completely freed me from the dominion of the devil; that He protects me so well that without the will of my Father in Heaven, not a hair can fall from my head; indeed, that everything must fit His purpose for my salvation. Therefore, by His Holy Spirit, He also ensures me of eternal life and makes me wholeheartedly willing and ready from now on to live for Him.

These age-old words remind us that God has purchased our lives; we no longer "own" ourselves. The purchase price was immense—the life of God's own Son (see 1 Cor. 6:19b-20). Since we no longer belong to ourselves, we ought no longer to live for ourselves alone, but should sacrifice ourselves for others (1 John 3:16).

These words also remind us of where we receive the strength to live sacrificial lives, the strength to minister even when we are tired or hungry or drained. For the Catechism says that God's Holy Spirit is the One who "makes us wholeheartedly willing and ready . . . to live for Him." On our own human strength, we cannot make ourselves "whole-heartedly" ready and willing to be servants. But God's Spirit can place within us a *desire* to give—even when the giving inconveniences us. And He alone can equip us—make us ready—for such service.

God has also encouraged me in the area of service by reminding me of His promise of full provision. The story of the widow of Zarephath in 1 Kings 17:7-16 illustrates this powerfully.

At a time of drought and famine, God commands the prophet Elijah to go to the town of Zarephath and to request food from a widow that he will encounter there. So at the town gate Elijah sees a widow gathering firewood and asks her for food and drink. She explains that she has virtually nothing to offer him. In fact, she was gathering sticks for a final cooking fire. Her little bit of flour and her few drops of oil will furnish her and her son with their last meal—and then, she says, they will die. Elijah, nevertheless, presses his request once more. He even asks that she feed him first and then feed herself and her son! He soft-ens this seemingly unreasonable demand by promising her that if she does as he says, God will bless her and provide for her family—even until the drought is over.

Bravely the widow obeys. The result? In verses 15 through 16 we read: "So there was food every day for Elijah and for the woman and her family. For the jar of flour was not used up and the jug of oil did not run dry, in keeping with the word of the Lord spoken by Elijah."

Sometimes we feel as though our physical energy—the proverbial jar of flour—is all used up. We feel our emotional energy—our jug of oil—has dried up too. We hear the call of God to sacrifice for another, and we take stock of our own provisions and find them wanting. God may sometimes make what appears to us as unreasonable demands. He promises, though, that He Himself will replenish our jars of flour and jugs of oil, providing us with the physical, emotional, and spiritual resources we need. If we are self-protective—holding back what time, energy, and material resources we have—we will miss the blessing of God's own rich provision. In 2 Corinthians 9 Paul reminds us that "whoever sows sparingly will also reap sparingly, and whoever sows generously will also reap generously." Some less familiar words then follow a few verses further—words we can rely on as we struggle to emulate Christ's servanthood: "And God is able to make all grace abound to you, so that in all things at all times, having all that you need, you will abound in every good work" (2 Cor. 9:8).

New Rhythms. In addition to combating the sin of our selfishness, we must also fight the battle of our busyness. We must ask our heavenly Father to help us reorder our priorities. We need heavenly wisdom for pruning back our schedules in ways that allow "margin" for us to be available to others.

In this process, we need to learn to think outside the boxes created by our culture. In his book *Wild Hope,* Tom Sine explains: "The dominant culture has not only largely defined the future for which many of us labor and the values we subscribe to. More than we recognize, the culture also has a great deal to do with the timestyles we adopt—the busyness that many of us succumb to."[6]

Sine goes on to argue for a reordering of the rhythm of our lives along biblical lines. While the culture has lost the art and practice of Sabbath rest, for example, we as Christians need to recapture it. Most importantly, this honors God. In addition, it can give us the refreshment we need so that we have energy for service.

We also should reevaluate our work styles. There is no law in the universe that says all people have to work forty hours a week—or more. Yet we typically assume that everyone should have a formal full-time job—and then we squeeze in time for ministry on the edges of our schedules. We may, though, be able to reduce our cost of living and cut back our formal work hours, thus opening up time for ministry. Not everyone will be able to shift from full-time to part-time work. But most people never even consider the question because they assume that they could "never make it" on a part-time salary. The question is whether, by simplifying our lifestyles, we could indeed make do with less. The answer will be different for every person, but we should at least ask the question.

Creative Design. Church leaders should keep in mind the barrier of busyness as they design their outreach ministries. While we shouldn't coddle volunteers, we do need to think creatively about how to help them make time for ministry. One very effective way is to offer couples opportunities to minister as couples and families the opportunity to minister as families. Ministry leaders can also encourage small groups who gather regularly anyway for fellowship, social activities, or Bible study to volunteer as a group. People will be more likely to make time to help a ministry if they get to spend time with their friends doing it!

We should also try to design the various aspects of our ministries around the skills and interests of our volunteers. We can't be so rigid in outlining a ministry program that we lose the potential involvement of people who would serve if they could use their talents in ministry. Obviously, the design cannot rest exclusively on the interests of the volunteers; it has to be relevant to the needs of the community. But there are many ways to bring these interests and needs together. In volunteer recruiting efforts, seek a balance between, on the one hand, asking volunteers to do tasks that need doing because of your predesigned plan and, on the other hand, asking people what they would like to do if given the chance. People will make more time to do those things for which they have a passion.

Receiver and Giver Transformed

When Jesus departed from the Samaritan woman at Jacob's well, her life was forever transformed. In John 4:28 a small but significant detail in the story is noted. The woman left her water jar at the well. We can speculate on the meaning of this.

Jesus' conversation with the woman focused on the topic of "living water." He announced Himself to her as the water of life, and after she has experienced this living water, she rejects any substitute—leaving behind her old water jar. One wonders whether this might also signify that she has renounced her old life of sin and embraced a new life in Jesus. In any event, through her testimony others are drawn to come and see Jesus, and then they invite Him to stay and teach in that community. As a result, John tells us in verse 39, "Many of the Samaritans from that town believed in him."

The promise held out for us if we, like Jesus, overcome the obstacles that hinder our outreach is great. The blessing is this: We will have the opportunity to share living water that can transform others' lives. But there is another less obvious blessing as well.

If we cross the divides that separate us from our needy neighbors, our lives will be shaped by those we touch. It is difficult to imagine that Jesus' disciples were not themselves transformed by their three days in Samaria. As they watched their Master preach and love the very people they had considered outcasts and heretics, their understanding of the kingdom began to deepen.

This was the first of several lessons God would teach the early church about the multinational character of His kingdom. Throughout the book of Acts we see the disciples gradually beginning to grasp that the Gospel really was to be proclaimed in Samaria—and to the ends of the earth. It took some divine intervention for them to get untangled from the barbed wire of prejudice and narrow-mindedness. Consider Peter's rooftop experience in Acts 10. Over time, though, the first disciples were changed by their interactions "on the other side" of the dividing walls of race and class. As we cross those walls, we too will be transformed.

Making the Shift to Relational Ministry

S ome readers of this book are familiar with the challenge of transforming an inward-looking congregation into an outreach-oriented church adept at serving the community. Other readers are members of congregations that are already active in helping the needy. The challenge faced by these church leaders lies in *redirecting* their church's outreach to go beyond conventional commodity-based ministries to more relational development-oriented ministries.

Many churches organize food pantries, provide emergency cash assistance to needy families, or have clothes closets on the premises where poor people can find free or low-cost secondhand clothing. Clearly, there is a place for commodity-based ministries. For instance, sometimes, as a result of natural disaster or house fire, people find themselves in need of emergency clothing, food, and money. Commodity-based ministries provide a valuable service for families in temporary distress—distress caused by disasters or by sudden unemployment or serious illness.

One common problem with commodity-based, relief-oriented, short-term ministries, though, is that people with longer-term, more complicated needs sometimes take advantage of them. Consequently, commodity-based ministries run the risk of further entrenching needy families in unhealthy dependency. The mother of two youngsters who consistently runs out of food stamps for her family each month may not need free food from the church's pantry as much as shopping advice, nutritional counseling, and money management training from church members.

A second problem with commodity-based ministries is that they usually require very little relational contact between the families served and church members. Their interaction might consist of a single meeting when the family stops by to pick up food or clothing. Thus, the opportunity for developing relationships with our needy neighbors through these ministries is severely limited. Bereft of such relationships, commodity-based ministries may well provide material goods, but they can never meet the needs of the whole person.

In short, while the traditional mercy ministries that many churches offer can be important in meeting specific, short-term material needs, they often mis-serve poor people. Sometimes the help they provide is not the help most needed. And they often fail to engage a significant proportion of the congregation in active face-to-face relationships with needy neighbors. Most conventional mercy ministries, when scrutinized according to the "how-to" guidelines outlined in chapter 5, fall short. Consequently, to conduct distinctive, biblical, holistic, and responsible compassion ministries, many churches will need to reform their current commodity-based approach or add new relationally focused ministries to complement their existing outreach programs.

Effecting this shift can be hard work, simply because churches—like most organizations—often resist change. To help your congregation make appropriate changes, you can encourage your fellow parishioners and church leaders to evaluate your church's current mercy ministries according to the questions raised in the previous chapters. For example, ask: Does this ministry truly empower people or just provide them with a temporary handout? Is this ministry distinctively Christian, or does it merely imitate secular social service providers? And does this ministry challenge us, as a congregation, to be personally involved in serving our needy neighbors? Marvin Olasky, author of *The Tragedy of American Compassion*, writes that in the 1800s schemes of help were judged according to whether they made "great demands on men to give themselves to their brethren."[1] The standard for nineteenth-century Christians should be applicable to us today.

Making the Shift

One possible first step in making the shift to relationally oriented mercy ministry is to reform existing commodity-based ministries so as to decrease their potential for abuse and increase their opportunities for relationship building.

At Oak Cliff Bible Fellowship in Dallas, specific mercy assistance guidelines protect the church against abusers of charity. One rule is that a family cannot receive more than $100 in financial assistance. In addition, a family cannot return to the church seeking further financial aid within the next three months. Individuals with emergency financial needs must meet face to face with a church counselor. During the interview, they must explain their situation and show relevant documentation—such as an eviction notice from the landlord or a "cut off" notice from the electrical power company. They also must disclose information about their sources of income—pay stubs from their jobs or documents describing their public assistance benefits. The counselor will then verify this information. If the need is genuine, the church will write a check to the person or company to whom the money is owed. No *cash* is given, and the church's check is never made out to the individual applicant directly. In this way, the church ensures that the money goes to whom it is owed.

These guidelines may at first seem harsh. They appear to suggest that not all people in crisis are entirely trustworthy. The key to implementing these rules is that every individual or family in need of help must be treated kindly. Explain to them why you are asking each question. Help those in need understand that you want to proffer aid but that that will require you truly to understand their situation. And let them know that you ask these questions of everyone; you're not singling them out for scrutiny. You may also want to explain that the church's benevolence funds are limited and that you want to make sure that you're helping those with the most pressing needs. Honest applicants with legitimate needs have nothing to fear from your inquiries and will likely understand why such safeguards against abuse and fraud are necessary.

In Phoenix, Neighborhood Ministries has designed programs that offer short-term assistance while facilitating long-term relational involvement. Everyone who visits Neighborhood Ministries's food pantry and clothing closet is briefly interviewed by a church volunteer. Applicants' addresses are kept on file so that church volunteers can also make follow-up home visits. Applicants complete a short questionnaire during the interview that helps the church learn about the applicant and his/her needs. The questionnaire asks: "What is your relationship with God like?" This question may prompt a conversation between a church volunteer and the applicant about spiritual matters and later may pave the way for introducing the applicant to other means through which the church can serve him/her.

Julianne Thompson, a physician who volunteers once a month at Neighborhood Ministries's food bank, relates a personal story about how a single contact at the food bank has grown into an ongoing friendship. During her first day "on the job," Thompson met Patti Gualajara. Señora Gualajara was like many of the poor Latino women who come to Neighborhood Ministries seeking assistance. Married to an alcoholic, she suffered physical and emotional abuse and lived in financial straits. Thompson interviewed Gualajara through a combination of English, Spanish, and sign language, and, Thompson says with a smile, "We just sort of clicked. I felt comfortable asking her some of those personal questions about whether she knew who Jesus Christ was and whether she read the Bible. I told her about the women's Bible study and what was available in church for the kids."

Thompson and Gualajara periodically ran into each other in the neighborhood over the next several months as Thompson continued her volunteer work. As the friendship developed, Thompson encouraged Gualajara to get involved in church. After six months Gualajara joined the Wednesday night Bible study and eventually converted to Christianity. Now Gualajara is one of the most effective volunteers at the food bank, since she can easily communicate with, and relate to, the women who go there for help.

RESTORERS in Phoenix and in Dallas view their commodity-based assistance as just one aspect of their broader outreach in the community. If counselors at Oak Cliff Bible Fellowship realize that a person requesting emergency aid also needs help finding employment, they can refer that individual to the church's job training/job procurement program. If volunteers in Phoenix learn that a woman seeking aid at the food bank is in an abusive relationship, they can invite her to the church's support group for such women. Both ministries have designed programs that increase the possibility that members of the church may develop deeper relationships with needy individuals in temporary crises.

Other churches as well have sought to transform their exclusively short-term mercy ministries into ministries that address both short-term and long-term needs. Broadway Presbyterian Church on New York City's west side, for example, began making the shift from a commodity-based ministry to a more relational development-oriented ministry in 1991.[2]

Throughout the 1980s, the church operated a soup kitchen that fed nearly 250 people each day. Key leaders in the ministry, however, were troubled. They continually saw homeless people sleeping in "cardboard villages" under bridges or in public rest rooms. They also realized that 85 percent of those eating at the soup kitchen were on drugs. By 1991 these leaders began to recognize that Broadway Presbyterian's efforts weren't really changing people's lives. Instead, the soup kitchen was unwittingly enabling aid recipients to continue in their self-destructive patterns.

To make the shift to a "responsibility-based" model of caring for the homeless, ministry leaders instituted a system whereby individuals had to obtain a ticket for each free meal. This meant that people in need of a meal had to plan ahead and take some initiative. Moreover, soup kitchen staff began encouraging the regular diners to volunteer to set tables, serve the food, and help with cleanup. In this way, the homeless were given the opportunity to feel that they were helping to earn their meal.

Moreover, under the church's new approach, responsible, punctual volunteers could be rewarded over time with paid positions in the kitchen; they could receive a small cash stipend plus food for their labor. Stipended kitchen workers could also be promoted to supervisors with larger "salaries" if they proved themselves. Incentives such as these help the homeless make the transition to regular daily work and provide them with the structure and discipline they'd lacked on the streets.

The church also began a "Street Smart" program, which offered homeless men jobs sweeping the streets in front of nearby businesses. These jobs pay a starting wage of $3.35 an hour. As the men demonstrate punctuality, dependability, and a positive work attitude, they can earn raises in twenty-five-cent increments. Thus, the church reinitiates these men into the labor force. The church also seeks to address the men's spiritual needs. It offers group counseling sessions for the homeless that "nearly always include Scripture readings and prayers."[3]

Big churches like Broadway Presbyterian in big cities such as New York are not the only churches that have learned how to restructure their community outreach efforts. In the small town of Warrenton, Virginia (population 18,000), the midsized Warrenton Baptist Church is pursuing some structural reforms as well.

About 450 white middle and upper middle class people are active in the approximately 150-year-old church. For many years the church's community outreach program, called the Deacons' Family Ministry, provided as many as fifty families with emergency cash and food each month. Often the church secretaries bore the brunt of the numerous phone calls from families in need. These secretaries typically referred the families to the church's food bank. Rev. Doug Harris, assistant pastor, says that during the six years he's been on staff, he has witnessed many of the same families come back repeatedly to the church for help. The church kept good records of the material assistance it provided, but follow-up—personal contact with the families—"was basically zero," according to Harris.

When Virginia enacted a series of welfare reforms that required able-bodied individuals on welfare to seek employment, the Fauquier County Department of Social Services put out a plea for community assistance. Mary Deeter, a Social Services official with the VIEW (Virginia Initiative for Employment, not Welfare) Team, explains that the AFDC women need "a lot of supportive services" as they try to find and retain jobs. "That's where the community comes in," she says. VIEW contacted every church and nonprofit organization in the county, explaining the new reforms and asking the community's aid in helping AFDC recipients make the transition from welfare to work. The Warrenton Baptist Church responded to this call and became one of the first three churches in the county to mentor families on welfare.

The church had already begun to better organize its Deacons' Family Ministry by recruiting a dozen volunteers who answer the phones every Monday and Wednesday mornings, taking calls from families in need. This reduced the burden on the church secretaries and allowed for greater conversation with needy families. The church's move to mentor two welfare families marked an even bigger step toward a more relational ministry.

Two groups in the congregation—the Women's Missionary Union (WMU) and the youth group—are especially active with the two families. Both families consist of a single African-American adult female and one child. Members of the WMU and youth group are in regular contact with these families by phone and make home visits frequently. When one of the mothers mentioned that she wanted to begin interviewing for jobs, the youth group purchased some new clothes for her. Congregants are involved in other ways as well.

Darlene Grimes, a thirty-three-year-old mother of four and part-time social worker, is one of the congregation's frontline lay ministers working with the two families. She relates that one of the mothers the church is helping is recovering from drug and alcohol addiction. Church members provide her a lot of emotional support and encouragement through friendly visits, phone calls, and cards. This mother is "gainfully employed," Grimes explains, and has limited material needs. Grimes is excited about the spiritual influence church volunteers seem to have had on this mother, who has remained "clean" and who has recently expressed interest in attending a Black church near her. "That may never have happened without the church's involvement," Grimes asserts.

The other mom lives in an old, run-down house with her child and other relatives. The church has helped this family repeatedly with groceries, and the youth group brings over hot meals on Wednesdays. This mother has secured a job at a local fast-food restaurant, but Grimes says she may not keep it. Because of the significant level of personal contact Grimes and other volunteers have had with this woman, they've learned that she has a serious medical disorder—of which the social services department was unaware. The woman suffers from seizures that inhibit her ability to keep a steady job. Church volunteers brought this problem to the attention of the appropriate case worker, and the case worker is now researching whether this mother is eligible for disability. If the mother ends up on disability, her overall income is likely to be less than what she receives from working. So Grimes says that church volunteers must help this mom make a plan for living within further straitened means.

Rev. Harris admits that the transition from conventional mercy ministry to relational ministry in Warrenton Baptist's benevolence program has not always been easy. Despite support from lay members like Grimes, Harris cites three key obstacles he's confronted—challenges other ministry leaders should expect. According to Harris, the first hurdle is that some of the church's phone volunteers are reluctant to join cooperative efforts with other churches—efforts that could avoid duplicating services and might minimize the abuse of charity. Harris has been meeting, for example, with a local nonprofit organization called People Helping People. The group recruits churches to join a helping network served by a single central clearinghouse. Harris wants Warrenton Baptist to donate its benevolence funds—and its Monday and Wednesday phone volunteers—to the clearinghouse. According to Harris, some of the volunteers are challenging this approach, asking him, "Why do you want to give up *our* ministry?"

A second hurdle faced by Harris is that some members of Warrenton Baptist disagree with his goal of serving fewer families more holistically. "The feeling of 'The more people you help, the better,' is there [in the congregation]," Harris reports. But this philosophy is misguided. "Over the past six years, the people we've 'helped' aren't really being helped," Harris argues. "They're becoming dependent upon us and on the other churches."

According to Harris, the third struggle in the transition of the church's benevolence ministry pertains to the attitudes of some church volunteers. "It's very difficult to move away from the mentality of 'Let's help them' to 'Let's help them help themselves,'" he explains. "When someone comes in asking for help, giving them assistance to pay their bill or giving them a way out is not really helping them. What [we] need to do is, in a very kind and understanding way, ask them: 'How are *you* going to pay this bill?' or 'How are *you* going to provide child care for your children?' You have to be there for the families, but helping means more than just finding the solution for them. It means helping *them* find the solution."

By reforming aspects of their existing outreach programs and adding new components, Broadway Presbyterian Church and Warrenton Baptist Church have embarked on a path toward more holistic, relational, and permanent-change-oriented social ministry. The transition hasn't always been easy, but it has proved possible. Your church can make it too. The rest of this chapter offers information about some national organizations that can help your church make the shift to relational ministry.

Resources That Can Help

Love INC (In the Name of Christ). A community training system of World Vision, this is a national church-based community ministry that helps churches help people. It teaches churches how to mobilize their members to effectively serve needy individuals and families in their local communities. Churches in various communities across the country come together to establish a local Love INC clearinghouse. The clearinghouse is staffed mainly by phone volunteers, who process requests from needy people. Volunteers attempt to verify the validity of each request by asking about the cause of the current problem, whether family and friends can help, and what assistance other agencies are providing. The clearinghouse then gathers all this information and discusses with the person who called what sort of help the churches could provide. Next the Love INC volunteer calls one or more Love INC-affiliated churches to inform them of the need.

All Love INC churches conduct annual "Time and Talent" surveys in which church members record their skills, the ways they'd be willing to help someone (e.g., delivering meals, providing transportation to appointments, being a budget counselor, serving as a tutor, providing temporary baby-sitting, completing minor home repairs, helping people move, etc.), and their availability (evenings, mornings, weekends, etc.). Staff at the church analyze the completed surveys and provide the church's Love INC contact person with a listing of all the individuals who've agreed to participate in the ministry. When the Love INC phone volunteer calls the church contact person about a need, the contact person can begin searching his/her lists of potential volunteers for the right match to meet the need.

Before joining Love INC, many participating churches report that community residents would routinely call their church offices asking for financial or other kinds of assistance. Usually such calls had to be fielded by the already overburdened church secretary or would be passed on to a deacon (who might or might not be immediately available). Neither the secretary nor the deacon would have had adequate time to investigate and verify the need or to ascertain whether the church's offer of assistance (especially money) would truly help. Also, though the church might have had a wealth of potential volunteers, it might not have had a mechanism through which to tap these volunteers for service. The Love INC model provides churches with a *system* for connecting willing Christian volunteers with people in need. And it helps to verify needs.

For more information, contact Love INC's national office at 1-800-777-5277 or write Love INC, c/o World Vision, P.O. Box 9716, Federal Way, WA 98001.

New Focus. Based in Michigan, New Focus was started by individuals active in Love INC who wanted to help churches better evaluate requests for assistance. Some individuals seeking the church's help truly desire to improve their lives if someone will show them how. Others, though, have no intention of eschewing self-destructive behaviors. New Focus has developed an innovative self-evaluation tool called the "Heart House" to help churches make accurate assessments. By completing the Heart House questionnaire, needy individuals identify the areas where they think they need help. The completed questionnaire also reveals to church leaders the person's readiness for making necessary changes.

New Focus's executive director, Jenny Forner, recognizes that traditional church benevolence, centered on cash assistance, can sometimes do more harm than good. "Money sometimes puts a Band-Aid on a broken leg," Forner says. "New Focus trains church leaders how to put casts on broken legs and bring about long-term change."

New Focus's comprehensive strategy for targeting the use of church benevolence funds embodies sound biblical principles concerning responsible compassion. Churches adopting the New Focus program must commit a specific percentage of their benevolence funds to the program, including monies to pay a part-time New Focus director at their own church. (Churches are, of course, free to find a church member willing to serve in this position without salary.) New Focus trains the church director to establish an incentive-based budget counseling program and mobilize the laity for involvement in "Compassion Circles" that befriend and mentor needy individuals. Participating churches agree to make space available in their own buildings for the weekly evening meeting and for a "store" at which New Focus members can redeem earned vouchers for clothing and food. New Focus calls itself a "change management system," since it seeks to help people in financial trouble take small, consistent steps toward positive change. Its core is the biblically based budget counseling program, but New Focus is about much more than just money management. The illustration below shows how New Focus works.

Let's suppose Sandy calls the local Love INC clearinghouse in her city and asks for $200. She needs the money to pay an electricity bill; she doesn't have the funds herself and fears her service will be turned off. During the assessment process at Love INC, the phone counselor learns that Sandy frequently runs short of cash to pay her utility bills. Given her income from part-time work, food stamps, and housing assistance, it seems that Sandy should be able to meet her monthly financial obligations. The clearinghouse volunteer tells Sandy that a local church may be willing to help her with this specific need if Sandy is willing to adopt a plan for managing her finances that will help her avoid this situation in the future. If Sandy is interested, she can attend a New Focus introductory meeting at that local church on Wednesday night, and she'll receive a free bag of groceries just for showing up. In addition, the phone volunteer lets Sandy know that the church provides free child care during the New Focus meeting and that refreshments will be served. If, after attending the meeting, Sandy decides she wants to join New Focus and get some help in taking positive steps toward change, church members will meet with her to design an action plan and figure out the ways their church can help.

So Sandy and her kids go the New Focus-affiliated church on Wednesday night for the introductory class. Her children join the other kids for a time of crafts, singing, Bible lessons, and games. Sandy and the other adults hear a presentation about the New Focus system. The church offers no-interest loans, small financial gifts, other material resources (food, clothing, household items) and services (budget counseling, prayer support, transportation) to individuals who become members of New Focus. Members, in turn, agree to attend weekly meetings with a personal budget counselor who helps them establish a workable spending plan. The budget counselor may hold the member's checkbook and credit cards if compulsive spending is a problem. Otherwise, the member keeps the checkbook but writes his/her checks once a week during the budget counseling session. Counselors and members discuss the small steps members can take to get back on their feet financially and eventually to become debt-free.

If Sandy decides to become a New Focus member, a small team consisting of the New Focus director, a trained budget counselor, and a deacon will meet with her in her home to help her design a strategic long-term plan for exiting the public assistance system and for enjoying greater financial stability. In the course of this discussion, the group will decide what steps Sandy needs to take and what resources—financial and nonmaterial—she needs. Basically, New Focus encourages Sandy to envision a better, healthier future for herself and her family, and then helps her to identify the steps to take to get there.

As members, Sandy and her family will continue to attend New Focus meetings once a week. Each meeting consists of two sessions. During the first session Sandy and other members will together listen to Bible-based teaching on money management, enjoy a "prayer and share" time, and eat together. Then during the second session Sandy will meet individually with her budget counselor. As Sandy accomplishes the various small goals she and her counselor have set, she will be rewarded with various incentives provided by the church—laundry soap, discounted goods, groceries. Sandy can also let her counselor know of any specific needs she has—such as a need for car repairs or a winter coat. The counselor then writes these requests on small pieces of paper resembling apples and hangs them on the church's "Giving Tree." The tree is placed in a public area in the church where lay people can look requests over and see if they can provide the goods or services needed.

After Sandy graduates from the budgeting class, she is linked with a "Compassion Circle" that will support her as she continues to take small steps to positive change. (Members of the Circle actually attend the graduation and celebrate with Sandy.) As noted earlier, the Circle is a small group of individuals (or couples) from the church who will meet regularly with Sandy to cheer her progress. Members of the Circle will have already completed a three-hour ministry training session and a twelve-week study on the book *How Can I Help?* by Skip Hunt.[4] New Focus recruits volunteers interested in being in a Circle and asks them to identify their ministry passion and unique life experiences and/or educational experiences they can draw from. Some volunteers may want to help a single mom; others may want to help an unemployed man; others may have a burden for the low-income elderly; while still others may feel they could best be used as mentors to young mothers. Then these volunteers are available to help a New Focus family when the need arises.

Perhaps a Circle that has requested to work with a single mom will be hooked up with Sandy. Sandy and her Circle will then start meeting twice a month for at least three months. During this time Sandy also continues meeting weekly with her budget counselor. Once a month Circle members will help each other complete a service project. One month they might repaint Sandy's apartment; another month they might resurface another member's driveway. This way Sandy has the opportunity to be a giver, not only a receiver, in these relationships.

Like Love INC's approach, New Focus's model is relational; it's aimed at long-term change, and it builds in accountability. New Focus's approach is also volunteer-friendly. Individuals are more likely to be willing to help Sandy when they understand that they are part of a whole team surrounding her. Also, each friend in the Circle makes only a twice-per-month time commitment. Budget counselors make a more significant commitment—a weekly meeting. Budget counselors, however, benefit from the fact that their instruction is reinforced by the weekly general teaching session and by the incentive/rewards system built into New Focus's program. Churches benefit because their benevolence funds now are tied to a variety of other supports (Bible-based teaching, budget counseling, emotional succor, and other practical aid) that help address the root problems underlying a person's immediate cash emergency. Moreover, church money helps individuals whom church members are getting to know personally.

Even more importantly, the New Focus program is evangelistic, overtly encouraging members to follow God's ways in dealing with their money, their family, their work, and their problems. While a member need not be a Christian to join the program, he/she is told that the Bible is the program's main textbook.

New Focus members benefit from the ministry because in addition to financial aid, they are given emotional support and taught the skills they need to live healthier, balanced, responsible lives. Often, people are dissatisfied with their current lifestyles, but feel that they lack the strength to take the steps necessary to improve their lives. New Focus provides them with a network of caring support and tangible incentives for taking those steps.

For more information, contact New Focus at 1-616-895-5356 or write New Focus, P.O. Box 351, 6837 Lake Michigan Drive, Allendale, MI 49401.

Kids Hope USA. This is a ministry founded by well-known author and church-based ministry expert Virgil Gulker. Perhaps your church is more interested in targeting its outreach ministry to children rather than to a particular neighborhood. Kids Hope can help your church "adopt" a local elementary school and, through one-on-one tutoring relationships, connect your congregants with at-risk kids. Each tutor agrees to meet with his/her designated child for one hour each week at the school. Tutors receive training designed by the Kids Hope national office, and a part-time Kids Hope director at each participating church provides ongoing support for the volunteer tutors.

According to Gulker, tutors provide an invaluable service to kids. During elementary school, children are at a critical age when they form their values, develop self-esteem, and acquire basic academic skills. Research shows that kids who learn to read by the fourth grade are eight times less likely to drop out of school and four times less likely to be unemployed and dependent on welfare later in life. Girls who learn to read by the fourth grade are four times less likely to have babies as teens. Consequently, Kids Hope targets children from kindergarten through fourth grade.

And, asserts Gulker, the one-on-one attention tutors provide is reshaping kids' lives:

> Initially, many of the kids are somewhat mystified by the relationship. This is a non-conditional, loving relationship for them. Essentially, the volunteer's presence contradicts the negative self-image the child has. If I stay with a child and constantly give positive input, I begin to shape that child's spirit and heart. Maybe that's the role of a Christian in our society: to contradict the negative forces that say, "You're not worth anything," and the reason I can say that is because I'm willing to give you my most valuable commodity, my time.

While developing the concept for Kids Hope, Gulker visited numerous churches, many of which were interested in serving needy children but lacked a system for coordinating church involvement. Consequently, Gulker's goal became to establish a "volunteer management system" that would recruit, screen, train, and place volunteers—a system that would "initially be used in relating to children but which could ultimately be used to develop relationships with other client groups and families."

Today the Kids Hope national office provides guidance to interested churches on how to get a tutoring program up and running.

According to Gulker, the development phase takes approximately eight to twelve months. It involves learning the ministry, establishing a leadership team within the church (composed of a pastor, lay members from various church committees, youth workers, a few high schoolers, a neighborhood school representative, and a few single moms from the targeted school), hiring a part-time Kids Hope program director, setting up the Kids Hope office, and identifying eligible students and interested volunteer tutors. Churches pay a one-time start-up fee to the national Kids Hope office for training and consultation services. (Average annual operating costs for the ministry depend on the size of the congregation and the number of "adopted" students, but most participating churches report spending between $8,000 and $16,000 a year.)

The national Kids Hope director assists the church's leadership team as it lays the organizational groundwork for the ministry and also trains the part-time director. The national office also helps to organize volunteer training sessions; these typically include a session with a child psychologist on how to relate to children, how to listen, how to affirm, and so forth. Finally, the national office guides the church in setting up an evaluation process by which the church can judge the effectiveness of its work in the school.

Tutors always work with the children during the school day on school property. The child's teacher sets various objectives for the tutoring sessions, and the volunteer works on these particular skills—usually reading. After each tutoring session, tutors complete brief reports about the session. One copy goes to the teacher and one to the Kids Hope director. The director regularly phones the volunteer tutors to address any problems mentioned on these progress reports. Once a month all the Kids Hope tutors meet at church for a potluck supper where they can talk with each other about their tutoring experiences and pray for their assigned students. Contact between tutors and the parents of the tutored children is encouraged during special events that occur throughout the year.

Churches that participate in Kids Hope send a powerful message to the community that they are willing to invest in the lives of the community's children. This is a positive Christian witness to school officials, kids' parents, and the world at large. In one town Kids Hope volunteers kicked off the academic year by forming a human prayer chain around the school, to give the school a "gigantic hug." The local newspaper gave the event front-page coverage!

For more information, contact Kids Hope USA at 1-616-846-7490 or write to Kids Hope USA, 17011 Hickory, Spring Lake, MI 49456.

✧

Each of the above organizations offers a well-structured model for how a church might establish a community ministry that makes a long-term impact on recipients' lives. The ministries highlighted here are designed to be replicated; they offer the benefits of a "turnkey" type program complete with consulting support. By seeking help from these groups, your church won't have to reinvent the wheel.

Many testimonies are available from churches that laud the merits of these organizations, but perhaps one church's story will suffice in depicting the advantages of collaborating with a tried and tested national ministry.

Calvary Church of Grand Rapids, a large middle class suburban congregation, has always been generous in terms of its assistance to needy families. Annually, it provides about $70,000 to people in need. Before the church restructured its benevolence program with the help of New Focus, though, much of that money failed to change in any significant way the lives of the families receiving aid.

In the days before New Focus, a team of two church deacons would meet with needy families. Given the huge number of requests for assistance and the time constraints on the deacons, there was little opportunity for accountability, personal contact, and adequate investigation of each petition. Consequently, many of the families sought aid time and time again. "We knew that we weren't doing a good job of addressing the problems," admits the church's business manager, Tom Bursma. "We were just helping to take care of the symptoms. We weren't able to get alongside people and encourage them, counsel them, and rebuke them if necessary. There just wasn't time to do that."

New Focus has helped the church mobilize the laity for greater involvement in outreach ministry. Thirty-five families are currently enrolled in New Focus classes, and they are served by some fifty to seventy church volunteers who help out as budget counselors, prayer partners, Compassion Circle participants, and children's ministry team affiliates. The deacons continue to play a crucial role overseeing the ministry but, in Bursma's words, are less "swamped."

New Focus has also provided structure and accountability to the church's benevolence efforts. Now, Bursma says, the church is "seeing a greater return on the investment" of its funds. "We have seen without a doubt that there's been visible change in people's lives. They say, 'This is the first time in years when I've had any hope,'" Bursma relates. "They feel good about themselves because they're making progress; they're getting out of debt, and they're feeling that someone cares for them." And beyond this, Bursma adds, "This [outreach] has made the families want to be a part of what's going on here at Calvary, to be a part of the different programs. [So] they're going to come under some teaching, and they're going to grow in their spiritual journey." That, of course, is the church's ultimate goal.

Despite the many benefits of making the shift toward a more relational ministry, many churches fail to make this transition because it's easier to keep on doing things the way they've always been done. This means, however, that the same old mistakes will be made, and the poor will not be genuinely served. The organizations listed above, and others like them, can offer invaluable counsel to churches willing to change to a more relational, holistic mercy ministry. Their comprehensive approach may appear a little overwhelming at first, but they may be able to assist you in starting a "scaled-down" version of their programs. Or your church may design its own imitation of their models, shaped to meet your congregation's unique vision for outreach. In any event, the bottom line is whether we're being faithful stewards of the resources, time, and talents God has given us for the purpose of loving our neighbors. If the old ways aren't working, it may be time for us to start pouring our love out of new wineskins.

Getting Going: Ten Steps to Building a Community Ministry

Once you've slogged your way past the barriers to outreach and begun to redirect the church's efforts away from conventional mercy ministry to relationally oriented ministry, you might consider establishing a church-based community development ministry that targets a particular neighborhood. This will involve tackling a variety of tasks both inside the congregation and in the targeted community. The ten steps listed below, while not exhaustive, provide a useful overview of how to get started. These steps are based on my studies of community ministries around the country, as well as on my personal experience in helping to launch a church-based urban ministry in my city.

But at the outset some caveats are necessary. The establishment of an effective Christian community development outreach is not simply a matter of taking the following ten steps. I want to avoid leaving the false impression that becoming a RESTORER is relatively easy. Frontline activists counsel Christians interested in urban ministry to plan on being involved in the chosen community for at least fifteen years. It takes considerable time to change lives and to make a lasting impact on a neighborhood. Inner-city ministry is not something to be done on a whim because it is fashionable or "hip." It must be viewed as a long-term commitment, one sure to bring heartache as well as tremendous joy.

Getting a ministry up and running is also no small job. The preliminary work of prayer, assessment, research, and building relationships can take a year or two—or more. Don't be discouraged by this. It's simply important to be realistic about the challenges ahead, counting the cost before committing to the ministry. Obviously these ministry challenges have been addressed and overcome by many, many churches and parachurch groups that are now RESTORERS.

Moreover, while the ten steps outlined below are important, they are not sufficient. Rather, prayer must be pervasive. We must pray to be empowered by God to take the necessary steps; we must pray to be guided by God as to when to move from step to step. And we must pray to be discerning. Not all the steps listed below are equally important. By far the most essential steps involve building friendships between church members and community residents, and establishing a working team whose members, cooperatively, will design and implement the ministry. Community development ministry is an organic approach to outreach; it involves entangling lives together so that the people in the church and in the community learn from one another and are shaped by one another.

Finally, the following ten steps are listed in the order that our church and many others have found effective. God may direct your church to follow a modified pattern.

Step One: Assess your church's strengths and weaknesses. Once ministry leaders have laid the foundation and have identified the barriers to outreach, they should assess the strengths and weaknesses of their church. This candid assessment will enable leaders to think realistically about the size, type, and scope of community ministry their church can establish. The assessment process should include the question: What financial resources can the congregation actually provide for the start-up of a new outreach ministry? Small churches, struggling to make their own annual budgets, may be unable to finance an ambitious new ministry. Money, however, is hardly the most important element of a ministry's success. Lack of money may even facilitate the design of an outreach program that specifically focuses on developing relationships with the needy, rather than on simply throwing money at the problems. Churches with limited financial resources are forced to think creatively about the *non*monetary aid they can provide.

Two further questions that should be raised in the assessment process are these: What skills do our congregants have? What do the demographics of our congregation imply for outreach? Congregations filled with professional people might consider beginning a Christian health clinic or Christian school for low-income families. Perhaps the congregation is composed principally of tradespeople—car mechanics, electricians, construction workers, plumbers. Such a church might do well to begin an outreach repairing cars and refurbishing homes. Possibly the congregation is dominated by senior citizens. In this case, the ministry might focus on matching needy elementary school students with an adopted "grandparent." Or the retired businessmen in the church might mentor promising inner-city entrepreneurs and future business owners.

Step Two: Learn about the community. This assessment of the congregation's strengths and weaknesses should be accompanied by a reasonable familiarity with the demographic and socioeconomic realities of the community. The ministry's targeted neighborhood should be thoroughly studied. How many people live there? What are the characteristics of the families there—working poor? single moms? low-income elderly? What is the community's history? Was it once integrated and now dominated by one ethnic group? Was it ever a prospering community? What are the principal needs, as identified by residents themselves as well as by outsiders who work in the community (e.g., social workers)? These questions can be researched through census reports, city planning reports, local history accounts, and by interviewing community leaders, social service personnel, and government officials. Conducting a community-wide survey can also be fruitful, but should probably be done at a later date (see Step Five).

Step Three: Identify what others are already doing. One key aspect of "learning the community" is identifying what other churches, private groups, and government agencies are already doing to meet the needs of the targeted neighborhood or population. Often organizations such as the local Department of Social Services or the United Way compile comprehensive directories of social service groups active in the community. These directories are an excellent resource for learning what existing groups are doing. Sometimes, though, such directories fail to include the outreach efforts of churches. Consequently, it can be useful to conduct a brief survey of local churches, asking them to identify their own community ministries. Finally, community residents themselves can provide information about who is active in their neighborhood. As you talk with them, they may inform you, for example, that some Good Samaritan—quite unknown by Social Services or the United Way—visits the community every Saturday and teaches arts and crafts to the local children.

Step Four: Begin building relationships. Perhaps the simplest way to build relationships in the targeted neighborhood is to ascertain if a neighborhood association or tenants' council exists and, if it does, contact its leaders. Describe your church's interest in partnering with community residents for the betterment of the neighborhood, being careful to emphasize that you desire their input on what initiatives would be most helpful. Attend the meetings, listen to the discussions, and get acquainted with the residents. Try to identify the Christians in the neighborhood and go and meet them. Start praying with them too. Ask them what they think the community needs most. Explain your church's fundamental philosophy of outreach, so they will know that you seek a distinctively Christian, relational, and holistic ministry.

Step Five: Gather together a core community team. One of the exciting things that will happen when your church begins building relationships with residents is that you will discover that God has already placed His people there and perhaps even given them a vision similar to your own. While coordinating our church's new urban outreach ministry, I experienced this very thing. The second person I met in our targeted neighborhood was Mrs. Lula Rogers. A devout Christian,

Mrs. Rogers has been living in Blue Ridge Commons, the neighborhood's main apartment complex, since it was built twenty-five years ago. Though always an active member of the community, in recent years numerous physical ailments have limited her mobility and energy. Roughly two years before our meeting, Mrs. Rogers began earnestly praying for Christians to come and help her reach out to Blue Ridge Commons' residents with the love of Jesus. When I first met her and explained what our church was thinking about, her eyes sparkled with excitement and enthusiasm. She believes we are God's answer to her prayers.

Identifying key individuals in the community, people who embrace the vision of Christian community development, is vital to the long-term stability of the project. This must be a priority before commencing outreach work. If local residents are not visibly involved in the work from the beginning, the ministry will lack credibility in the community. Gathering a committed team of community residents can be a difficult and lengthy process. But it is well worth the effort. Participation by residents in the design and implementation of the outreach assures that the ministry will belong to the community.

Pray that God would raise up people eager to partner with your church. And then invest in those people, building strong friendships characterized by openness, willingness to listen and learn, and mutual respect. For the long-term sustainability of the ministry—and more importantly, for the community's own long-term prospects for development—indigenous leadership must be developed and empowered.

Conducting a survey of the neighborhood can build unity among the core community team members, get the word out about the forthcoming ministry, and gather the opinions of local residents as to the most pressing needs. In Charlottesville our community team divided into pairs, consisting of one person from our church and one person from the Blue Ridge Commons community, and conducted a brief house-to-house survey. Since everyone on the leadership team from the community is Black and everyone on the team from the church is

white, the survey pairs sent a visible message that the ministry is a partnership that transcends the race barrier. Our survey questionnaire
asked respondents about their family life, their educational background, their work life, and their spiritual life. We also listed several
possible initiatives and asked respondents which they thought made
the most sense in light of their household's needs and their perception
of the neighborhood's needs.

While you are busy building the team and meeting more people
in the neighborhood via the community survey, your church's life goes
on—holding special holiday services, youth rallies, church suppers and
picnics, hymn sings, and concerts. Such events on the church calendar
can serve as excellent "low maintenance" opportunities for getting
your congregants together with new acquaintances in the target neighborhood.

Our community team conducted our survey of Blue Ridge
Commons in early fall. Every year our church organizes a fun-filled
night of games that we call the All Saints Fair, an alternative to
Halloween. For a few dollars, we printed up flyers explaining the event
and then, while we went door-to-door with the survey, invited families
in the neighborhood to attend the Fair in the company of a host family
from the church. In this way, church families and neighborhood families got together in a relaxed, low-pressure, fun atmosphere. In the
spring our church holds an annual congregation-wide picnic we call
the Spring Fling. Once again we invited families from Blue Ridge
Commons to attend the event in the company of a host family.

Step Six: Determine your unique niche. Armed with a general
knowledge of the community, a sense of what is being done by others
(and not being done), and an understanding of the felt needs expressed
by community residents, you are ready to design a ministry. The design
will build on your church's strengths and relevantly address the community's needs, without duplicating others' work. To determine your
unique niche, a planning team within your church should hash out preliminary vision and mission statements for the new ministry. The vision

statement specifies what sort of future the ministry ideally would engender. The mission statement briefly describes the purpose of the ministry and includes answers to the questions: Who is going to be served? What services are going to be offered? Where will this all take place? Both the vision and mission statements should reflect the fundamental principles of your church's theology of outreach.

At this point, the planning team must carefully avoid the danger of overextending the ministry by trying to do too much. The team must be on guard against a "bigger is better" philosophy and the temptation to increase the program's scope so as to boast about the large numbers of people served. Big programs can be more convenient, but often they are not better. For example, it's easier to feed 100 homeless individuals a Thanksgiving meal than it is to befriend one homeless family for one year, helping that family overcome the problems that led to homelessness in the first place.

Once the planning team has completed rough drafts of the vision and mission statements, group leaders should share these with their partners in the targeted neighborhood. Neighborhood residents on the community team can then assess whether the ministry's proposed vision and mission adequately address the felt needs of the community. If not, they can offer modifications. In this way, both church members and community residents participate in finalizing the ministry's vision and mission statements, giving both groups a sense of ministry ownership.

Step Seven: Learn from other models. Once the vision and mission statements are complete, the community leadership team should define goals for the ministry (based on the team's mission) and design a strategy for achieving these goals. This process will determine the actual shape of the ministry—its schedule, its programs, its staffing and volunteer requirements, etc. At this point, it is beneficial to examine other ministries whose missions are similar. The Christian Community Development Association (CCDA), a national network of evangelical church-based and parachurch community development ministries, publishes a directory. (See Resources, page 251, for information on how to contact CCDA.) This directory briefly describes the programs of each of CCDA's 250-plus member organizations. It is likely that several organizations in other locations have created ministries similar to the one you hope to establish. Contact these groups for information and, if possible, visit them on-site. They can help you avoid reinventing the wheel as you design your outreach.

Step Eight: Decide on basic organizational policies. Early on in the design phase of the ministry, the planning team within the church should settle various administrative and programmatic issues. First, how will the ministry be structured administratively? Will it operate as an "arm" of the church, under the authority of church government and reliant on the church budget, or will it be incorporated separately as a nonprofit organization with its own board and budget? Second, what will the ministry's hiring practices be? Will only professing Christians be hired? Third, what will the ministry's fund-raising policies be? Will the ministry seek funding only from the church, or also from foundations, businesses, secular organizations, or government? The potential complexity of initiating a relationship between the ministry and government agencies is so critical that I've devoted three chapters to this topic in Part Three.

In addition to administrative questions, programmatic policies should also be hammered out between the church's planning team and the community leadership team. What behaviors—by staff, volunteers, and program participants—will not be tolerated? What sort of disciplinary methods will be used? What will be expected of the parents whose children participate in the ministry's programs? Will the ministry charge a fee for any of its services? Will the ministry set limits on the number of people it will enroll in its programs? Volunteers, staff, and program participants will all be more comfortable if such policies are clearly delineated and everyone understands what is expected.

Step Nine: Establish a system for recruiting, screening, training, placing, and affirming volunteers. Whether seeking volunteers for existing ministries or new ministries, church leaders must construct a system to coordinate lay involvement. Sometimes this need for an effective mechanism to connect interested laity with service opportunities is underappreciated. But, as many churches have learned, simply publicizing available service opportunities is not sufficient. Below are some suggestions from frontline workers for recruiting, training, placing, and affirming volunteers in ministry.

Recruiting. RESTORERS have found that the more specific they can be about the ministry's vision and purpose and about volunteer opportunities and the time commitment required, the better. Volunteers want to know what is being asked of them, what kinds of people they will encounter, what training they will receive, and how much time they must give. People are especially interested in knowing if they can serve in a way that capitalizes on their particular skills, life experiences, and spiritual gifts. Consequently, ministry leaders may find it helpful to think of their ministry's work in terms of various volunteer jobs. Rather than putting out a general call for assistance, ministries can list the different volunteer roles they hope to fill—such as tutors for children, tutors for adults, instructors to teach computer skills to single moms, budget counselors to work with low-income families, Bible study leaders for small groups of teenagers, and so forth.

One key element in recruiting is convincing people that they have relevant skills to make a difference in someone's life. Jenny Forner, founder of the New Focus ministry mentioned in the previous chapter, employs a particularly effective technique in recruiting volunteers. New Focus's slogan is "You Can Make a Change in Someone's Welfare." The ministry aids churches to help welfare recipients exit the welfare system. When Forner addresses a church group, she brings along a large ball of twine. She asks the church members to stand up and form a large circle. Then she tosses the twine ball to someone and asks the person to specify one interest or skill he or she has that could help someone get off welfare. One person might offer to help with resumé preparation or transportation to job interviews or baby-sitting.

Then the person hangs on to a thread of twine while throwing the ball
to another person in the circle—who identifies what he or she can do
to "make a change in someone's welfare." After the twine ball has been
tossed to everyone in the circle, it has created a crisscrossing web. Then
Forner explains that a woman trying to make the shift from welfare to
work takes a big risk in jumping from the protection of the "social safety
net" of public assistance to the unknown workaday world. The church
members' time and talents, though, as represented by the web of twine,
provide a new safety net to undergird that woman.

Screening. Ministries also need to establish procedures for
screening volunteers—especially if the ministry works with children,
the disabled, or others vulnerable to abuse. One way of screening is to
ask potential volunteers to fill out a brief job application. The application should include a request for references (not friends or family)
whom the ministry coordinators can contact to verify the suitability of
the volunteer. In highly sensitive situations, such as where volunteers
are asked to provide temporary lodging for abused children, a criminal
record check may be appropriate. If these precautions are carefully
explained to potential volunteers and the necessity of protecting ministry participants is emphasized, volunteers are unlikely to be offended.
The general rule of thumb is that the intensity of screening should cor-
respond to the demands of the volunteer job. Someone asked to work
alone with small children in unsupervised settings outside of the ministry should be screened more carefully than the volunteer who offers
to make snacks for the children's Bible club once per month.

Training. Nonprofit organizations report that their volunteers
are highly interested in receiving training appropriate to their volunteer
positions. Some ministries may fear that requiring potential volunteers
to participate in training programs will decrease their pool of interested
workers. This, however, seems not to be the case. Volunteers who know
training will be provided feel more comfortable about accepting
responsibilities and make better, more effective servants.

The training, like the screening, should be commensurate with the volunteer job. Some activities will require no specialized training. In such instances, an orientation session that introduces the volunteers to the ministry staff; presents information about the ministry's vision, goals, policies, and participants; and answers any particular questions new volunteers may have (where to park, whom to call if they cannot make a meeting, etc.) may be sufficient. In other cases, more specialized training may be required. Volunteers who will be working with children may benefit from a short presentation about child development. Similarly, those working with senior citizens can learn much from a brief session on the aging process and related key issues (loss of independence, grief, loneliness, coping with physical limitations).

In order to design training sessions effectively, it is helpful for ministries to identify what kind of training they hope to provide— training that increases the volunteer's knowledge, that improves the volunteer's skills, or that seeks to affect the volunteer's attitudes.[1] In the first instance, lectures, discussions, field trips, readings, and video presentations may work well. In seeking to teach a volunteer new skills, the best teaching methods may be demonstrations, role-playing, simulations, and on-the-job practice sessions. When trying to affect volunteer's attitudes, role reversals, playacting, and reading case studies may be effective teaching tools.[2]

Placement. Next comes the task of placing volunteers in appropriate roles. Some churches have found it useful to do a church-wide "Time and Talent" survey. Congregants are asked to indicate which of the church's ministries interests them and what kinds of tasks they are willing to do (e.g., delivering meals to shut-ins, tutoring a high schooler in math, befriending a refugee family, visiting the sick in the hospital, leading music once a month in the children's Sunday school, or conducting mock interviews with job seekers). Congregants are also asked to indicate their time availability (once a week, once a month, once per semester, etc.) and to provide general information about their schedules. Do they consistently work weekends or the night shift? Do they leave town every summer? Are they only available on certain nights of

the week? Information from the survey is then passed along to the ministry leaders, who now have the names and phone numbers of potential volunteers, as well as information on the ways in which these
people are interested in serving. (To obtain a sample "Time and Talent"
survey, contact Love INC.)

Affirming. Finally, effective ministry leaders emphasize that it is
essential to affirm volunteers consistently and repeatedly. Some ministries demonstrate their gratitude to their volunteers at an annual volunteer appreciation banquet; other ministries regularly say thanks with
words or with well-timed cards. Volunteers also feel affirmed and
important when they are allowed to have a voice in decisions affecting
their volunteer jobs. Ministry leaders may want to meet with each volunteer personally at least once a year to evaluate the volunteer's work
and to hear the volunteer's thoughts about how the ministry's work
could be improved. This approach helps the volunteer to feel a stake in
the ministry, to be reassured that his or her work is important and valuable, and to feel that ministry staff are interested in encouraging the
volunteer's spiritual development.

Step Ten: Establish an evaluation system. Time invested in carefully defining the church's philosophy of ministry and the ministry's
vision and mission will pay off when it comes to evaluating the ministry. Planning for an evaluation may seem premature when a ministry
has just barely begun, but periodic reviews are essential if the ministry's
daily work is to live up to and reflect the philosophy and goals of the
vision and mission statements. Thus, ministry leaders should regularly
evaluate the outreach both in terms of its *faithfulness* to the church's
philosophy of ministry and in terms of its *effectiveness* in accomplishing the goals it set for itself.

Some important questions to ask regarding the ministry's faithfulness are listed below:

1) Is the ministry relational, seeking to transform people's lives
by providing them with personal contacts? Or is the ministry commodity-based, providing poor people primarily with things?

2) Is the ministry's approach truly holistic, seeking to address people's material and spiritual needs? Does the ministry challenge participants to grow spiritually?

3) Is the ministry promoting self-sufficiency or giving people handouts?

4) Does the ministry's approach treat recipients of care with respect, protect their dignity, and exhort them to take personal responsibility for improving their condition?

5) Is the ministry "doing much but changing nothing"? In other words, is its reach scattershot and diffuse, permitting only limited contact between recipients and the church; or is the ministry targeted and focused?

6) Is the ministry's approach to outreach wise and discerning, with built-in systems to protect against abusers of charity? Is the ministry discriminating, ensuring that its aid is truly helpful, rather than merely enabling needy people to continue on in self-destructive patterns?

7) What percentage of the laity are mobilized in service to others? Are the same few people doing all the church's outreach? If so, it may be time to return to the basics, teaching the congregation about the Gospel's demands and equipping the saints for service.

8) Is the ministry adequately drawing on the unique strengths and gifts of the congregation?

The best questions to ask regarding the effectiveness of the ministry are those suggested by the ministry's goals. Consequently, it is important to establish what Rev. Gerald Austin of the Center for Urban Missions calls "SMART" goals. These goals are specific, measurable, achievable, results-oriented, and time-bound.

Remembering Our First Love

Clear thinking. Careful organization. Strategic planning. Despite their importance, these are all insufficient for conducting an effective church-based ministry. Even the most deliberate and orderly plan for implementing an outreach won't get far without love—love of God and of others.

Our love of God must be sustained in the midst of our service, and this love must motivate all we do. In Revelation 2:2-3 the glorified Christ commends the church of Ephesus with these words recorded by the apostle John: "I know your deeds, your hard work and your perseverance. . . . You have persevered and have endured hardships for my name, and have not grown weary." Surely we long to hear such words of praise regarding our own lives, to be commended for our service and good deeds. But Jesus goes on to warn the Ephesians in verse 4: "Yet I hold this against you: You have forsaken your first love." The church of Ephesus grew slack in its devotion to God and in its love for Him. One significant danger we face in outreach ministry is that in our zeal for doing good works, we will lose our passion for God Himself. It is easy to become overwhelmed with the physical and material needs we see and to get so busy addressing these needs that we forget to spend time with the One whose love is supposed to be motivating us. But if we lose our "first love," quickly our service to others becomes mechanical, our touch efficient but cold.

In addition, we must rely on Jesus' sacrificial love to work through us in helping others. It is His love—not our competency or our programming, even though these are important—that empowers people to transform their lives. Certainly we can meet needs without sharing His love; indeed, this is what secular social service organizations do. But if we fail to maintain our first love and draw others to that love, we will likely effect no substantial lifestyle changes. A solid foundation for ministry, an effective strategy for overcoming barriers to outreach, and prayerful consideration of the ten steps listed above are important but are insufficient without love. For love transforms lives.

Part
Three

Collaborating with Government: The Benefits

Two Views from Detroit

Mary Jackson is a cheerfully maternal middle-aged African-American woman who eleven years ago moved into the Smith Homes, a crime-infested, drug-ridden public housing project on Detroit's west side. Love for the ghetto's children has motivated her to endure crack-peddling neighbors and stray bullets. The *Detroit News* once called her the "Mother Teresa" of the Smith Homes. Her cramped living room is a refuge each week for the thirty to forty neighborhood youngsters who attend her Bible club. Jackson is also trying to improve their home life by challenging the kids' parents and by connecting Smith Homes' families with her church, Rosedale Park Baptist.

Mary Jackson is a *feisty* Mother Teresa, known for her willingness to challenge the government bureaucrats who oversee the Smith Homes. For her, government is largely a frustrating, unresponsive force that impedes her ministry.

Several months ago Jackson took me on a tour of the Smith Homes in her 1984 Ford station wagon. We crawled through the complex's narrow alleys, waving hello to the children and averting our eyes from the groups of young men huddled in shady corners of the buildings. Jackson was eager to show me a small, nondescript rust-colored building—the complex's community center. Pointing to it with a disgusted look on her face, she fumed: "They [the housing authorities] have so much red tape about using this facility. It just stands there most of the time closed and locked with nothing going on. It's just the bureaucracy trying to keep the people oppressed." Jackson has requested use of the center for the Bible clubs and recreational activities she plans. Each time the authorities have turned her down, citing the need to keep church and state separate. "I'm a resident here, and this center is supposed to be for the residents. So I don't see why it's such a problem to use it," Jackson reasons. She says she'd be willing to limit her use to recreational activities. "This place would give the kids a place to burn off that excess energy, instead of watching all those negative things on television and listening to that demonic music." But her efforts have been to no avail.

Throughout the rest of the tour, Jackson raised other complaints about the government agencies overseeing various aspects of the residents' lives. Pointing to the newspapers plastered on many apartment windows, she explained that while housing authorities promise to provide residents with curtains, they never come through. We walked to the community's "playground"—a trash-littered site sporting only a rusted swing set with no swings and an unstable slide. Grimacing, Jackson reported that for ten years she's been trying to get the appropriate governmental entity to replace the swings. That afternoon she went to city hall for an appointment with a new bureaucrat with responsibilities touching on the lives of the Smith Homes residents. She was stood up. Later an undaunted but weary Jackson told me that she'd try again to get an appointment.

Don DeVos's encounters with government have been considerably more pleasant than Mary Jackson's. DeVos is the seventy-six-year-old fireball who directs the Detroit Rescue Mission Ministries (DRMM). He glows with enthusiasm about Jesus, about the ministry—and about public-private partnerships. DeVos's office is located just off the "Cass Corridor," perhaps the most notorious strip in inner-city Detroit. Like

Jackson, DeVos takes me on a tour. I haven't time to visit all of DRMM's twenty-one facilities that serve some of the toughest individuals in the state's welfare system—homeless families, gang members, drug addicts, juvenile offenders. So we travel only to the Genesis House, a unique rehabilitated shelter for recovering female drug-abusers and their children.

For DeVos, Genesis House is a visible example of how cooperation with government entities has enhanced the ministry. DRMM purchased the property in early 1990. It needed extensive repairs and remodeling before it could be used, and the city government contacted DeVos to find out how much the refurbishing would cost. They then put up nearly $400,000 in 1992; this, combined with DRMM's funds from private sources, enabled the Mission to complete the remodeling and open the facility.

DRMM's relationship with city officials and government representatives at the state and federal level stretches back some eight years. DeVos's own collaborations with the public sector during the five years of his tenure as president have been, in his estimation, uniformly positive. Government grants—which made up nearly 50 percent of the ministry's $5.2 million in 1995—have helped DRMM serve far more individuals than it would otherwise have been able to help.

Unlike some who complain about the "strings" accompanying government grants, DeVos argues that the regulations imposed with state funding sometimes "make [religious social service providers] do what we might not otherwise do, salary-wise and program-wise." DeVos is particularly supportive of the certification and training requirements that often accompany the grants. He worries that some Christian ministries have incompetent staff members who "would not make it in the secular work world." Therefore, state-mandated certification requirements can "weed out" unqualified people and improve overall service delivery to the poor. "Too often because we're in Christian ministry, we feel we're supposed to be untouchables," DeVos argues. "I don't buy that at all. I think our program should exceed what the secular realm does; we shouldn't try to get by on less because we're Christians."

There are nonfinancial perks to public-private collaboration as well, in DeVos's opinion. He reports that his staff have benefited from training they have received from experts working in various state agencies. His staff members also improve their skills by attending various state-sponsored seminars and conferences. And, he says, governmental staff help keep DRMM informed about additional resources available for the Mission's clients.

Mary Jackson and Don DeVos, committed Christian frontline workers among the poor, have clearly had very diverse experiences with government. Governmental entities have hog-tied Mary Jackson's ministry while enabling Don DeVos's. Ministries across the country report all sorts of experiences in their relationship with government— some that approximate the difficulties Jackson has faced, some similar to the fruitful collaboration DeVos has enjoyed, and some characterized by a mixture of benefits and hassles. Most new community ministries—regardless of whether they plan on collaborating with government—will at some point butt up against state entities. The encounter might be initiated by something as simple as needing a license or as complex as applying for government funds to underwrite some part of the ministry's programming. The issue of funding is ubiquitous. Every Christian nonprofit I visited, regardless of whether it accepted state funds or not, had had to wrestle with the matter.

The Current Climate

The current welfare reform debate, characterized by frequent and typically positive discussions of the potential role of faith-based ministries to address the problems of the poor, makes the issue of governmental relations all the more pressing for Christian leaders. The present enthusiasm for faith-based groups has some political leaders eager to channel more tax dollars to such ministries. The federal government already provides some 350 grant programs for social service nonprofits,[1] and most nonprofits receive considerable public-sector financing.

Professor Stephen Monsma of Pepperdine University recently conducted a survey of 766 nonprofit organizations involved in education, children and youth services, and overseas relief and development. He found that almost 70 percent of the organizations with a religious orientation accepted public tax dollars. Monsma concluded from his study that "one of the best kept secrets in the United States is that when it comes to public money, church and state mix."[2]

Some GOP legislators want to go even further in providing funds for faith-based groups. Senator Dan Coats has proposed legislation allowing individual citizens a dollar-for-dollar tax credit (up to $500 total) for donations made to charities—including religious groups—that serve the poor. Senator John Ashcroft has proposed a tax credit of up to $500 for individuals who spend fifty hours a year in volunteer work with a charitable organization serving poor people.

Ashcroft was also responsible for the inclusion of the "Charitable Choice" provisions in the 1996 federal welfare reform law. Charitable Choice encourages states to involve community and faith-based organizations in providing federally funded welfare services to the poor and needy. The provisions are designed to protect the religious character of faith-based organizations that choose to accept federal funds to help the poor (as well as protect the religious liberty of beneficiaries of welfare services). Under Charitable Choice, religiously based social service providers retain their institutional autonomy and control of their mission. A faith-based group accepting government funds does not become a "state actor"; rather it retains its autonomy and control "over the definition, development, practice, and expression of its religious beliefs."[3]

The initiative is "unprecedented," according to welfare policy analyst Stanley Carlson-Thies of the Center for Public Justice. He explains that typically legislators sympathetic to religious social welfare ministries favor funding mechanisms such as vouchers. In these schemes poor people receive government vouchers worth a specific amount of cash and can "redeem" them at secular or religious organizations offering the services they require. In this way, religious organizations receive government funding indirectly, staying at arm's length from the state. According to Carlson-Thies, Charitable Choice "presumes that religious providers ought to be no less eligible to participate in offering public services with governmental funds than any secular provider, but that special protections are needed so that religious groups are not pressed to secularize themselves."

In short, substantial government funds are already available to religious nonprofits serving the poor, and Charitable Choice may encourage states to provide even more money. Indeed, the flurry of legislative initiatives related to government funding of religious nonprofits indicates that "public-private partnerships" are today's hot topic in welfare reform circles. The challenge of such partnerships is that they must be structured to preserve the very things that make the faith-based ministries so successful—such as their personable, relational style; thrift and programmatic flexibility; volunteer strength and credibility in the communities they serve; and, most importantly, their caring spiritual witness and moral challenge. In today's climate ministries working among the poor will be faced increasingly with the question of whether or not to seek government funding. Consequently, this chapter and chapter 10 provide an accounting of the promises and potential pitfalls of government funding and begin to sketch guidelines for fruitful public-private partnerships.

Benefits of Government Funding

Faith-based ministries that receive government funding cite several reasons for its attractiveness. The most obvious is that with increased resources, ministries may be able to expand their efforts and help more people, or continue a valuable program for which private funding has been inadequate.

In some instances, seeking government funding rather than private support can be cost-effective. If the grant applied for is large enough, the staff time expended in preparing the application may produce a higher rate of return than the same amount of staff time spent in fund-raising efforts with the ministry's individual donors. Also, government grants usually provide a specific, known amount annually, whereas private donations are unpredictable and usually cyclical. As one ministry staffer put it, such guaranteed funding "can free the organization to concentrate on service delivery rather than on fund-raising and donor maintenance."

In addition, many government grants are set up as matching funds. This can be an incentive for private donors. As they recognize that their gifts will be multiplied because the ministry has secured such an arrangement with government, donors may decide to give to this ministry rather than to another one, since they believe their giving will have greater impact.

Some ministry directors also report that the process of soliciting and receiving government grants has expanded their network of funding sources. Pamela Martin Turner, executive director of REACH, Inc., a faith-based community development organization based in inner-city Detroit, says her collaboration with government has introduced her to potential funders she otherwise would not have met. Her organization participates in city commissions and other government-sponsored meetings where she meets new contacts and is kept informed about grant programs for which her agency might be eligible.

Ms. Turner adds that important "cross-learning" occurs in public-private partnerships. "If there isn't opportunity to work together, organizational cultures develop which each member doesn't understand. If you're in the government, all you know is the government's way of doing something, and vice versa; if you're in the private business sector, and you've never worked with government, you don't understand how government works." Turner says she has found that some Christian ministries lack necessary technical skills to conduct their outreach effectively. Contact with government agencies can provide some necessary training. She reports that REACH "has learned a tremendous amount about the actual implementation of community development programs by virtue of our seeking funding outside of the church."

Turner and others also note the discipline that comes from writing grant proposals and completing reports for government officials. "Part of what happens when you [write] reports," Turner explains, "is that it makes you think about what you're doing. And that's usually a good thing."

Ministries that receive government funding may also find that their contractual relationships with public officials provide them opportunity for regulatory relief. Leonard Krugel, Divisional Services Director for the Salvation Army in Michigan, explains that the Army's contract with the state government to oversee homeless shelters exempts the Army from some highly detailed regulations passed by the city government. These include the mandates that homeless shelters in the city provide a registered dietician in every shelter, offer special meals to people with special dietary needs, cooperate with local schools in providing transportation and tutoring for the children staying in the shelters, and even provide staff to ensure that residents on medication take their pills when they are supposed to. "All [these regulations] are outside the scope of our contract," Krugel reports.

Before this arrangement with the state government, the Army's programs were "overburdened" with regulations. The partnership was attractive to the Army, Krugel explains, because it increased the Army's flexibility. "The homeless problem was there anyway, and so we were going to face it whether or not we participated in the partnership. We were appreciative of the opportunity to be consulted about how to handle the problem. This was historic in that it was a partnership instead of having policy dictated to us—'You do this service in this way, and we will manage you.'"

Some organizations receiving substantial funding from governmental sources argue as well that they are able to influence public policy because of their relationships with state actors. William Blacquire of Bethany Christian Services, a large evangelical adoption and family services agency, reports that his group "sits on task forces and committees. We testify in front of state representatives and local boards. We have an influence on policy and procedures, how things should be done in adoption and foster care." Most importantly, he says, "We can give a Christian perspective to policy." Blacquire believes that Bethany's influence in public policy circles would be more limited in the absence of its contractual relationships with the state government.

In sum, many faith-based ministries have found that accepting government funds and cooperating with governmental entities is beneficial. In a survey of over 700 directors of nonprofit charitable organizations (both religious and secular), most said that they believed the benefits of governmental funding outweighed the potential costs.[4] And some individuals on the front lines favor taking government grants for a reason that goes beyond the specific benefits described above. These individuals pursue government funding because they believe it is a way to ensure that their tax dollars get reinvested in their own communities. As Charlene Johnson of the Michigan Neighborhood Partnership (a network of private social service organizations) puts it, "I think that because we contribute to the government through our taxes, we have a right for those funds to come back to support our efforts in the community."

Some Positive Partnerships

Positive relationships between faith-based ministries and governmental entities are characterized by several important elements. Bethany Christian Services's work with the Kent County Department of Social Services and the Detroit Rescue Mission Ministries's partnership with its local DSS reflect these elements. These two examples of fruitful collaboration set a standard by which other ministries can judge the effectiveness and desirability of their own public-private partnerships.

As mentioned above, Bethany Christian Services (BCS) works with governmental entities to provide foster care for at-risk children and residential care for abused and neglected children and for juvenile sexual offenders. Its relationship with government is cordial and long-standing. John Cole, program manager for the local DSS, is the ministry's principal governmental contact. Cole takes a results-oriented and respectful approach to the partnership. Cole says he "doesn't implement any policy without first developing it in draft form and asking the private groups [with whom the department partners] what they think about it." He says his relationship with BCS is not just an arms'-length, businesslike one. His staff meet with BCS staff monthly, and he meets personally with BCS leaders quarterly to discuss policy design and implementation.

Don DeVos's Detroit Rescue Mission Ministries (DRMM) provides emergency shelter for homeless men and women and runs substance abuse recovery programs. As noted earlier, the ministry enjoys an excellent relationship with Wayne County welfare chief Sam Chambers and has collaborated for decades with Chambers's Department of Social Services. Chambers has established a community-wide planning board, on which several faith-based ministries (including DRMM) sit, to discuss policy formation and share ideas and information. Chambers says he doesn't think the state has all the answers and welcomes input from the religious nonprofits. These groups, he explains, are closer to the needs, more "user-friendly," and less bureaucratic and intimidating. Noting that Detroit has 4,000 churches but only thirty-three welfare offices, Chambers says it is obvious that he can meet needs more effectively by tapping into the religious sector. More than this, he asserts that faith-based ministries "do a better job because they tend to treat the whole man."

Aware of some of the church-state issues involved, Chambers says his evaluations of the religious nonprofits with whom his department partners are "outcome-based." His office enforces health and safety regulations and conducts financial audits but does not interfere with ministries' internal policies and procedures. There is no attempt to force groups to change their holistic approach or extirpate their religious sensibilities. Chambers says he works with DRMM because the ministry's track record is stellar. It has helped turn around the lives of some of the toughest clients in the welfare system.

These partnerships work well because the governmental officials involved, for their part, are willing to forge a genuine, respectful, pragmatic working relationship marked by much dialogue and close interaction. They appreciate the ministries' religious character and do not insist that the groups compromise their vision and mission.

For their part, BCS and DRMM do three important things that maintain them in a healthy position vis-à-vis their relationship with the state. First, they enjoy strong leadership. Second, they have a clear sense of purpose and vision. These things help the ministries avoid being sidetracked or co-opted into projects that would distract them from their mission or threaten their religious integrity. Third, while both ministries receive significant governmental funds, they are not dependent on those funds. Instead, they have diversified their donor base so that they could continue essential operations in the absence of governmental grants.[5]

These two partnerships are also based on many years of patient relationship-building; now a mutual trust and respect exists that makes the collaboration truly one between equals. Don DeVos says that his age and experience have won him respect from governmental staff, and that his personal interest in the state workers with whom he interacts has even led to opportunities for him to minister to them spiritually. DeVos also thinks these bureaucrats sense his brokenness over the plight of the needy. "They recognize what we're doing and that we're concerned about these needs," he says.

Moreover, DeVos believes DRMM's unique approach with various agencies has made the Mission's collaborations with the public sector more fruitful than those experienced by other nonprofits. He explains: "We aren't only out here asking them for help. We're saying, 'What can we do to help you?' . . . I don't go to them with the idea of: 'What can you do for me?' I go to them, ask them their goals, where their greatest needs are, and what we can do to help. And they look at me as if I was crazy! Because every other organization says they'll do such and such, but that they need help."

DeVos has provided specific, tangible help to governmental agencies. A few years ago, the Department of Social Services wanted to establish an office on the east side of Detroit near one of DRMM's facilities, and DeVos let them have space in the building. He also granted office space to the police department, which wanted to establish a small substation in that neighborhood.

Another clear sign of the strength of DRMM's and BCS's partnerships with government is that the ministries influence the policy agenda and have input into program design. In both cases, the ministries are not treated merely as subcontractors carrying out the state's wishes, but as partners in implementing policies both have helped to shape.

Unfortunately, according to Kent County's John Cole, this kind of genuine broad-based collaboration is rare in his state. Most Michigan county welfare offices are biased against purchasing welfare services from private nonprofits, Cole says. They believe that they themselves should provide their own services. And even when local welfare departments do purchase services from nonprofits, Cole maintains, they do not do so as part of a broad, genuine partnership. "They may purchase services, but I don't think they really believe that that's the way they ought to go. I've been in meetings where they [governmental officials] are very critical of the [private] agencies," he reports. Often the arrangements are "very businesslike and one-sided," even "adversarial" at times.

Because some interactions between faith-based ministries and state entities are "adversarial," or at least frustrating, many religiously grounded groups simply avoid accepting government funds and partnering with governmental agencies. Other groups choose to cooperate with government, but they report that they have had to navigate around numerous potential pitfalls presented by state funding. Several of these pitfalls are described in the next chapter.

Collaborating with Government: The Potential Pitfalls

R ecently I attended the inaugural meeting of a city task force that plans to target initiatives on the low-income neighborhood my church "adopted" for its new ministry. I went because I wanted to learn about the local government's plans and because I hoped to network with officials who might be helpful in our church's efforts. I met a young man from the mayor's office who said he'd see what he could do to get our group some reserved time at a city pool near the neighborhood during our two-week summer camp. And a woman from the housing department invited me to send her a "wish list" from our ministry, and she'd see what her agency might be able to do to help.

I was encouraged by these conversations, as well as reminded that government bureaucrats are real people—often individuals who really do care about their constituents. This chapter tells some sad stories about ways ministries have been hampered by cooperating with government. While such accounts must be taken seriously, I do not wish to leave the impression that *all* bureaucrats are inept or that agencies actively seek to frustrate the efforts of Good Samaritans.

The pitfalls described below are rooted in part in the nature of governmental institutions themselves. These institutions are inherently bureaucratic, sometimes more "process-minded" than "results-minded," and often inflexible and unimaginative. Their lumbering pace and tradi-

tion-bound internal culture can make them a drag on a ministry's inno-
vation and efficiency. More seriously, some bureaucrats (some, not all)
manifest a condescending view of small faith-based nonprofits. This attitude of "government knows best and private groups must conform" is the
most worrisome obstacle to fruitful public-private collaboration.
Thankfully, as the anecdote above reveals, many governmental officials
are eager to serve private nonprofits rather than to merely exploit such
groups for their own ends. But the challenges of cooperating are real.

Stifling Creativity

Many private ministries work hard to provide personalized attention to
needy families. Whereas governmental social services programs tend to
be standardized and inflexible, treating everyone alike, faith-based
ministries try to design helping strategies for the particular situations
of different individuals. And many analysts claim that such flexibility is
an important reason for these groups' high success rates.

Unfortunately, governmental regulation of certain fields of social
service can stifle this flexibility and creativity. In addition, when private
groups apply for public funding, the bureaucrats administering the
grants sometimes seek to shape the private agency into the government's mold. Eve Crossman formerly worked with Covenant House, a
Christian home for runaway youth in New York City. According to her,
government bureaucrats seem to forget that "people aren't run by
computer programs." Covenant House avoided soliciting public funds
for its ministry because it feared the stifling conditions such aid would
entail. "For example, if Covenant House would have gotten this one
grant from the government of New York City, we would have had to
restrict the stays of kids for our long-term program to exactly eighteen
months, and on the day after the eighteen months, these kids would be
kicked out. But you can't run these kids like a computer. You can't say,
'Okay, you've done your eighteen months. Now take off.'"

Martha Hamstra, volunteer coordinator for the Washington,

D.C.-based Samaritan Ministries, agrees with Crossman. She tells of applying for a grant from the city government in the District of Columbia for Samaritan's employment training program:

> They [the city] just could not understand that our training was not six hours a day, five days a week. We have a much more flexible program than that. People participate in the classes they need. For example, maybe two people need a workshop on interviewing, so they do that. Another person doesn't need it, so he doesn't take it. At the end of the training everybody is pretty much in the same place; they all just took a different route to get there. But [the city agency] just couldn't understand this. They didn't get it that our program wasn't six hours a day, five days a week. They weren't ready to give us the money if we didn't do things their way. But that's not how we work, and our program is successful exactly because we don't do the program that way, because we don't demand the same things from everyone who participates. People are tired of being a number and appreciate so much that we deal with them on an individual basis. . . . I can't help asking: Our program works and theirs doesn't, so why are they trying to make us look like them?

Unrealistic Regulations

In addition to regulations that stifle creativity, government entities sometimes impose unrealistic and extremely expensive regulations—regulations that can even put a ministry "out of business." Rev. James Holley, pastor of the Little Rock Baptist Church in Detroit, had to close down his church's homeless shelter after two years of operations because the church couldn't afford the $300,000 that would be necessary to bring the facility into compliance with a new ordinance passed by city officials. The ordinance requires homeless shelters to provide dietician-approved menus, quiet rooms for children in which to do their homework, and fire-suppression sprinkler systems. Holley says he agrees with the intent of the new rules—to provide safe and adequate shelter for the homeless—but comments, "I'm not quite sure the people in the ivory towers really understand what it's like out here. . . . The ordinance wants me to provide all the amenities that a hotel provides. It's totally ridiculous."

Gary Bayer, a former Salvation Army employee who oversaw a Detroit homeless shelter, says that some of the building codes on which the government insisted were "excessive," such as the rule that bedroom doors be equipped with view sites (or "peepholes," in average American parlance).

Excessive regulations can especially hurt private citizens who decide personally to join the fight against poverty and hunger. Carol Doe Porter, a Houston resident, was called a "quintessential point of light" by the *New York Times* because each month she and her family deliver 18,000 meals, mostly sandwiches handmade in her kitchen, to the poor. The city's Health Department once tried to shut her down because her stove lacked a ventilated hood and she didn't have a separate mop sink in the kitchen. Porter summoned television cameras into her kitchen to prove its cleanliness, asserting to government officials: "Are you going to tell me it's better for [poor children] to eat garbage-can cuisine than out of my kitchen? If the kids of America are going to get fed, then the Health Departments of America are going to have to relax those regulations to accommodate the surge of volunteerism."[1]

In Atlanta the nonprofit group Summerhill Neighborhood Inc. (SNI) is trying to revitalize a poor section of the city through massive housing rehabilitation and redevelopment efforts. According to board member German Cruz, SNI generally has avoided public sector funding even though the extra money can appear attractive. He explains that the strings attached to government monies would cripple the organization's ability to provide affordable housing: "Public sector funding imposes on the receiver a lot of conditions in terms of who builds the houses. We can build houses for $40,000 and sell them to a low-income person for a $250 a month mortgage payment, and they own it. If the house had to be built according to the Davis-Bacon Act, with union labor, nobody could afford it because then the home built for $40,000 with volunteer labor will cost $80,000 with union labor."

Hassles and Headaches

Of course, some forms of governmental aid can multiply the effectiveness of a private group's efforts. For example, suppose a woman graduates from a Christian group's job-training program and lands a job. The ministry may not be able to provide the graduate with affordable day care or money for transportation to reach the work site. The government, however, may have a program offering subsidized day care or transportation. In this way, the state aid supplies what's needed to keep the woman on a trajectory of self-improvement. Consequently, many ministries see themselves as bridge builders between needy individuals and the governmental programs that can offer them a "hand-up."

But playing this bridge-building role can be extremely tiresome and difficult. The problem, say frontline activists, is that public assistance programs are often in flux, changing from year to year, if not more often. Moreover, government bureaucrats inconsistently apply the rules of the programs, telling clients one thing one day and another thing another day. This produces uncertainty and confusion for clients and ministries. Hamstra from Samaritan Ministries reports that keeping abreast of the continual changes in government policy and personnel can be a maddening full-time job: "The government doesn't have consistent policies. . . . Each time we send someone over to the Department of Employment Services, some clerk has a different idea as to what needs to be done to get through the system. It's so inconsistent, and that is terribly frustrating."

Ministry staff also report enormous annoyances in trying to identify the appropriate government officials with whom to speak about various matters. Charlene Johnson of the Michigan Neighborhood Partnership reports that her group collaborates in conferences with state governmental departments and provides advice to officials regarding welfare policies. The state government assigned her organization a specific liaison within the bureaucracy, but Ms. Johnson reports that she still has "to play the yellow page phone tag and find out who you need to talk to to make something happen. . . . With this tremendous state bureaucracy it's really a daunting challenge to get to all these people we need to get to."

Late Reimbursements

Other headaches besides those imposed by "phone tag" can accompany state funding. Sometimes community ministries receive reimbursement grants from local governmental bodies to support their programs. In this scenario, a ministry applies for a project grant, is approved, uses its own cash funds to pay for the project, and then submits receipts to the government for reimbursement. The problem with this is twofold: first, often ministries are requesting aid specifically because they do not have funds on hand to pay for their proposed project, and second, the government often does not pay the ministries back in a timely fashion, thus creating a potentially devastating cash flow crunch.

Samaritan Ministries' Hamstra says her organization hasn't pursued support from the District of Columbia "because it is notorious for not paying on time. Other nonprofits in the city have had a large percentage of their budgets based on governmental contracts and haven't had enough money in the bank to cover expenses because the D.C. government is often four to five months behind on paying its bills. We can't afford to take a risk like that."

Impersonalization

One attraction of faith-based social service groups is that they tend to be more personable than their secular counterparts. This may be because workers in these ministries come from the local neighborhood and can relate well to clients. Moreover, ministry staff are often volunteers or are underpaid; they are there because they view their work as a calling rather than as a job. Nearly everyone on the front lines of social service agrees that a friendly, supportive environment helps produce positive behavioral changes among welfare recipients. Consequently, the impersonalization or bureaucratization of a ministry can severely undercut its effectiveness. Some leaders of faith-based groups worry that that is exactly what can occur when government grants are accepted.

The process of impersonalization unfolds in a variety of ways, some more obvious than others. Ministries complain that government requires an immense amount of paperwork that steals time away from face-to-face ministry. Charlene Johnson calls the reporting process for government grants a "horrendous bureaucratic monster." And everyone laments that the grants do not come with adequate funds to pay for the additional personnel needed to ensure compliance with the regulations and complete monthly reports and annual audits. Rev. Thomas Laymon, executive director of the Mel Trotter Ministries in Grand Rapids, Michigan, reports that the elaborate reporting requirements imposed on groups who receive state funding for substance abuse treatment programs limit the impact of such groups. "You can't deal with as many individuals," Laymon says, "not because you couldn't do a good job with them, but because you cannot do all the paperwork associated with those higher numbers of clients."

Moreover, government sometimes dictates that ministries receiving public funds hire only staff with specific educational degrees, such as a Masters of Social Work (MSW), or with certification in professional substance abuse counseling programs. While this may reduce the number of unqualified people offering services, it can also bring a professionalization that produces a new distance between staff and recipients of care where once an informal, relational style existed. Gary Bayer, who formerly oversaw a Detroit homeless shelter serving substance abusers, argues that ex-clients who have overcome their addictions make some of the best employees. They have walked the same streets that the clients currently walk and can relate to them, challenge them, and teach them how they managed to get clean. But under the government's credentialing requirements, such homegrown leaders often are not eligible for employment as licensed counselors.[2]

And there is a further issue for religious agencies. Bayer explains, "My concern is that you [end up] building ministries more upon individual credentials as opposed to character. The restrictions can do us a disservice," he adds, "because we're required to be seeking the MSW or the individual who 'has the training,' but may in turn not have the character nor the same Christian underpinnings."

Tom Laymon agrees. "You may have a social worker who is doing, by definition, good social work, but who is not responding to the real needs of the individual—especially if 'good social work' demands that it be nonreligious," Laymon argues. "If our professionalism runs counter to our philosophy [of ministry]," he adds, "then it becomes a problem." Laymon refuses governmental funding for Mel Trotter Ministries. If he did accept state aid, it's unlikely Mel Trotter himself (if he were still alive) could work there. Trotter's principal credentials were as a recovered alcoholic, ex-barber, and evangelist—yet he left behind sixty-seven rescue missions still in operation today.

Credentialing requirements can also limit the number of volunteers a ministry can use. This reduces the available manpower and can alter the casual "accessible" atmosphere of the organization. As Linda Smith of Detroit's REACH, Inc. put it: "Part of the criticism of us now is that we're too professional, too polished, that we can't relate to the things that [local residents] are going through. Because some of us have a couple degrees, people tend to judge you."

Delays and Frustrations

REACH, Inc.'s evolution over the last nine years offers additional insights about the pitfalls of government funding. REACH began as the brainchild of several lay members of 12th Street Baptist Church who started an outreach to senior citizens in the neighborhood. Eventually, the group established a day care center, purchased and rehabilitated some crack houses, and even opened up a local restaurant.

Rev. Lee Earl pastored the church then, and REACH's offices were located physically within the church building. In the initial years, church members and private foundations financed the ministry's work. As the group's vision for community renewal expanded, though, some members wanted to pursue government funding. Rev. Earl disagreed but was outvoted.

Government funding did allow REACH to expand its efforts in housing redevelopment and small business training. But headaches accompanied the dollars. Governmental sluggishness delayed REACH's efforts. "Their turnaround time might be a month, and your turnaround might be a day," Earl fumes. "But you've got to move by their timetable." Even worse, local government officials overseeing REACH's work lacked both technical skill and "street sense."

When REACH was rehabilitating homes with private monies, it had to deal only with the city government's building authority. "The building authority was flexible to the realities of rehabbing," Earl said. "For example, the houses have to have gutters and doors and other parts made of aluminum. But you can't put that stuff on until the house has people in it because the crack heads will steal the aluminum and sell it for drugs." Since the building authorities recognized this, they would approve the building inspection as long as the materials were purchased and ready to be put on. Then with the approved inspection, the family could move in, and the church within twenty-four hours would put on the aluminum.

Once REACH received government funds, other actors in the local government in addition to the building authority, including the community development department, assumed various responsibilities for oversight. According to Earl, these additional officials did not "understand the realities" of rehabbing in the inner city. "They wanted [the aluminum] on the house before they would even come out and inspect it. They said, 'Put it on the house, and we'll be out within seven working days.' Well, it wouldn't stay on the house for seven working hours!"

To make matters worse, church members could watch the druggies sell the aluminum to unauthorized street dealers down on the corner. When they'd complain about these dealers to local officials, they'd be told that such dealers had no business permit to do work in the neighborhood and so "didn't exist." "The government would say that there was nothing they could do against the guy because he wasn't licensed," says Earl with disgust. "So I took my church staff and had them look out the window at the man buying the stolen aluminum, and I said, 'The reason that man's business is profitable is because he doesn't take government money!'"

Displacement

Rev. Earl says government funding of REACH brought about an even more painful problem than the frustrations of dealing with out-of-touch bureaucrats. It might be called "displacement." Once REACH began receiving substantial government funds, church members decreased their personal giving and argued that it was no longer necessary for the church to finance REACH. And once the financial tie was loosened, the congregation's overall involvement with and commitment to REACH and its vision waned. "The church was assuming full responsibility for turning the neighborhood around, using its dollars, using its assets," Earl reports. "But as governmental dollars came in, then there were members in the church that were very adamant that 'now that the government is doing it, then we shouldn't [have to].'"

Eroded Credibility

Earl believes that REACH also lost credibility in the community by accepting governmental funds:

> The community has a strange relationship with anything that's affiliated with the government. They think that once you get affiliated with the government, you've got it made. So when

REACH was seen as being of the people, then the people felt a lot closer to it. But when the government came in, then we got some of that baggage. In other words, the perception was that the government wouldn't be funding [REACH] unless we had an "inside track." They didn't believe anymore that we perform[ed] based on our merit, because their experience is that you can do very well with the government and not be concerned about results [in the community]. Because they felt that government doesn't serve them very well, they thought REACH wouldn't either. Accepting government[al] funds can be a nightmare in terms of your credibility with the citizenry.

Rev. Eddie Edwards of Joy of Jesus, a Christian community development organization in Detroit's Ravendale neighborhood, cites a further dimension to this issue. "When we are working with people in the community, helping them become self-sufficient, helping them get off welfare, it would have been extremely difficult to tell them to get off welfare if we [ourselves] were on some kind of public assistance." This perception restrained him from accepting government grants.

Moreover, when local citizens no longer invest in the ministry because they believe government is adequately funding it, the ministry loses donors uniquely qualified to keep it accountable, says Joel Samy of American Family Hope, a Michigan nonprofit that helps the working poor. Government keeps organizations accountable only in the sense of requiring the timely submission of reports and financial statements, Samy argues. The local residents are the ones best positioned to monitor and evaluate the organization's actual impact in the community and keep it accountable to high standards of cost-effectiveness.

Organizational Drift

In fact, the kind of evaluation government does of an organization receiving grants can encourage a shift in the ministry's work—one that may start somewhat unconsciously. At the heart of a faith-based ministry is its goal of transforming lives. That goal can be difficult to measure by objective, quantitative data. That's why when ministries report to their supporters in the private sector, they typically tell stories. Progress in an individual's transformation is often judged by such things as changed language, reformed attitudes, faithful attendance in education/training programs, increased punctuality and personal responsibility, willingness to work, improved social relations with staff, reaffiliation with family, avoidance of drugs, commitment to financial accountability, greater reliability, and increasing initiative and enthusiasm. These often intangible and qualitative changes are the very ones linked to permanent socioeconomic improvement.

Government reporting, by contrast, focuses on objective, measurable statistics, usually related to the number of commodities provided to a needy person or neighborhood. Consequently, ministries receiving government funds start counting numbers and recording statistics. *And to ensure continued receipt of state dollars, they may start investing more effort in programs that produce easily quantifiable results rather than in holistic ministry that produces qualitative change.*

REACH's Linda Smith reports that the tone of the group's mission statement has changed, as has the thrust of its programs. Before receiving public funds, the ministry was more holistic. Former director Charlene Johnson says the "core element" of REACH's ministry was "human development," which involved great attention to moral and spiritual matters. "We saw very clearly that the spiritual aspect of [people] needs to be developed in order to sustain economic development. . . . Our experience showed that if we didn't do this, we could move people into a house, but they'd trash it and not make the mortgage payments. REACH," Johnson argues, "unlike some community development corporations which focus on physical development and business development to the exclusion of human development, really concentrated on human development."

Now the ministry's help is more commodified (providing people material goods such as houses), and its work is more project-oriented, rather than relationship-oriented. REACH's primary focus is housing rehabilitation and construction; these are programs for which the group can access major federal and state grants. Recently REACH secured a $1.7 million grant for a major housing initiative; by contrast, under Johnson's tenure the ministry's total budget reached $1 million, distributed across youth, family, and economic development programs.

"Government[al] funding will not realistically finance your Christian, holistic, or evangelistic purpose," says Virgil Gulker, a guru for the faith-based ministry community who founded Love, INC and Kids Hope USA. "So you end up evaluating quantitative things—how many houses did you build, how many meals did you serve, how many jobs did you find—that will have no impact on your organization's original purposes, other than to diminish that original purpose or mission."

"Organizational drift" can also arise from the temptation of large grants available for purposes other than those for which an organization was originally founded. Virgil Gulker reports that most ministries he's familiar with have passionate and precise mission statements—but "no one ever reads them." Consequently, ministries may begin to allow their programming to be directed by the dollars available, rather than by their own sense of calling. "It's very easy to do what funding is available to do," Gulker says wryly.

Of course, groups can be tempted by private donations in the same way. But the public funds do pose a particularly dangerous temptation for faith-based ministries, Gulker maintains. "Government[al] funding calls into question the distinctiveness or 'value-added' of the church-based organization," Gulker argues. According to him, church-based ministries too often replicate the activities of secular welfare agencies rather than emphasize what they, as faith-based groups, can most uniquely offer—spiritual transformation and moral challenge. "We get into difficulties sometimes because we neglect to understand what we do best. Groups that accept government[al] funding can compromise their original evangelistic purposes," he continues. "It's very easy to take a government grant, but the question is value-added. What should church-based organizations do? If it's evangelism, the government[al] funding will kill them."

Secularization

Gulker's comments approach the real heart of the issue of governmental funding of faith-based ministries—the potential danger of secularization. REACH's current executive director, Pamela Martin Turner, admits quite openly that REACH has "evolved into a more secular, more ecumenical organization than in past years." She elaborates: "To some large extent, the work of the past was primarily based on faith, on a commitment to spiritual and religious values. Whereas now, on the staff level, there may be some internal spiritual value that compels people to come to work, but that's not the explicit understanding. People come to work because it's their job and they're expected to do a good job. [The spiritual motivation] was more explicit in years past."

The deemphasis on the spiritual comes with a cost: It makes it less likely that REACH staffers will bring their religious convictions to bear in addressing, confronting—and meeting—the needs of the needy. "We do not talk about the spiritual needs at all," says staffer Linda Smith. "When we worked out of the church, I knew every day, without a doubt, why I was there. Now some days I come to work and people come in, and I feel like I can't help them because they need more than to just talk about putting them in a house. It's a struggle for me."

People of faith, of course, are concerned about the threat of secularization. But others ought to be worried as well, for the dilution of a ministry's religious distinctiveness may remove the very key that makes it so effective in addressing social problems.

For example, the ministry Joy of Jesus on Detroit's east side accepts no governmental funding. But financial problems led it to incorporate a separate, not explicitly religious, nonprofit partner organization called R-3 that could solicit state funds. Such monies are used principally in the group's housing redevelopment program. But the ministry also moved its job-readiness/job-training program under the rubric of R-3 because private donations were insufficient to maintain the program. Instructor Kevin Feldman reports that he used to integrate biblical principles in the training curriculum but had to stop once the organization received governmental funding. In Feldman's view, the result has been that "our success rate has dramatically declined." Fewer individuals are completing the program, and fewer are finding and retaining jobs. In this instance, governmental regulations prohibited R-3 from putting up religious pictures in the classroom, praying during the class sessions, or making explicit references to the Bible. Fortunately, the new Charitable Choice provisions will, if correctly interpreted and implemented by Michigan state officials, terminate such secularizing pressures.

Looking the Other Way

Prior to Charitable Choice, many faith-based providers reported that they had experienced the "wink and nod." Satisfied with their religious partners' performance, government officials simply looked the other way when those partners engaged in any religious activities that state officials thought might compromise the principle of the separation of church and state.

Stephen Monsma's survey of religiously based nonprofits found that a strong majority of organizations receiving governmental funding reported no problems, pressures, or threats from government overseers. (A significant minority of groups that rated high on a "religious practices" scale developed by Monsma, however, did report problems.)

Many of the frontline activists I interviewed who receive governmental funding asserted that they have found that as long as they dutifully fulfill their monthly or quarterly reports and do not do anything patently evangelistic with governmental funds, they have little or no problem with governmental officials.

Some faith-based groups have invented creative ways of getting around the restrictions on religious activities imposed by state funding prior to Charitable Choice. One ministry holds a children's Bible club during the hour before its state-funded recreational program. Still other organizations sidestep the hiring nondiscrimination rules. They ask no pointed questions about the religious beliefs of potential employees but gather enough information through indirect questions to know whether the candidate shares their faith commitments.

Some of the ministries I visited are very straightforward about their religious identity. Staff members report that they make no bones about who they are, and governmental entities fund them anyway—because of their proven track record. "They are interested in results," Frederick Hill, chief financial officer at the Center for Urban Missions, states directly. Others agree. Gary Bayer acknowledges that there is always a danger of secularization in partnerships between faith-based ministries and government, but that secularization does not *have* to occur. "My experience has shown that the governmental agencies are more concerned with seeing the results of a program and less concerned with the process by which those results are achieved."

Comments like these are reinforced by the testimonies of some social workers and public officials I've spoken with in several inner cities across the nation. These individuals admit that they have looked the other way when they see things that, in their opinion, probably breach the church-state divide. They expressed feeling so completely overwhelmed by the scope of ghetto woes that they were delighted to work with any group, religious or secular, that was making headway. Principals at inner-city elementary and high schools in Phoenix and Birmingham said they permitted faith-based groups to use school facilities even though they were aware of the religious content of some of these groups' programs. One ministry director told the story of a government official who approached him suggesting that his group accept a governmental grant to establish a special program for hard-core juvenile offenders. The director said he wouldn't take the money if he had to tone down his organization's Christian identity, and the official replied that the government would give the grant *only* to a group that included a spiritual component in its program.

Despite these stories of *de facto* cordiality between governmental officials and faith-based ministries, though, the legal regime under which public-private collaboration has taken place (prior to Charitable Choice) has been a precarious one for religious nonprofits. The degree of institutional autonomy currently enjoyed by some faith-based groups receiving governmental funds results from cordial, long-standing relationships with pragmatic state officials who are more interested in enabling faith-based ministries to transform lives than they are in rigorously enforcing a church-state divide. (This is clearly the case in the partnerships described in the previous chapter between Wayne County DSS and the Detroit Rescue Mission Ministries and between the Kent County DSS and Bethany Christian Services.)

This is a shaky foundation for such public-private partnerships, though, since such individuals could be replaced by less sympathetic officials. Clearly, a stronger foundation for collaboration was needed—and Charitable Choice is a giant step forward. It remains to be seen how carefully the Charitable Choice provisions will be implemented by state officials. The rules for collaboration between governmental agencies and faith-based groups have changed for the better. If states acknowledge Charitable Choice and bring their own practices in relating to religious nonprofits into conformity with the new rules, some of the problems highlighted in this chapter should be eliminated.

In short, the climate for collaboration between state agencies and faith-based groups has improved. The next chapter examines some innovative examples of recent collaborations between churches/faith-based groups and governmental entities. These examples suggest several steps both groups can take to forge healthy, workable, effective partnerships.

Toward More Fruitful Collaboration

The most important step toward a more fruitful collaboration between the government and faith-based groups is to redefine public-private partnerships beyond the prevailing "delivery system" model. This model is principally concerned with saving money, not with transforming lives. According to this arrangement, the state decides what services to offer and then pays private groups (including religious nonprofits) to deliver these services. The "delivery system" model leaves the government in charge of program design, thereby limiting the creative potential for community-based groups to formulate their own solutions to poverty. It opens the way for private nonprofits simply to assume responsibility for and run previously government-operated services as these services are currently configured. But the point is not to change who hands out the same prepackaged welfare goodies. The point is to change the package itself, thereby transforming the lives of those who receive it.

The governmental welfare system has failed not only because it is an unsatisfactory mechanism for delivering the standard welfare benefits package, but because the benefits package itself is flawed. Welfare currently focuses on the distribution of cash and commodities, but these are not the things that truly transform poor people's lives. RESTORERS have a better track record in changing lives not only because they deliver services more effectively, but because their package of services is different. They provide "goods" like love, emotional support, spiritual instruction, trust, accountability, moral authority, hope, character training, and basic life skills in the context of personal relationships with the poor. They suffer with and walk alongside needy people until those people are able to walk out of the underclass. Any arrangement with state agencies that fails to maintain the faith-based ministries' focus on relationship building and moral education will not, in the long run, help the poor to help themselves.

What's needed, therefore, is a model of collaboration that builds not only on the cost-effectiveness of faith-based ministries and churches, or even on their efficient delivery systems, but on their unique strengths as religious organizations ministering holistically. Governmental officials must acknowledge the value of the churches' holistic approach to serving the needy and take action to ensure that ministries agreeing to work with the state do not stumble into the traps discussed in the previous chapter.

At least three states—Mississippi, Maryland, and Virginia—are taking important steps in the right direction. All three have initiated collaborative programs in which churches are asked to provide considerable personal, ongoing, multidimensional support to families enmeshed in the public assistance system.

Collaboration in Mississippi, Maryland, and Virginia

Mississippi's "Faith and Families" initiative, launched in October 1994, asks churches to "adopt" families on welfare and provide them with the emotional support, practical training, and moral counsel to make the shift from welfare to work. The Department of Human Services (DHS) provides churches with "blind profiles" of welfare families living within a ten-mile radius of the church. These profiles describe the educational and work background of the head of the household and the ages, number, and special needs of the children; they also include relevant comments about the family from the social services caseworker.

Only AFDC recipients enrolled in Mississippi's JOBS program can volunteer to be matched with a participating Faith and Families church. (The JOBS program requires able-bodied AFDC recipients to attend school or to participate in job-training or "work experience" programs in order to maintain their public aid benefits.) The participants continue to receive monthly welfare payments, food stamps, rent subsidies, Medicaid, and any other benefits for which they may be eligible during the time they are mentored by the church (usually between six and twelve months). The DHS does not expect the churches to provide financial assistance to the participants (though many have). Rather, the churches' primary responsibility is to help the participants find stable full-time employment.

In Maryland the Anne Arundel County Department of Social Services began a pilot program called C-DAP (Community-Directed Assistance Program) in June 1994. Welfare recipients can volunteer for the program and be matched with a support team from a participating church. One year's worth of the recipients' AFDC benefits are paid in a lump sum to the church. Church volunteers and program participants then decide jointly how to manage those funds over a six month period. During this time, the participant and volunteers design a strategic plan for achieving independence from welfare. Church members teach budgeting skills, provide transportation and baby-sitting, help participants complete job applications, and generally serve as a personal support network.

In Virginia the Department of Social Services is phasing in over the next three years a comprehensive welfare reform package (i.e., stiff working requirements, a family cap, a two-year cutoff for benefits). Some of the pilot counties targeted for the initial implementation of the new welfare laws are experimenting with church-state collaboration. Most of these experiments are not as developed as Mississippi's Faith and Families initiative; indeed, some are still in the conception stage, and it is impossible to determine what their impact will be. Still, the discussions occurring between religious groups and county-level governmental entities in Virginia are just the kind likely to produce healthy partnerships.

In (mostly rural) Fauquier County, Virginia, the DHS has invited churches to mentor welfare families and provide the same sort of help that Faith and Families churches provide AFDC recipients in Mississippi. In Orange and Culpepper Counties, the regional United Way office is spearheading an initiative to recruit adult mentors from the community to work in one-on-one relationships with welfare recipients. Hampton, Virginia, has experimented with a similar program since 1993.

In Fairfax County, Virginia, many churches that had participated in a homeless family resettlement initiative called "Project HOMES" are now training mentor teams to serve welfare families. This new partnership between the Fairfax County Department of Social Services and local churches is brokered by Community Ministries. Community Ministries was founded by a group of mainline Protestant churches that wanted to establish a small clearinghouse to research policy issues of concern to the churches and provide training to congregations that wanted to engage in outreach efforts among the poor.

Another interesting partnership is Richmond's "Spiritual Family Development Program." It links families of repeat juvenile offenders with local churches that provide them with family counseling, mentoring, religious education, and personal support.

It is too soon to say conclusively how well these examples of public-private cooperation will work. Initial evidence from the three states, though, is promising. These endeavors illustrate a new approach to collaboration that surpasses the delivery system model. Although these fledgling partnerships are not yet fully solidified, they demonstrate several elements critical to producing better, healthier, more fruitful public-private collaboration. These are discussed below. Churches considering whether to collaborate with government entities should evaluate proposed partnerships according to the presence or absence of these critical factors.

"Ground-Floor-Up" Involvement

The first element is "ground-floor-up" involvement. As noted earlier, one of the most significant problems with the delivery system model of public-private cooperation is that it often presents private groups with prepackaged plans designed exclusively by the government. State agencies do not ask nonprofits to help shape a given program, only to implement it in a timely, cost-efficient manner. The private group may have valuable firsthand experience that could inform the program's design. But if the DHS does not solicit the group's participation from the ground floor up, this worthy input is lost.

A more fruitful partnership would invite nonprofits to participate in shaping the program. This is likely to increase the degree of private sector involvement in the initiative. Groups are more likely to participate in initiatives in which they feel some ownership.

Richmond's Juvenile Justice Department adopted this laudable approach in designing its "Family First" program. This program helps families of repeat juvenile offenders aged fifteen or younger to strengthen family relationships, improve communication, and guide their children onto more productive paths. Juvenile court judges can sentence juveniles and their families to mandatory participation in the six-month program. Among other elements, the program requires parents to take fourteen weeks of parent education classes and assigns a Family Mentor who meets with them weekly.

According to Family First project director Jane Talley, however, "there was a general recognition that a spiritual component is helpful" in strengthening the families of juvenile offenders. Consequently, Family First staff invited ministers in Richmond's impoverished East End (the Family First program targets families residing in this community) to a discussion on what role the churches might play in assisting participating families. The ministers met with governmental staff and brainstormed about the goals they might achieve and the sort of program that would be distinct from, but related to, the overall Family First initiative. According to Talley, the ministers were "extremely enthusiastic" about designing a "piece" of the program they could call their own. Their "ground-floor-up" involvement in designing the initiative has strengthened their commitment to addressing the problems of juvenile offenders. And it has increased the program's credibility in the eyes of East End residents.

The mentoring initiative in Fairfax County, Virginia, is another good example of ground-floor-up involvement. John Wells, executive director of Community Ministries, came up with the idea and then presented it to county welfare officials. Wells and the county employees then met regularly to fashion the mentoring program. In this way, Wells was able to address from the beginning issues he knew would be of concern to participating churches.

Contrary to these examples of "ground-floor-up" involvement, in Mississippi government staff designed the Faith and Families program and then presented it to churches "as a prepackaged thing," according to Rev. Phil Reed of Voice of Calvary Church in Jackson. This is one reason why the churches' initial reaction to the initiative was lukewarm. Faith and Families field coordinator Rev. Ronald Moore admits candidly that it would have been better to have solicited the churches' input during the design stage. "If we could have gotten the grassroots involvement at the beginning of the project," Moore acknowledges, "we would be much further along." Nonetheless, Moore is making inroads in recruiting churches—207 have signed up so far. And he reports that he is encountering less resistance and suspicion from church leaders—partly because the program now has a track record of some successes and partly because Moore emphasizes that participating churches can be flexible in designing their own particular strategy for helping the participants. Indeed, the DHS may have "prepackaged" the Faith and Families program, but the package was not highly detailed. Thus, even though churches initially had no role in shaping the program, they do not find themselves boxed in to a rigid model once they agree to participate.

Connected Autonomy

A second critical element in fruitful partnerships is "connected autonomy." In all three states, some religious leaders and nonprofit directors have worried that "welfare reform" may be a governmental code word for "dumping" welfare responsibilities on churches and private charities. Even individuals who argue that the government ought to reduce its role in serving the poor and make room for private groups to do more do not want state officials to wash their hands completely of welfare clients. Many churches are willing to help, but are not prepared to take *full* responsibility for the care of disadvantaged and dysfunctional families. Justifiably, these churches want the freedom to help poor people in their own unique, holistic ways—without excessive governmental interference that would squelch the spiritual character of their outreach.

But many churches also want the assurance that the individuals they are serving are linked as well to government-sponsored programs that address needs the church cannot meet. Many churches that decide to work alongside governmental agencies helping families on public assistance want to be able to pursue those things that they do best while not being expected to do everything. They want, in short, "connected autonomy." This means being a part of a team surrounding the family—a team on which they play a significant, largely unfettered, and unique role—but a team nonetheless.

Virginia's Spiritual Family Development program, Maryland's C-DAP initiative, and Mississippi's Faith and Families program are structured to provide churches this "connected autonomy." In all three partnerships, churches work with families that are simultaneously involved in a state-mandated reform program. Thus, the churches provide one key piece of a larger package of support. In their own sphere, the churches have tremendous latitude in working with their adopted families. By agreeing to partner with government in these initiatives, participating congregations have not had to follow endless bureaucratic regulations or mold their helping strategy according to guidelines imposed from secular agencies. Indeed, they have retained so much autonomy that state officials in Mississippi do not call Faith and Families "a government program," and Virginia officials refer to the Spiritual Family Development initiative as "the ministers'" program.

Still, none of these initiatives are cut adrift from the social services system. This is important because of the need for leverage. Churches can encourage, persuade, and cajole participants in their programs to take the steps necessary for self-improvement. But clients' participation is totally voluntary. In the Faith and Families program, for example, participants can consistently reject the advice of their church mentors, and the churches have no way to discipline them—except by terminating the relationship. Government agencies, on the other hand, wield a diverse array of effective sanctions. They can hold clients accountable by reducing or eliminating benefits. Consequently, it helps that Faith and Families is one piece in the "total pie" of Mississippi's welfare reform project. Though DHS officials have not yet determined exactly how to keep Faith and Families clients accountable to their end of the bargain, all Faith and Families clients are bound by the rules of the JOBS program, which can discipline clients for noncompliance with the expectations of that program.

Remy Agee, special programs manager for Anne Arundel County DSS in Maryland, is available to "play the heavy" with C-DAP participants who are not living up to their agreement with their sponsoring church. This relieves church volunteers of an exercise they do not find particularly pleasant. Agee reports that in a few instances, she and the C-DAP participant would review the original contract, discuss areas for improvement, and add specific action items to the contract that the participant needed to fulfill (by expressed deadlines) in order to remain in the program. "I'd tell them," Agee explains, "that this is a voluntary program, and you don't have to be in it, but if you're going to be in it, then you've signed an agreement and need to keep it."

In point of fact, few churches involved in C-DAP or Faith and

Families have reported problems with the program participants. Most of the welfare recipients in the programs are the "cream of the crop"— they are highly motivated, teachable, and willing to take the necessary steps to transition from welfare to work. Nonetheless, churches who take seriously Jesus' instruction to "be wise as serpents" know that all people, because of sin, sometimes need to be held accountable or even coerced to do what is right. A program that lacks any "teeth" or leverage is likely at some point to encounter serious frustrations. Consequently, churches that agree to partner with governmental agencies should expect those agencies to employ disciplinary measures when necessary. Otherwise an aid recipient who is unwilling to take steps toward independence may take advantage of a church's generosity.

Effective Recruitment Systems

Obviously, welfare-to-work mentoring programs will only work if welfare recipients are willing to join them and if volunteers are willing to serve as mentors. In most of the initiatives I studied, officials had had more trouble recruiting clients than they had recruiting volunteers. In Fairfax County's Project HOMES initiative, mentioned earlier, governmental officials were able to offer a very attractive incentive to potential candidates. All the candidates were living in homeless shelters, and most were on the waiting list to receive Section 8 housing vouchers (for subsidized rent). The average time families had to wait to receive their vouchers was two years. Project HOMES officials were given authority to move up to the top of the list any homeless family willing to enroll in Project HOMES. Many families jumped at the opportunity. None of the other initiatives I studied, though, used such an attractive incentive. Governmental agencies and private nonprofits should brainstorm about feasible incentives, since it is difficult for welfare recipients used to the security of the old entitlement system to "take the plunge" and enroll in a new, unfamiliar program.

"Connected autonomy" made recruiting churches an easier task than recruiting participants. It provided a crucial reassurance to the churches that they wouldn't be out there all alone. For successful recruitment campaigns, it is also useful for the governmental partner to screen potential program candidates for substance abuse problems. Nearly all the church volunteers I interviewed admitted that they would not be willing to work with drug addicts. This was something that they simply did not feel qualified to do. Providing churches substantial freedom in designing their helping strategy also facilitated church enrollment. C-DAP officials in particular were careful to give a substantial autonomy to the sponsoring churches and required of them very little in the way of reports. "We didn't want to burden the churches with a lot of paperwork," Remy Agee explains. "We wanted them to spend their time with the participants—that was the whole goal of the program."

C-DAP church volunteers also credit Agee with being a good listener. They felt she and other county officials were "extremely accessible." Agee organized exit interviews with the church volunteers at the end of the six month sponsorship, solicited their suggestions for further improving the program, and implemented those suggestions. All of this strengthened the church volunteers' commitment to, and enthusiasm for, the C-DAP initiative. Then these volunteers could encourage friends in other churches to consider joining the C-DAP effort.

In Mississippi Faith and Families field coordinator Ronald Moore initially experienced difficulties in recruiting churches. Some were suspicious of the program because they did not like the governor's politics. By contrast, John Wells has had success recruiting churches for the Fairfax County welfare-to-work mentoring program. One important reason is that Community Ministries serves as a "third party bridge" between the county DSS and the churches. Community Ministries is not a church but is supported by and well-connected to the faith community. Community Ministries' endorsement of the new mentoring effort gave local pastors confidence that this was something they should do. Wells explains that Community Ministries plays a crucial role in communications: "There's a natural reluctance on the part of some [church] people to listen seriously to a government group approaching them for help. The [County] saw Community Ministries as a vehicle for learning where the churches were and how to get in touch with them. In addition, CM could say to the churches, 'We've heard this idea, evaluated it, and we think it makes sense.' So there's a vouchsafing. And we have the manpower to call meetings and get out mailings, and simply make it happen."

Sympathetic Respect

For connected autonomy to work, governmental bureaucrats and ministry staff must adopt the proper attitudes toward one another. For their part, governmental officials must display "sympathetic respect." They should eschew the elitist perspective that only highly educated professionals are equipped to help poor people. Instead, governmental staff should acknowledge that their clients may be greatly served by "lay" volunteers who can speak to the clients' emotional and spiritual needs while offering moral direction. Social workers must genuinely believe that church members have something valuable to offer welfare clients—something that the government, by its very nature, is unable to provide. They must respect churches and faith-based organizations enough to allow them flexibility and creativity in meeting the clients' needs—even if the strategies religious groups employ are different from those typically utilized by governmental entities. And they need to be willing to listen to, and learn from, the Good Samaritans on the front lines.

Here again Richmond's Spiritual Family Development program is illustrative. Churches define and control their own program, which the Juvenile Justice Department both respects and appreciates. Department staff view their role as facilitators and enablers, rather than regulators and controllers.

Churches participating in the C-DAP initiative say that they have been very pleased with their interactions with county officials. As mentioned previously, they sensed that officials genuinely valued their input. The C-DAP staffers trusted the church volunteer teams and respected the role that these teams played in assisting program participants.

Mississippi Faith and Families staff are working hard to foster strong relationships with mentoring churches. They allow churches great flexibility and autonomy. I interviewed leaders in about half of the participating churches, and most were very satisfied with their relationship with the Department of Human Services. These church leaders felt that the DHS had given them wide latitude in designing their outreach to the program participants. In the first year of the program, some participating churches had difficulty maintaining frequent contact with the DSS. This problem, however, has diminished as the state has hired additional program staff.

Attitudes toward church involvement in welfare reform initiatives vary from bureaucrat to bureaucrat. This was brought home to me one day when I conducted interviews with two Virginia social services officials, one from Fauquier County and one from Culpepper County. The staff member from Fauquier was eager for the churches' help in implementing Virginia's new welfare programs. Church members could be "key players in the creation of families able to live independent of outside support," she asserted. They can be those "necessary supportive friends" AFDC recipients need. Consequently, this staffer had organized a regional summit at which ministers were invited to give their ideas about how churches could partner with the Department of Social Services (DSS) in serving welfare families.

The official from the Culpepper DSS spoke enthusiastically of a new initiative to recruit volunteer mentors from the community to befriend AFDC recipients. But she was hesitant about *church members* serving as mentors. She was interested in recruiting individuals from business associations and secular nonprofits. "You have to be careful with the churches," she confided. "What's their *real* motivation? We don't want them preaching their beliefs on the clients."

Clearly, church leaders will have to determine the prevailing attitude held by the governmental officials with whom they consider partnering. If the key staff people at the DSS do not show sympathetic respect, the church is likely better off avoiding close collaboration.

Discerning Teachableness

Just as governmental officials must display sympathetic respect, their church/faith-based nonprofit partners should exhibit an attitude of "discerning teachableness." Many governmental bureaucrats have good counsel and practical wisdom to offer Christians desiring to begin or enhance community outreach. The failure of the government's war on poverty does not imply that every DHS caseworker is incompetent. Many have long experience in working cross-culturally. Some are well-acquainted with life in low-income neighborhoods. They are familiar with the obstacles welfare recipients face. Ministry leaders should be willing to listen to their input and open to receiving specialized training from them.

On the other hand, churches must be careful to discern where secular values and philosophies underlie bureaucrats' understanding of the appropriate ways to interact with the poor. As one minister involved with the homeless notes, sometimes bureaucrats define "good social work" in a way that deliberately excludes attention to religious considerations.

Secular experts may be able, for example, to instruct churches in techniques for helping substance abusers quit drinking and drugging. But as one former addict who had repeatedly relapsed during his time in government-sponsored recovery programs explained, "Those programs generally take addictions from you, but don't place anything within you. I needed a spiritual lifting."[1] These comments demonstrate that while churches may benefit from cooperating with secular specialists, to the extent that the specialists neglect to treat individuals as whole persons, their strategies are inadequate.

Moreover, churches must be alert to the moral relativism of secular state agents. Scholar Gertrude Himmelfarb tells an illuminating anecdote that highlights this problem. While doing research for a book, Himmelfarb wrote to a federal agency to inquire about the latest statistics on illegitimacy. "I received a letter firmly rebuking me for using that term; the proper term, I was told, is either 'nontraditional childbearing' or 'alternative modes of parenting'—hence legitimizing illegitimacy."[2] Churches ground their outreach among the poor on certain truth claims. Governmental entities refuse to say definitively which behaviors are morally right and which are wrong. Churches must never forget this fundamental distinction between themselves and their governmental partners.

Strategic Internal Organization

In their justifiable concern to avoid replicating the welfare system's impersonal bureaucratic structures in their own benevolence activities, some churches and faith-based ministries err too far on the side of informality. Typically, governmental officials pursue cooperation with churches because churches can engage in relational, time-intensive ministry. This is, indeed, a strength churches offer. Even relational ministry, though, requires some level of internal organization. While the emphasis should be on developing personal friendships with individuals in need, churches should define, with some precision, the concept of "mentoring" a welfare family. Churches (and clients) must know what they are trying to accomplish, be able to articulate tangible goals, and establish a system or structure through which to pursue those goals. In Mississippi some Faith and Families churches have had greater success in transforming participants' lives than have others. One reason is that the successful churches have a stronger internal organization. The following brief examples illustrate this point.

Covenant Presbyterian Church in Greenville, Mississippi, joined Faith and Families in late 1995. Covenant's pastor Jim Holland has invested enormous personal time in developing relationships with the three welfare families the church is mentoring. The participants attend weekly luncheon meetings at the church where they discuss everything from resumé preparation to child-rearing.

"Rev. Holland has given us the get up and go," says program participant Jennifer Lockett enthusiastically. "We have better attitudes." Holland won credibility in the participants' eyes by transporting them to job interviews, being available to talk by phone at all hours, and helping two of the women enroll in a certified nurse's assistant program.

Lockett reports that Holland's biblically based teaching has "helped me spiritually, as far as my being too carnally minded." She's appreciative of the emotional support she's received, the new friendships she's forged, and the positive influence these relationships have had on her family. "I want my children to see me doing right," Lockett says. "I don't want them to come back and say, 'Mama, you fussin' at me about this, but everything I'm doing, I'm doing because you're doing it.' I want them to be able to say, 'My mama raised me well.'"

Covenant's approach provides for regular face-to-face contact between church volunteers and participants. It requires participants to show some initiative by requiring them to attend weekly meetings. And it ensures that a degree of formal instruction occurs wherein Rev. Holland covers some topics he believes are essential to the participants' future success. Plenty of informal conversations also take place throughout the week as volunteers call and visit the participants. But at least once a week, the relationship is framed in a training format, and a place is provided for participants to report on their progress.

Stronger Hope Baptist Church in Jackson follows a similar approach, combining informal, friendly, and spontaneous interaction with more structured weekly tutorials. In addition, Stronger Hope organizes its volunteers into specialty groups that assist the participants in specific areas such as computer skills training and personal and family health and hygiene. The church has the best record statewide in helping participants move from welfare to work. It has placed nineteen individuals in full-time jobs in the two years since it joined Faith and Families.

Crossgates Baptist Church in suburban Brandon, Mississippi, has enjoyed one major success story and endured one failure during its participation in Faith and Families. It has not established a structure for regular compulsory interaction with its participants. In the successful case, this did not matter. The participant was eager for involvement with church members and allowed the team of volunteers assigned to her to "get close." She returned their phone calls, kept her appointments, openly stated her needs, accepted godly counsel, and was willing to be held accountable.

The other participant, however, kept church volunteers at a distance. She accepted the church's material and financial aid but made no efforts to respond to the church volunteers' attempts to build a genuine relationship with her. Church aid was not made contingent on her taking initiative to improve her condition. Volunteers were dismayed when they learned she had quit the GED program in which she'd been registered when initially "adopted" by the church. In this instance, a structure for regular interaction might have helped church members influence this woman's life and encourage her to take responsibility for herself.

The church's internal organization doesn't have to conform to some set model. But the evidence from the Faith and Families program suggests that at a minimum it should involve established times for face-to-face interaction, a clear understanding between volunteers and participants as to what responsibilities they each accept, and some level of formal training/teaching.

Intentional Volunteer Support and Affirmation

Serving as a mentor is time-consuming and sometimes emotionally draining work. Consequently, churches that have been most effective have their volunteers work in teams. In this way, no one person has to feel overwhelmed. The team approach also enables volunteers to work in pairs, and this provides an extra measure of protection. In the case of providing child care, for example, this buddy system insulates volunteers from accusations of improper care.

The C-DAP program, Hampton DSS's mentoring initiative, and the Fairfax County family mentoring program all do a good job of supporting, encouraging, and affirming their volunteers. C-DAP officials host occasional meetings in which volunteer teams from the different participating churches gather together to share ideas, learn from one another, and encourage each other to "not lose heart in doing good." Volunteers were uniformly fervent in their praise for such gatherings. New teams felt they gained from the wisdom and trial-and-error experience of mentor teams that had already completed some "adoptions." By meeting other teams, volunteers were able to expand their network of contacts further; in one instance, a team whose participant needed car repairs was able to link up with a mechanic from a different team's church.

The Hampton DSS organizes monthly "mentor support group" meetings for all volunteers involved in the Family Mentoring initiative. In Fairfax County, Community Ministries plans to host monthly volunteer team meetings where social workers can provide in-service training tips. John Wells hopes the gatherings will promote supportive relationships among the teams. He plans to produce a volunteer handbook that will summarize helpful information about available community resources and codify the lessons learned by the volunteer teams. The handbook will then be available to each new team that joins the effort.

Clear Communication

The final critical element in fruitful public-private collaboration is clear communication between the church (or faith-based ministry), the client, and the governmental agency. When this is lacking, an unfortunate "disconnect" can occur that reduces the effectiveness of the partnership. The story of Cynthia Hollins, a Faith and Families participant matched with the Cade Chapel Baptist Church in Jackson, illustrates this problem.

Cade Chapel is a large African-American congregation located in inner-city Jackson. It is currently working with three Faith and Families participants, including Hollins, a thirty-two-year-old mother of three. She lives a short drive from the church—up from Martin Luther King, Jr. Street off Medgar Evans, a thoroughfare of despair begrimed by trash-riddled lots and boarded-up three-room "shotgun" houses. I spoke with Hollins just after interviewing Hank Anderson, Cade Chapel's principal volunteer with the Faith and Families initiative. The juxtaposition of the two conversations highlighted the disconnect between Hollins and Anderson.

Hollins wants more personal contact with church members and feels that the church is letting her down. "How can I put this," Hollins wonders, struggling for words. "Like, I'm 'adopted,' right? Me and my family. But what do we do? I mean the Faith and Families—what are they doing? I haven't seen them." Hollins is quick to express appreciation for the fact that the church has offered to help her find employment. She calls the church people "sweet" and says it "feels good" that they're trying to help her. But she also complains that they haven't lined up any job interviews yet. And, she says, "They adopted me *and* my children. But they haven't even met my children." She wants the church to provide her sons a "big brother" and offer them tutoring. But she admits that she hasn't actually asked for this: "I just sit back and wait for them to call me."

Earlier Hank Anderson described to me the variety of services Cade Chapel is willing and able to share with its "adoptees" if they or their children need them—counseling, transportation, tutoring, job skills classes. He reports that he tries to be in phone contact with the participants twice a month, that he's been actively seeking job interviews for them, and that, as far as he knows, none of them are having any problems with their kids.

"We want to be there for them," Anderson emphasizes. "Whatever they need, we'll try to do it." But he is concerned about taking too much initiative and being "overbearing." Anderson is not worried that the families will be reluctant to seek assistance: "These families will ask for anything," he claims. Indeed, Anderson thinks Faith and Families staff could do a better job educating participants on what they should and should not expect from their church mentors.

Thankfully, this disconnect can be rectified with improved communication. Hollins needs to be more vocal about her needs, and the church needs to be more assertive in explaining the various helps it is willing to provide. In addition, Faith and Families staff ought to help Hollins understand that she should take a more aggressive role in finding employment; she must not expect the church to do all the work for her.

Faith and Families staff report that soon they hope to have adequate personnel to make monthly follow-up calls to participating churches and clients, so that they can troubleshoot any misunderstandings and facilitate clear communication between the churches and the participants. This should strengthen the program substantially. Frustrated volunteers from Crossgates Baptist church, who worked unsuccessfully with the aforementioned participant who dropped out of her GED program, report that during the entire year they were trying to help that woman, no one from DHS contacted them to check on their progress or offer suggestions. Now that the Faith and Families staff has expanded, and DHS has promised Faith and Families its own central office space, bureaucrats will be better able to provide support to participating churches. In fact, significant improvements in communication have already been made, and most of the church leaders I interviewed were presently satisfied with the accessibility and helpfulness of Faith and Families staff members.

Clear Definition of Expectations

Officials overseeing the Fairfax and Hampton County mentoring programs and the C-DAP initiative have done well in clearly communicating to volunteers and program participants what is, and what is not, expected of each. They provide information to potential program candidates that helps them understand what assistance they can expect from the support teams/mentors. The family mentoring initiative in Fairfax County, for example, printed brochures describing the program and stating that the mentoring teams are not intended to provide emergency financial aid or find the participants new jobs. Other programs produce similar literature. This clear communication avoids misunderstandings that can occur if participants feel that the church volunteers are not doing something they want them to do but that is, in reality, outside the team's proper role.

Recapitulation

When critical elements such as "ground-floor-up" involvement, connected autonomy, and sympathetic respect are absent from public-private partnerships, "working together" can mean that faith-based ministries accomplish less with governmental "help" than they would have without it. When big government imperiously issues decrees from on high, its private partners sometimes bust their budgets trying to conform. Genuine collaboration means involving ministries in program design so that the partnership will not stifle the ministries' creativity or their religious expression.

Genuine collaboration also requires mechanisms of leverage that will hold participants accountable and will persuade churches that they will not be taken advantage of. And it requires that both partners respect each other's unique strengths and work together as equals.

Effective recruitment systems are also important. Governmental agencies should think of creative incentives they could offer to encourage welfare recipients to participate in mentoring initiatives. For successful recruitment of church volunteers, a "third party bridge" is tremendously helpful. The "bridge" organization can facilitate communication between church leaders and governmental staff. It can assess the partnership, recommend (or discourage) church participation, and train volunteers in mentoring skills.

When strategic internal organization, intentional volunteer support, and discerning teachableness are absent from the partnership, the churches' good intentions likely will not translate into effective ministries. While the churches' relational ministry cannot be "programmed"—indeed, over-organizing such ministries strips them of their personableness—neither should they be haphazard. The relationship between the participating church and the needy family should be intentional and directed. Churches must be able to define just what exactly they mean when they say they will mentor a welfare family. Lay volunteers need to know what they are trying to accomplish through their relational ministry. Church leaders should establish a regular schedule of meetings to facilitate the development of genuine, face-to-face relationships wherein participants are held accountable. Over time, participants and church volunteers should develop genuine friendships and contact each other outside such formal meetings.

To protect against volunteer burnout, church leaders should design systems of volunteer support, ongoing training, and affirmation. Volunteers remain more committed to their ministries when they perceive that they are appreciated, when they feel they have received adequate training, and when they sense that their input and suggestions are welcome. Programs like C-DAP that bring together volunteer teams from different churches enable volunteers to share ideas and learn from each other. Such meetings can refresh volunteers who feel weary. When others share their success stories, everyone feels encouraged. And when volunteers express their frustration or confusion and receive practical suggestions from others who can truly empathize, it boosts their confidence and reinvigorates them.

Some churches that enter partnerships with governmental agencies may initially feel like the "new kids on the block." And they may indeed have much to learn from professionals in the social services field who have more experience in relating to poor people. Church volunteers, therefore, should listen and be willing to learn. But they should also realize that they bring valuable strengths to the table—not to mention philosophical beliefs that may be at odds with the presuppositions of secular experts. Healthy cooperation means that the church will not allow itself to be the weaker partner and will carefully weed out advice from secular entities that contradicts a biblical worldview.

Finally, regular, clear communication about roles, goals, and expectations marks all fruitful collaboration. Each partner must be accessible to the other. Churches and governmental entities need to send consistent messages to the clients they are serving; if clients hear one thing from the state and another from the church, confusion, disappointment, or frustration may follow. Regular follow-up, information sharing, and strategy discussions are all essential to a public-private collaboration that is genuinely a team effort.

Some of today's public-private partnerships—because they are not characterized by flexibility, teamwork, clear communication, mutual respect, and equality of strength—aren't really partnerships at all. The critical elements discussed in this chapter will mark genuine cooperation, and only collaboration of this sort is worth the church's investment.

Conclusion

Reviving Church, Relearning Community

Making the Inquiry

Many of the RESTORERS profiled in these pages look to the book of Nehemiah for inspiration. For Nehemiah himself was a RESTORER, called by God to rebuild the wall of Jerusalem—and to reinvigorate the spiritual and social lives of the Israelites. In the opening chapter of the book, Nehemiah inquires into the well-being of people far distant from himself. He is concerned for the welfare of the Jews in Israel and is grieved by the sad report he receives. Immediately he takes action—praying, confessing his own sins, and vowing to help his brothers. In the next chapter, Nehemiah asks permission to go to Jerusalem. Clearly his inquiry had not been made from mere curiosity. He was prepared to give himself. He was willing to go to those in need.

The work of all RESTORERS begins with this kind of concerned inquiry into another's welfare, an inquiry accompanied by a willingness to take personal action and assume personal responsibility in bearing the other's burden. Most of this book has described the way followers of Jesus are making these inquiries and taking actions that are transforming poor people's lives. As we bring our discussion to a close, though, I'd be remiss if I failed to mention the profound ways in which reaching out will also change those who do the reaching.

Transformed by Outreach

Reaching out to the poor and needy through relational, holistic ministry transforms us as churches, as individuals, and as families. As a church, we improve our financial stewardship. Instead of benevolence monies going to strangers, without follow-up or accountability, these are given as part of a package of assistance tailored to help the recipients break free of economic dependency. The return on our investment is improved because the financial aid actually helps needy people to change their lives, instead of merely making it a bit easier for them to cope with their dysfunctional lives.

Relational ministry also increases the congregation's sense of ownership of the church's benevolence outreach. In congregations that offer conventional, materially based mercy ministries, often only a small segment of the membership is personally involved. But congregational interest is piqued when churches begin to work closely with a few families—families that have real names and faces and histories. Suddenly mercy ministry becomes more real, more tangible, more personal. As mentioned in chapter 7, when the Warrenton Baptist Church decided to mentor two families on welfare, groups within the church who had previously had little involvement in community outreach came forward. Church members saw the needy families as "our" families, and this personal connection spurred greater enthusiasm for helping. A small group of elderly women, for example, offered to make curtains for one of the families.

Outreach also serves the congregation by contributing to its diversity. As the people we serve come to know Christ, some may choose to join our church. If our congregations are homogeneous, these new members may bring a wonderful blessing of heterogeneity. Our church body will be more colorful, more varied socioeconomically, and more enriched with cultural diversity. All this is good because our church life is impoverished to a degree when it does not reflect the multicultural character of the kingdom of God.

The blessing of diversity, though, stretches beyond the cosmetic changes it brings to the congregation. Being multicultural is not an end in itself. The point is that diversity enriches our conception of God's multifaceted "gracing" of His people. Too often our churches are composed of people just like us. One unfortunate consequence is that we have a too-limited view of God's providence. The struggles we experience and the trials and temptations we face are often very similar, because our life situations are similar. In a white, middle class church, for example, we learn how God intervenes, equips, provides, and graces us for the trials of white, middle class life. Certainly those trials are different for various congregants, depending on their backgrounds and ages. But the litany of prayer requests one hears in a homogeneous congregation has a familiar ring. Our spiritual lives are diminished in some measure because we are exposed primarily to our own experiences with God—and the experiences of those like us.

Cut off from people with entirely different life situations, we fail to learn how God gifts and graces those in circumstances unfamiliar to most of us (for example, the experience of being persecuted or discriminated against, the experience of being healed from drug addiction, or the experience of living at the financial margin). As a result, increased diversity in the body helps us all to see more vividly the multifaceted grace and providence of our heavenly Father. Our knowledge and adoration of Him is deepened.

Reaching out relationally also transforms us as individuals and families. We learn some important lessons from economically poor but spiritually rich fellow believers. I have learned more about what it means to "be content in all circumstances" through my elderly friend Mrs. Rogers than I have from anyone else. Despite the discrimination she endured as a young black woman in Jim Crow Virginia; despite the opportunities foreclosed to her because of her race and economic standing; despite the hardships of painful broken relationships; despite the challenges of living in a decaying and increasingly crime-ridden neighborhood; and despite the physical discomforts of arthritis, heart disease, diabetes, poor vision, and chronic respiratory problems, Mrs. Rogers is content. She smiles more than anyone else I know. She praises God more regularly, effortlessly, and fervently. She has perfected the art of seeing the silver lining inside the black cloud. Her sufferings have produced character, and her character, hope. The hope glistens in her eyes and radiates in her smile. It prompts people to ask her the secret of her happiness, a question she is only too glad to answer. She says if she's given five minutes to talk to anyone, she'll spend three of them talking about Jesus!

Those of us with rainy day savings accounts and relatives who could help out in a pinch also learn from our poor brothers what it really means to pray, "Give us this day our daily bread." God's promise to provide and protect has an immediacy for many low-income inner-city believers that it lacks for comfortable suburbanites. Randy Draughon, our church's former youth minister, tells about sitting in on a widow's prayer group in inner-city Chattanooga and witnessing this immediacy:

> What we saw was that for these ladies, God was their strength just to hang on. They have very strong faith. One lady [prayed], "Lord, I woke up this morning, and I went to my first bedroom and everything was okay and You protected me. And I went to my second bedroom and looked around, and everything was okay and You protected me. . . . " She walked through her whole house in prayer and realized that nobody had broken in, nobody had stolen anything, and she said, "Praise Jesus!"

Reaching out also exposes us to people and places with which we might otherwise have no contact. Such exposure beyond our comfort zones reminds us that many in our society are experiencing profound brokenness, oppression, and misery. Seeing the needs firsthand softens our hearts and makes them "break for the things that break God's heart." As one volunteer who works with impoverished Latino kids in Phoenix put it:

I must admit that when I started being involved in Neighborhood Ministries, I was very naive. Yes, I knew that there was an inner city, a poor area, in the valley. But short of driving past the area, I had never gotten to know it. I still can't say I really know it, but I know a whole lot more now. . . . Life has changed quite a bit for me. . . . I miss the kids when I don't have contact with them. I spend time wondering and worrying and praying for those I know by name—and those whose names I don't know.

Relational ministry also deepens our discipleship. It can help to reveal prejudices that we need to confess and eschew. It can also "spur us on" to love those who are unlovely or exasperating. And how will we grow in the love Jesus calls us to—the love that surpasses "loving those who love us"—unless we pursue such stretching relationships? Moreover, as our service begins to be less sterile, less clinical, and more costly of our time, energy, and emotions, we grow in our appreciation of Jesus' servanthood, forbearance, and mercy. One teenage volunteer with a RESTORER profiled in this book says:

> The relationship between me and the kids I work with has been a picture of Christ's relationship with me. I may sacrifice a small amount of time for the kids. However, Christ sacrificed everything for me, and instead of always responding with love, I reject and rebel against Him. Also, unlike me, He never gives up or loses His patience. [The ministry] has taught me that just as I want the kids to respond to my love, so I need to respond to God's love. His love needs to flood the cracks and dissolve the hard places in my heart just as much as the hearts of the kids I work with.

Our exposure can also serve as a check on our materialism, as we recognize more clearly the many blessings God has given us. By looking down the economic ladder instead of up, we see how abundantly

God has provided. We offer prayers of thanksgiving for what we already have instead of petitions for more.

Relational ministry can also transform our children. It gives them an opportunity to develop interracial friendships. It teaches them to appreciate other cultures. It tempers their materialism as they learn that other children do not have all the wonderful toys and possessions they have.

It also exposes them to real life lessons about the consequences of poor decisions. Rev. Phil Reed, who pastors a church in inner-city Jackson, tells how his kids have learned to "just say no" to drugs. The Reeds have invited recovering drug addicts to live with them at various times. Some of these individuals do well; others relapse. Reed's two teens have witnessed this firsthand and have told him that they never want to do drugs—they've seen with their own eyes how it ruins lives.

Finally, children learn something about the "true religion" the apostle James speaks of by watching their parents "walk the talk" of Christianity. Godly parents want nothing more than that their children embrace their Christian faith. Especially as children grow older, they watch their parents closely. Kids want to know if this "Jesus talk" is real, if it makes a difference in their parents' workaday lives. When they see their parents imitating the servant life of Jesus, they receive a powerful signal that this "Christianity thing" is not so much God-talk. It's genuine.

Witness to the World

Just as children watch their parents to see if they will truly "walk the talk" of Christianity, so the larger society watches the church to see whether it will practice what it preaches. Especially in this moment of public dissatisfaction with the governmental social welfare system, when the call to shift welfare responsibilities to private charities is increasingly loud, many are asking whether the church will rise to the challenge.

There are some hopeful signs. In the six years since the Christian Community Development Association was founded, for example, it has increased in membership from 37 organizations to over 250. In my own denomination, the Presbyterian Church in America, six new urban ministries have been established, and three existing urban ministries have been greatly expanded since 1993.

In chapter 7, I discussed the work of Love INC, a national network of community-based clearinghouses that mobilize church members to serve needy individuals in the local community. Love INC's impressive growth since it started in one city in Michigan in the mid-eighties is one very hopeful sign of increased awareness among churches of their responsibility to serve their communities. Over 3,000 churches have joined Love INC. I randomly contacted a dozen Love INC clearinghouses scattered throughout the country and learned that all but one had experienced impressive growth in the number of churches affiliated with their ministries. Eight of the twelve clearinghouses had tripled or quadrupled their memberships. Some of this growth has been very recent and has come at least in part as a response to the rhetoric of welfare reform. As Carolyn Eyerman, program director for Love INC in Redbank, New Jersey, reported: "As time moves along, people are looking to the churches to fill the gaps left by welfare reform. They see the value of what we are doing. Reform is coming, and some people are going to drop out of the system. Churches are looking to us to help them meet the needs."

Pat Johnson, director of the Love, INC ministry in Charlotte, North Carolina, agrees. "We've seen a leap in the number of churches responding to the needs around them. These churches are beginning to realize that our country is not going to make it unless the churches get involved."

Outside observers of church activity also assert that the church's involvement in outreach is growing. Ann Caplan of the American Association of Fund-Raising Counsel, a group that helps nonprofits do fund-raising, asserts that "the human service mission is of increasing importance to local congregations. Religious organizations are big players [in the welfare arena] and are getting bigger." Independent

Sector, the premiere research organization on the nonprofit world, issued a study entitled *From Belief to Commitment* in 1988. It described the activities and finances of American religious congregations, based on a survey of over 4,000 churches. In the study's foreword, Independent Sector President Brian O'Connell wrote: "This study . . . makes clear how very large [religious institutions'] community services are, dwarfing all funds contributed to and by other voluntary organizations for local human services. The report documents that religious congregations are the primary volunteer service providers for neighborhoods. It is my experience that the poorer the community, the larger that role and impact."[1]

According to the study, religious congregations spent about $17 billion on education, human services, community development, and health programs in 1986—and 36 percent of the churches' volunteer resources were expended on such areas. Fully 87 percent of the churches reported having one or more programs in human services and welfare.[2]

Moreover, several Christian relief and development agencies that previously focused exclusively on social welfare needs overseas have begun programs to minister to the poor here at home. The move comes in part from increasing interest on the part of foundation and individual donors to such ministries to address the needs of America's underclass.

Of course, there are also signs of persistent inertia within the church community. Last fall I interviewed a number of pastors while attending a summit on community responses to Virginia's welfare reform initiative. While half reported that their colleagues in the ministry shared their interest in expanding the churches' community programs, the other half said that other ministers in their cities were "blind" to the upcoming changes and the possible increase in people needing help. Additionally, one of the Love INC clearinghouse directors was extremely discouraged and frustrated by the lack of outreach by churches in her Michigan town: "There's been absolutely no response to the rhetoric [about welfare reform] in the last few years. Getting churches involved is like pulling teeth. . . . People say, 'We don't have poor people in Charlotte,' or, 'If they're poor, it's their own fault for being lazy.' Churches are in for a rude shock when these welfare reforms hit the state."

Mississippi's executive director of the Department of Human Services, Colonel Donald Taylor, complains that inertia within some churches is a major obstacle to the success of the Faith and Families program. "It's one thing to sit down and write a check for needy people," Taylor comments. "It's quite another to commit yourself personally to work with someone one-on-one, see to their needs, and try to boost them from economic slavery to economic freedom. It requires a lot more commitment than simply writing a check."

Larry Temple, Taylor's colleague at the Mississippi DHS, argues that part of the problem is that government's expansion into the social welfare arena reduced private citizens' involvement with the poor to the sterile obligation of paying taxes each April 15. Temple's view is shared by many who believe that an encroaching "nanny state" has weakened civic institutions—and thus contributed to social breakdown. Senator Dan Coats articulates the dilemma with particularly compelling prose:

> America's cultural decay can be traced directly to the breakdown of certain institutions—families, churches, neighborhoods, voluntary associations—that act as an immune system against cultural disease. In nearly every community, these institutions once created an atmosphere in which most problems—a teenage girl "in trouble," the rowdy neighborhood kids, the start of a drug problem at the local high school—could be confronted before their repetition threatened the existence of the community itself. When civil society is strong, it infuses a community with its warmth, trains its people to be good citizens, and transmits values between generations. When it is weak, no amount of police or politics can provide a substitute. . . . Government clearly has had a

role in undermining civil society. Families, churches, and community groups were forced to surrender their authority and function to bureaucratic experts. Fathers were replaced by welfare checks, private charities were displaced by government spending, religious volunteers were dismissed as "amateurs," whole communities were demolished in slum-clearance projects. The power to replace an institution is the power to destroy it.[3]

The growing acknowledgment that the state has enervated civil society, and the ensuing call for a "re-limiting" of government, is just one step, however, toward remedying the situation. As Coats says, "The retreat of government does not automatically result in the rebirth of civil society."[4] Fortunately, the RESTORERS have something to teach us about how to reinvigorate civil society. Their holistic, relationally based strategy can be a catalyst to spark the increased civic conscientiousness among churchgoers that must accompany a viable shift of welfare responsibilities from the state to society. Two stories from Mississippi illustrate this.

The first comes from Mississippi DHS staffer Kim Turberville, an assistant with the Faith and Families program. She describes a friendship between a church member and a former AFDC recipient. Tamia[5] was working on her GED and living with an abusive boyfriend when she volunteered for Faith and Families. She had no family support and was an emotional wreck. She was adopted by a church and linked with Ellen,[6] a retired schoolteacher. "Ellen talked with Tamia and helped her work through many of her emotional problems; she was like a caring aunt," Turberville relates. As the friendship grew, Tamia severed the abusive relationship, sailed through the GED program, and, with some help from Ellen, learned about various financial aid programs, and enrolled in community college. Meanwhile, Ellen was introduced to the "other side" of Jackson.

When one of Tamia's aged neighbors needed eyeglasses, Ellen called Turberville to learn whether there was a community program that might help. There was, Turberville recalls, her speech quickening with excitement. "So the church became interested in that program—which they saw help someone they knew—and then church members started supporting it with their money and their volunteer time." What started out as a single friendship became a bridge between Ellen's church and Tamia's neighborhood. This is the key, Turberville argues, for changing the prevailing "it's *their* problem, not *my* problem" attitude. Since the elderly neighbor's problem affected Tamia, it touched Ellen's life too—and by extension, the lives of Ellen's co-congregants.

The same kind of bridge building is happening between Christ United Methodist Church and North Midtown, an inner-city neighborhood in Jackson. Christ Church signed up for Faith and Families a year ago but hasn't yet been matched with an AFDC recipient. But it began making the shift from what Missions Director Martha Walton calls "Band-Aid" material-aid ministry to relational ministry a few years earlier. Christ Church, a conservative, upper middle class white congregation of 4,200 members, agreed to help build several Habitat for Humanity homes in Midtown and urged its black janitor, Earl Owens, to apply for one of them. Several months ago, Owens moved his wife and three kids from their one-bedroom apartment to the bright three-bedroom house. Church enthusiasm for helping Owens was "overwhelming," according to Walton.

Excitement for the new urban ministry has increased further since Christ Church hired a black minister, Rev. Leon Collier, to join the all-white staff and spearhead the church's outreach in Midtown. Owens says the church has gained credibility with the residents because congregants have "come into the neighborhood and gotten eyeball to eyeball with the people and really seen the needs."

Long-time resident Dorothy Davis catalogued those needs as we chatted in her invitingly cluttered living room—streets so full of drug pushers you could hardly drive through, shootings, crack houses, old folks and children afraid to traverse the streets. Davis credits the church with reinvigorating the community's long dormant neighborhood association. She reports that fifty kids and a dozen adults are involved in various programs put on by church volunteers in an apartment the church has rented in the neighborhood. The church's Bible study and parenting class have "given residents a place to come together," Davis and Owens say. And they assert that the new hope and the new Habitat for Humanity homeowners are driving out the drug dealers. "For many years nobody on these streets gave their kids bikes, because we couldn't let them ride them here." Davis grins. "Guess what I bought my children for Christmas this year?"

Authority and the Restoration of Community

North Midtown is on its way to restoring its lost sense of community. One terribly important reason why is that a core group of its residents have come to share a "moral consensus" and have accepted Rev. Collier's exercise of legitimate moral authority. Cultural critic Ken Myers has argued that societies cannot achieve the common good unless the citizens hold an idea of the good in common. North Midtowners have decided what they will and won't tolerate in their neighborhood; this gives them a common vision for the community and a common standard for acceptable behavior.

Such norms, though, must then be enforced. In his penetrating analysis of the community enjoyed in the Chicago of the 1950s—and lost in our times—commentator Alan Ehrenhalt writes: "Stable relationships, civil classrooms, safe streets—the ingredients of what we call community—all come at a price. The price is . . . rules and authorities who can enforce them."[7]

Ehrenhalt describes how moral authority was effectively exercised in one working-class community in Chicago, called St. Nick's parish, by the senior priest, Father Fennessy:

> For decades Fennessy had walked the neighborhood day and night, dressed in a black cassock that reached down to

his shoe tops. He greeted people on their front stoops and handed out dimes to children. . . . "He glided around like a ghost," one child of the parish remembers. "He would appear everywhere. It was his personal fiefdom. He was in the playground, in the hallway, in class. He appeared on the playground, and the grab-ass would stop. He had that effect. He was lord of the manor, and there was no mistaking who was in charge." *Fennessy represented authority of the most natural and unaffected kind, based neither on persuasion nor coercion, but simply on the identity and credibility of the person exercising it.*[8]

RESTORERS like Rev. Collier are able to exercise this kind of authority in neighborhoods like North Midtown because they, like Fennessy, are *known* by the residents. They are frequent fixtures in the community. And they have earned the respect and trust of the residents. They have earned it by heeding the timeless wisdom of the ancient church father Gregory of Nyssa. Gregory taught that "mercy is a voluntary sorrow that joins itself to the suffering of another." When helpers accept helpees' woes as their own, helpees are more likely to consent to the helpers' moral counsel. But a genuine "owning" of another's sufferings must be a concrete and tangible act if it is to lay the foundation from which moral authority can be legitimately exercised and consistently accepted. The genuine mercy Gregory speaks of is not a vague "I feel your pain." RESTORERS have won respect because the mercy they have demonstrated has cost them dearly. It has required of them their time, their money, their hearts, their lives. In return, however, they have earned respect from even the most subversive elements of the underclass.

One of the more surprising things I discovered in visiting America's ghettos was that most of the frontline workers in the ministries I studied displayed little fear of the streets. They certainly wouldn't barge into the middle of a gang fight or get too close to crazed gunman high on crack cocaine. But these frontliners could walk easily by the pimps and pushers because often such bad guys gave them sincere respect. In fact, the bad guys see the RESTORERS as "godmen."

Wayne Gordon from Lawndale Community Church in Chicago tells an amusing—and revealing—story about his prized flags that flutter from atop a pole in the church's parking lot. One day he walked into the lot and noticed to his dismay that someone had stolen the flags. He barely had time to grieve their loss though. Later that afternoon one of the most notorious gang leaders in the area showed up at Gordon's office, holding three carefully folded flags. The gang leader placed them gently on Gordon's desk and apologized for the "punk" who'd been so "ignorant" as to steal them. The gangster assured Gordon that the punk had been informed who Gordon was and what the church was trying to do for the community, and that the regrettable incident would not be repeated.

As I visited other ministries and listened to more frontliner talk, similar anecdotes abounded. Pastor Randy Draughon tells of playing basketball with some rough teens in inner-city Chattanooga who chastised one another for swearing "in front of the godman." Rev. Skip Ryan went to work with Redeemer Presbyterian Church in New York, a congregation well known for its community outreach. He was verbally harassed on the street during his first day, and then he noticed a dramatic change the following day. Everyone was deferential. Word had gotten around that he was a minister helping out with Redeemer, and thus a "godman" not to be molested. Earl Owens from North Midtown says the drug dealers have moved their selling stations down several blocks out of respect for Rev. Collier and the other Christians active in the neighborhood. "They would stop [their dealing] when the church people came," Owens relates. "They would respect them. They saw that somebody had something good in mind, that [these Christians] wanted to do something for the community. And the bad people, they knew that was needed," Owens explains.

Come Worship the Restorer

Of course, the punks' respect for the "godmen" doesn't usually terminate their dealing, drugging, and shooting for good. In most cases, they just reduce their activities somewhat or move them. The gangster who returned Wayne Gordon's flags didn't get religion that day and quit the gang. But the fact that "the godmen" have been able to command some measure of respect from the bad guys is remarkable. No one else seems to have accomplished this. And in some instances, what begins as respect grows into curiosity and eventually into friendship. The Wayne Gordons of the world can share testimonies of the bad guys who've even gone on to become "godmen" themselves.

Indeed, getting the addicts and gangsters to respect the "godmen" is one important step in bringing them to accept the God Man, Jesus, Himself. Luis Osoy, the young Latino profiled in the opening pages of this book, saw something intriguing in the "godmen" that work with Neighborhood Ministries in Phoenix, and he hungered to possess what they had. Leslie Miller felt the love of the God Man through the human hands and hearts of the congregants at Rosedale Park Baptist Church. Osoy's and Miller's transformed lives give testimony to the power of God's love and grace transmitted through the often fragile earthen vessels that RESTORERS are.

To repeat, though, it's not just the Osoys and the Millers who are transformed. The RESTORERS themselves and the volunteers who assist them watch such transformations unfold and are moved to an even deeper worship and adoration of God. Amy Malouf, a high school student who volunteers with Neighborhood Ministries, says her work on the front lines has spurred such a deeper relationship with God that she plans a lifelong involvement in ministry. She explains, "It seems as though once you have experienced the amazing power of God through servanthood, you can't settle for anything less."

The ultimate result of the work of restoration, it seems, is reinvigorated worship. The poor who never knew God are brought into relationship with Him through the holistic ministry of the RESTORERS, and that leads them to praise. The disciples of Christ who serve as RESTORERS on the front lines, in face-to-face relationships, experience firsthand the amazing power and provision of God, and they are awed and moved to more vigorous praise. Rev. Ronnie Crudup of New Horizon Baptist Church in Jackson, Mississippi, says the urban ministry volunteers in his congregation have been indelibly marked by their work. "It's made their faith not just words in a book; they've [seen] the reality that there is life in these words. People on the front lines not only say 'God is able,' but 'God is willing,'" Crudup says. "They've seen His power. They're fired up." He continues, "They've gotten beyond their doubts as to what the Gospel can do, because they *know* it changes people's lives."

Seeing the Heavenly Restorer's miracles does fire us up to worship Him who alone is able to do beyond all that we ask or imagine. It certainly fired up the Israelites in Nehemiah's day. God empowered the people to rebuild the ruined wall of Jerusalem in an unbelievably short time and in the face of significant opposition. But God's work wasn't finished when the restoration project was completed. The rebuilding of the wall met the people's physical needs and gave them a new security and improved their living conditions substantially. There was a real restoration of their city. But the *ultimate purpose* God had in mind was for a restoration of the people's *hearts*, a revival of their relationship with Him. And so in the latter chapters of Nehemiah we see a glorious revival take place after the wall was finished. The Scriptures were read, proclaimed, and explained to the people. And the people submitted before God's Word, and they celebrated His goodness, praising Him and singing from atop the wall.

This must be our ultimate purpose as well—to bring about a restoration that leads us, and those we serve, to praise and worship King Jesus from atop the wall of rebuilt lives.

Notes

Introduction

1. Glenn C. Loury, "Ghetto Poverty and the Power of Faith," address to the Center for the American Experiment (Minneapolis, Minn., 8 October 1993).

2. William Raspberry, "Organized Religion Neglecting Its One Key Strength," *Washington Post,* 12 February 1995.

3. Nicholas Lemann, "The Origins of the Underclass," *Atlantic Monthly* (July 1986): 55.

4. Ibid., 56.

5. Charles A. Murray, *Losing Ground: American Social Policy, 1950-1980* (New York: Basic Books, 1984).

6. Carl Esbeck, "Government Regulations of Religiously Based Social Services: The First Amendment Consideration," *Hastings Constitutional Law Quarterly,* 19 (Winter 1992): 365.

7. For an in-depth description of Perkins's model of Christian community development, see John Perkins, *Beyond Charity: The Call to Christian Community Development* (Grand Rapids: Baker Book House, 1993) and John Perkins, ed., *Restoring At-Risk Communities: Doing It Together and Doing It Right* (Grand Rapids: Baker Book House, 1995).

PART ONE

Chapter One
The Challenge of the Streets

1. Elijah Anderson, "The Code of the Streets," *Atlantic Monthly* (May 1994): 82.

2. Ibid., 83.

3. Ibid.

4. Ibid., 82.

5. Ibid.

6. Ibid.

7. Ibid., 86.

8. Greg Donaldson, *The Ville: Cops and Kids in Urban America* (New York: Ticknor and Fields, 1993), 27.

9. Anderson, "Code of the Streets," 88.

10. Ibid.

11. Donaldson, *The Ville,* 61-62.

12. Ibid., 82.

13. John Perkins, *Beyond Charity: The Call to Christian Community Development* (Grand Rapids: Baker Books, 1993), 11.

14. Donaldson, *The Ville,* 139.

15. Ibid., 140.

16. See Charles A. Murray, *Losing Ground: American Social Policy, 1950-1980* (New York: Basic Books, 1984) and Robert Rector and William F. Lauber, *America's Failed $5.4 Trillion War on Poverty* (Washington: The Heritage Foundation, 1995).

17. William Julius Wilson, *The Truly Disadvantaged: The Inner City, the Underclass, and Public Policy* (Chicago: University of Chicago Press, 1987), 58.

18. Daniel Coyle, *Hardball: A Season in the Projects* (New York: HarperCollins Publishers, 1993), 77.

19. Ibid., 79.

20. Richard John Neuhaus, *America Against Itself: Moral Vision and the Public Order* (Notre Dame: University of Notre Dame Press, 1992), 83.

21. Jonathan Kozol, *Amazing Grace: The Lives of Children and the Conscience of a Nation* (New York: Crown Publishers, Inc., 1995), 57.

22. Chris Wood, "Inner-City Pain: Chicago Is a Test for Clinton's Reforms," *Macleans* (16 November 1992), 48.

Chapter Two
Transforming Culture

1. Glenn C. Loury, *One by One from the Inside Out: Essays and Reviews on Race and Responsibility in America* (New York: The Free Press, 1995).

Chapter Three
Reforming Hearts, Renewing Minds, Refreshing Spirits

1. Brad Wilcox, "Tough Love Isn't Enough," *Stewardship Journal* (Spring/ Summer 1994): 5.

2. Anthony Marciano as quoted in ibid., 12.

3. Quoted in Cathy Lynn Grossman, "Should Religion Be Involved in Welfare Reform?" *USA Today* (8 December 1995): 11D.

4. Jonathan Kozol, *Amazing Grace: The Lives of Children and the Conscience of a Nation* (New York: Crown Publishers, Inc., 1995), 230.

5. Glenn C. Loury, "Ghetto Poverty and the Power of Faith," address to the Center for the American Experiment (Minneapolis, Minn., December 1993), 3.

6. Cornel West, "Nihilism in Black America: A Danger That Corrodes from Within," *Dissent* (Spring 1991): 222.

7. Milbrey W. McLaughlin, Merita A. Irby, and Juliet Langman, *Urban Sanctuaries: Neighborhood Organizations in the Lives and Futures of Inner-City Youth* (San Francisco: Jossey-Bass Publishers, 1994), 50.

8. Ibid., 52.

Chapter Four
Enlarging Worlds

1. Reported in *Reader's Digest* (December 1995): 190.

2. Daniel Coyle, *Hardball: A Season in the Projects* (New York: HarperCollins Publishers, 1993), 134.

3. Ibid., 14.

4. Jonathan Kozol, *Amazing Grace: The Lives of Children and the Conscience of a Nation* (New York: Crown Publishers, Inc., 1995), 122.

5. Alex Kotlowitz, *There Are No Children Here: The Story of Two Boys Growing Up in the Other America* (New York: Doubleday, 1991), 13.

6. Ibid., 12.

7. Darcy Frey, *The Last Shot: City Streets, Basketball Dreams* (New York: Houghton Mifflin Company, 1994), 4.

8. Milbrey W. McLaughlin, Merita A. Irby, and Juliet Langman, *Urban Sanctuaries: Neighborhood Organizations in the Lives and Futures of Inner-City Youth* (San Francisco: Jossey-Bass Publishers, 1994).

9. Ibid., 5.

10. Ron Suskind, "Poor, Black and Smart, an Inner-City Teen Tries to Survive M.I.T.," *Wall Street Journal* (22 September 1994): A-1.

11. Kozol, *Amazing Grace*, 125.

12. Douglas G. Glasgow, *The Black Underclass: Poverty, Unemployment, and Entrapment of Ghetto Youth* (San Francisco: Jossey-Bass Publishers, 1980), 21.

13. Ibid., 59.

14. Kotlowitz, *There Are No Children Here*, 13.

15. William Julius Wilson, *The Truly Disadvantaged: The Inner City, the Underclass, and Public Policy* (Chicago: University of Chicago Press, paperback ed., 1990), 38.

PART TWO

Chapter Five
Laying the Foundation

1. Bob Moffitt, "Biblical Versus Secular Development," paper prepared for the *Stewardship Journal* Conference on Holistic Ministry (San Jose, Costa Rica, 11-15 January 1994), 2.

2. Ibid., emphasis mine.

3. Phil Reed, "Toward a Theology of Christian Community Development," in *Restoring At-Risk Communities: Doing It Together and Doing It Right*, ed. John M. Perkins (Grand Rapids: Baker Books, 1995), 28. What follows is a summary of Reed's helpful essay.

4. Ibid.

5. Ibid., 30.

6. Ibid.

7. Peter C. Phan, *Social Thought*, Vol. 20, *Message of the Fathers of the Church*, gen. ed., Thomas Halton (Wilmington: Michael Glazier, Inc., 1984), 67.

8. From Ambrose, *Duties of the Clergy*, quoted in Thomas C. Oden, "Two Thousand Years of Caring for the Poor," *Stewardship Journal* (Spring 1993), 52.

9. Timothy Keller, pastor of Redeemer Presbyterian Church in New York City, has written several helpful articles on intentional, sacrificial giving. See, for example, chapter 4 in his book, *Ministries of Mercy: The Call of the Jericho Road* (Grand Rapids: Zondervan, 1989).

10. Phan, *Social Thought,* 129, 131.

11. Ibid., 45.

12. Ibid., 46.

13. Marvin Olasky, *The Tragedy of American Compassion* (Wheaton, Ill.: Crossway Books, 1992), 101-103.

14. Jeannine Olson, *Calvin and Social Welfare: Deacons and the Bourse Francais* (Selingsgrove, Penn.: Susquehanna University Press, 1989), 39.

Chapter Six
Overcoming the Barriers to Reaching Out

1. Richard A. Swenson's book *Margin: Restoring Emotional, Physical, Financial, and Time Reserves to Overloaded Lives* (Colorado Springs: NavPress, 1992) offers helpful insights for controlling our schedules.

2. Mark R. Gornik and Noel Castellanos, "How to Start a Christian Community Development Ministry," in *Restoring At-Risk Communities: Doing It Together and Doing It Right,* ed. John M. Perkins (Grand Rapids: Baker Books, 1995), 211-235.

3. Ibid., 218.

4. Spencer Perkins and Chris Rice, *More Than Equals: Racial Healing for the Sake of the Gospel* (Downers Grove, Ill.: InterVarsity Press, 1993).

5. Gerald Austin and Tim Ritchie, "The Best Way to Improve Community Race Relations Is One-to-One," *The Birmingham News,* 11 July 1994.

6. Tom Sine, *Wild Hope* (Dallas: Word Publishing, 1991), 269.

Chapter Seven
Making the Shift to Relational Ministry

1. Marvin Olasky, "Beyond the Stingy Welfare State," *Stewardship Journal* (Winter 1991): 54.

2. This story was first reported by Gerald Wisz in "Giving Their Regards to Broadway: A New York Soup Kitchen Goes Back to Basics," in *Loving Your Neighbors,* ed. Marvin Olasky (Washington, D.C.: Capital Research Center, n.d.), 35-44.

3. Ibid., 38.

4. W. H. Skip Hunt, *How Can I Help? A Christian's Guide to Personal Counseling* (Nashville: Thomas Nelson, 1994).

Chapter Eight
Getting Going—Ten Steps to Building a Community Ministry

1. See Rick Lynch, "Training Volunteers: Choosing the Right Training Method," *Voluntary Action Leadership* (Fall 1980).

2. Ibid.

PART THREE

Chapter Nine
Collaborating with Government: The Benefits

1. Carl Esbeck, "Government Regulations of Religiously Based Social Services: The First Amendment Consideration," *Hastings Constitutional Law Quarterly* 19, No. 34 (Winter 1992).

2. Stephen V. Monsma, "The Mixing of Church and State: Religious Nonprofit Organizations and Public Money," *Calvin Center Pamphlet 1* (Grand Rapids: Calvin College, June 1994): 1.

3. The Center for Public Justice has published a succinct nontechnical guide to the Charitable Choice provisions. Christian ministries working in the social services field will find it extremely useful. Titled *A Guide to Charitable Choice: The Rules of Section 104 of the 1996 Federal Welfare Law Governing State Cooperation with Faith-based Social-Service Providers,* it is available at a small price from The Center for Public Justice, 2444 Soloman's Island Road, Ste. 201, Annapolis, MD 21401.

4. Stephen V. Monsma, "Public Money and Religiously Based Nonprofit Organizations: The Church-State Dance," paper prepared for the 1994 Annual Meeting of the American Political Science Association (New York, 1-4 September, 1994), 9-10.

5. Bethel New Life, a large, multifaceted Christian outreach in Chicago that accepts a considerable amount of governmental funding, has actually defined a specific action plan that ministry leaders would put into effect if the organization decided to reject such funding. This plan prioritizes Bethel's various programs and outlines which would be curtailed and/or diminished. Religiously based nonprofits that receive state monies would do well to imitate this example of contingency planning. The Charitable Choice provisions make it less likely that faith-based providers would unexpectedly suffer pressure from governmental entities to diminish their religious expression. Nonetheless, it is possible that at some time governmental funds would come with objectionable "strings"; consequently, organization leaders should, like Bethel's board of

directors, carefully think through what they would do if they suddenly faced a significant cut in their budget by refusing state grants.

Chapter Ten
Collaborating with Government: The Potential Pitfalls

1. Sam Howe Verhovek, "'Mother Teresa of Houston' Fights Hunger and Government Aid," *New York Times (2 June 1995), Section A, 12.*

2. There are promising signs in Texas that state officials are becoming more receptive to permitting faith-based groups—for example, the wildly successful Teen Challenge ministry—to hire substance abuse counselors who lack professional certification. In its 1996 report, "Faith in Action: A New Vision for Church-State Cooperation in Texas," the Governor's Advisory Task Force on Faith-Based Community Service Groups recommended that Texas "exempt from licensure requirements rehabilitation or treatment programs operated by a religious institution or social ministry that employs spiritual or religious methods of treatment and whose primary purpose is to propagate the organization's religious beliefs."

   The report further recommended that Texas officials should reevaluate credentialing standards that act to deny federal drug treatment funds to faith-based facilities. Such standards should be removed, argued the Task Force, so long as the requirements for education and training of personnel effectively barred religious groups from receiving federal funds.

Chapter Eleven
Toward More Fruitful Collaboration

1. Quoted in Dan Coats, "Can Congress Revive Civil Society?" *Policy Review* (January-February 1996): 27.

2. Gertrude Himmelfarb, "Remoralizing Civil Society," *Policy Review* (January-February 1996): 29.

Conclusion
Reviving Church, Relearning Community

1. *From Belief to Commitment: The Activities and Finances of Religious Congregations in the United States* (Washington, D.C.: Independent Sector, 1988), p. iii.

2. Ibid., pp. 4-5.

3. Dan Coats, "Can Congress Revive Civil Society?" *Policy Review* (January-February 1996): 25.

4. Ibid., 27.

5. Not the client's real name.

6. Not the volunteer's real name.

7. Alan Ehrenhalt, *The Lost City: Discovering the Virtues of Community in the Chicago of the 1950s* (New York: Basic Books, 1995): 2.

8. Ibid., 121 (emphasis mine).

Resources

RESTORERS *Profiled in the Book*

Anacostia Gospel Chapel/
DC Christian Ministries
1100 Savannah Street S.E.
Washington, DC 20032–4515
(202) 574–3053

Center for Urban Missions
P.O. Box 2482
Birmingham, AL 35201
(205) 252–8286 Fax: (205) 252–8243

Christ United Methodist Church
5301 Old Canton Road
Jackson, MS 39211
(601) 956–6974

Detroit Rescue Mission Ministries
150 Stimson
P.O. Box 2087
Detroit, MI 48231–2087
(313) 993–4700 Fax: (313) 831–2299

Lawndale Community Church
3848 W. Ogden Avenue
Chicago, IL 60623
(312) 762–6389

Neighborhood Ministries
301 W. Indian School Road, Ste. A-119
Phoenix, AZ 85013
(602) 263–7611 Fax: (602) 234–0209

Oak Cliff Bible Fellowship/
Outreach Center
1320 W. Camp Wisdom Road
Dallas, TX 75232
(214) 228–0872

Rosedale Park Baptist Church
14161 Vaughn
Detroit, MI 48223
(313) 538–1180 Fax: (313) 538–0002

S.T.E.P.
4206 Springhill Avenue
Richmond, VA 23225
(804) 233–0533

Voice of Calvary Ministries
1655 St. Charles Street
Jackson, MS 39209
(601) 353–1635
Fax: (601) 944-0403

HELPFUL ORGANIZATIONS

American Family Hope
4694 Spartan Industrial Drive
Grandville, MI 49418
(616) 249–8277
Fax: (616) 534–9190

*American Family Hope helps church
and community members to serve
the working poor.*

Christian Community
Development Association
3827 W. Ogden Avenue
Chicago, IL 60623
(312) 762–0994
Fax: (312) 762–5772

*CCDA is a national association of
Christian community development
organizations. CCDA's annual conference offers hundreds of practical seminars led by some of the best
practitioners in urban ministry.
CCDA's membership directory is a useful guide to the more than 250 organizations in the network.*

Christian Community
Health Fellowship
P.O. Box 12548
Philadelphia, PA 19151
(215) 877–1200

*CCHF is a national network of
Christian health care professionals
concerned about the health needs of
the poor in the United States.*

Habitat for Humanity
National Headquarters
121 Habitat Street
Americus, GA 31709–3498
(912) 924–6935

Habitat's mission is to provide "decent housing in decent communities" for God's people in need.

Kids Hope USA
17011 Hickory
Spring Lake, MI 49456
(616) 846–7490

See chapter 7 for a description.

Love, INC (In the Name of Christ)
c/o World Vision
P.O. Box 9716
Federal Way, WA 98001
1–800–777–5277

See chapter 7 for a description.

National Center for Neighborhood Enterprise
1367 Connecticut Avenue, N.W.
Washington, DC 20036
(202) 331–1103 Fax: (202) 296–1541

The National Center for Neighborhood Enterprise is a nonprofit research and demonstration organization that provides consulting help to community organizations in low-income neighborhoods, assisting such groups in devising workable solutions to local economic problems. It is not an explicitly Christian organization, though it has collaborated with Christian ministries and ministry leaders.

National Congress for Community Economic Development
1875 Connecticut Avenue, Ste. 524
Washington, DC 20009
(202) 234–5009 Fax: (202) 234–4510

The NCCED is a national trade association of organizations engaged in the revitalization of distressed urban and rural communities. It provides technical assistance to member organizations, sponsors conferences and seminars, and publishes studies of interest to community development organizations. It is not a Christian organization, although about 5 percent of its members are religious nonprofits.

New Focus
6837 Lake Michigan Drive
Allendale, MI 49401
(616) 895–5356

See chapter 7 for a description.

PICCD (Partners in Christian Community Development)
8205 East 93rd Terrace
Kansas City, MO 64138
Tel/fax: (816) 767–8493

PICCD provides technical assistance and training to CCDA-member churches and faith-based ministries working in distressed rural and urban communities.

Urban Family Magazine
P.O. Box 32
Jackson, MS 39205
(601) 354–1563 Fax: (601) 352–6882

Urban Family is published by the John M. Perkins Foundation for Reconciliation and Development and addresses issues of community development and racial reconciliation.

Urban Ministries, Inc.
1350 W. 103rd Street
Chicago, IL 60643
1–800–860–8642

Urban Ministries, Inc. produces high-quality, biblically-based multicultural Vacation Bible School curricula (grades pre-K through 12) designed for use in urban settings.

Index